Tackling the Tough Stuff

A Home Visitor's Guide to Supporting Families at Risk

by

Angela M. Tomlin, Ph.D., HSPP, IMH-E (IV)

and

Stephan A. Viehweg, M.S.W., ACSW, LCSW, IMH-E (IV)

Indiana University School of Medicine
Indianapolis

·P·A·U·L·H·
BROOKES
PUBLISHING CO.®

Baltimore • London • Sydney

Paul H. Brookes Publishing Co.
Post Office Box 10624
Baltimore, Maryland 21285-0624

www.brookespublishing.com

Typeset by BMWW, Baltimore, Maryland.
Manufactured in the United States of America by
Versa Press, Inc., East Peoria, Illinois.

Cover image ©istockphoto/Straitel

Library of Congress Cataloging-in-Publication Data

The Library of Congress has cataloged the printed edition as follows:

Names: Tomlin, Angela M., author. | Viehweg, Stephan A., author.
Title: Tackling the tough stuff: a home visitor's guide to supporting families at risk /
    by Angela M. Tomlin and Stephan A. Viehweg.
Description: Baltimore : Paul H. Brookes Publishing Co., [2016] | Includes bibliographical
    references and index.
Identifiers: LCCN 2015036413 | ISBN 9781598579277 (pbk.)
Subjects: LCSH: Home-based family services. | Developmentally disabled children—
    Services for. | Early childhood education—Parent participation. | Family social work.
Classification: LCC HV697 .T66 2016 | DDC 362.82/53--dc23
LC record available at http://lccn.loc.gov/2015036413

British Library Cataloguing in Publication data are available from the British Library.

2020   2019   2018   2017   2016
10   9   8   7   6   5   4   3   2   1

Contents

About the Forms

Purchasers of this book may download, print, and/or photocopy the materials in the appendixes and Figures 9.1 and 10.1 for professional use. These materials are included with the print book and are also available for print and e-book buyers at **www://brookespublishing.com/tomlin/materials.**

About the Authors

Angela M. Tomlin, Ph.D., HSPP, IMH-E (IV), is Associate Clinical Professor and Director of the Riley Child Development Center (RCDC) LEND Program, a nationally recognized interdisciplinary leadership training program supported by the Maternal and Child Health Bureau and located at the Indiana University School of Medicine. At the RCDC, Dr. Tomlin provides clinical services and supports the training of interdisciplinary learners. She is the author or coauthor of 20 publications on topics that include infant mental health, autism spectrum disorder, and work force development. Dr. Tomlin serves on several state-level committees, is the chairperson of the Indiana Association for Infant and Toddler Mental Health, serves on the Board of Mental Health America Indiana, and is Past President of the Board of the Autism Society of Indiana. With her husband of more than 30 years, Dr. Tomlin is the proud parent of two adult daughters and has two grandchildren.

Stephan A. Viehweg, M.S.W., ACSW, LCSW, IMH-E (IV), is Assistant Research Professor and Associate Director of the Riley Child Development Center, a nationally recognized interdisciplinary leadership training program supported by the Maternal and Child Health Bureau, and faculty member of the Indiana University (IU) School of Medicine, Department of Pediatrics, and the IU School of Social Work. He also helps direct the Center for Translating Research Into Practice at Indiana University–Purdue University Indianapolis. He currently serves as the Centers for Disease Control's Learn the Signs Ambassador to Indiana. He is Founding Chair of the Indiana Association for Infant and Toddler Mental Health and Founding President of Family Voices Indiana. Mr. Viehweg's experience as a social work provider with families and their children with delays as well as adults with disabilities, and his ability to communicate in Spanish and American Sign Language, make him a well-respected, sought-after therapist, presenter, and consultant. With his wife of nearly 30 years, he is the proud parent of an adult son and daughter and Papaw to two grandchildren.

Foreword

Relationships are at the center of this very illuminating and practical book that integrates developmental and clinical theories with many examples for home visitors to support effective service with families and, most important, healthy outcomes leading to growth and change. Connections between parents and child, parents and providers, and providers and supervisors provide the central theme throughout the book, with continuous reminders that relationships offer the cornerstone for effective service provision and the instrument for optimal growth and change.

PARENT AND CHILD

Beginning with the early developing relationship between parent and child, the authors describe the importance of attachment to a baby's health and growth and provide strategies for home visitors to consider during visits to a family's home. These include working with the parent and baby together, showing interest in the baby's development, speaking for the baby, responding with empathy to parental stories and concerns, recognizing and responding to feelings that parents have about the care of the baby, and commenting on the baby's efforts to connect.

PARENT AND PROVIDER

The parent–provider relationship is of equal concern to home visiting practice. Building a working relationship with parents, founded on mutual respect and trust, is essential for family engagement and positive outcomes. According to the authors, strategies that support the parent–provider relationship include persistence, consistency and empathy, and follow-through (i.e., following the parent's lead, remaining fully and emotionally present, inviting the parent to talk and listening carefully to his or her wants and needs, responding to each parent's concerns about the baby and about him- or herself). In response to the question, "How is this helpful to the child?" the authors' response is simple. By filling up the parent's "emotional fuel tank," the parent has the energy to respond and relate more sensitively and effectively to his or her very young child. An explanation of why parents seek help is equally informative, encouraging home visitors to think deeply about the meaning of a very young child's behavior as well as the challenges and stressors that many families face when raising very young children.

It is clear that Tomlin and Viehweg have a commitment to the understanding that parents need and welcome supportive relationships as they learn to nurture and respond appropriately and lovingly to their child.

PROVIDER AND SUPERVISOR

The third relationship, the guiding relationship between provider and supervisor, offers a context for reflection that leads to greater understanding of the work with children and families as well exploration of personal responses to the vulnerabilities and challenges of home visiting work, leading to personal and professional growth and change. Time for reflection includes *mindfulness*, the skill that allows a practitioner to have and share thoughts and feelings with someone who cares about the work with families and also about his or her own personal growth. The authors remind us that reflective skills can help the home visitor find ways to make sense of the situations that face many families (Weston, 2005). This practice can help the home visitor better integrate and make good use of the often competing emotional and cognitive processes inherent when addressing complex situations (Mann, Gordon, & MacLeod, 2009).

Together, these three relationships—parent and child, parent and provider, and provider and supervisor—are at the heart of Tomlin and Viehweg's wonderfully informative new book.

REFLECTIVE PRACTICE

Reflective practice goes hand in hand with relationship-centered service. The authors recognize the tremendous stressors families face and that home visitors must understand how stress affects parents' capacities to care sensitively and effectively for their very young children. Stressors may include a diagnosis of significant mental illness, parental depression, a motor or sensory impairment, an intellectual disability, substance use or addiction, or domestic violence. Past and present experiences of trauma and loss, as well as economic struggles and severe poverty, exacerbate these risks.

After describing barriers, challenges, and risks, the authors offer practical tips and strategies for home visitors to use when entering into relationships with very vulnerable young children and families. Among the most creative strategy is a problem-solving framework, PAUSE, that blends relationship and reflective skills. The acronym for PAUSE is Perceive, Ask, Understand, Strategize, and Evaluate. The authors offer illustrations for each component, exploring ways to think deeply and reflectively in partnership with families.

As described in the text, "The process organizes thinking about the behavior or issue, helps providers respond appropriately and effectively, and uses reflection to assess the experience."

In summary, reflective practice is uniquely embedded within a relationship-centered approach for early intervention and the home visiting staff. Tomlin and Viehweg celebrate this collaborative union in a book that is certain to profoundly and positively affect practice with babies, very young children, and their families for years to come.

Deborah J. Weatherston, Ph.D., IMH-E (IV)
Executive Director
Michigan Association for Infant Mental Health

REFERENCES

Mann, K., Gordon, J., & MacLeod, A. (2009). Reflection and reflective practice in health professions education. *Advances in Health Science Education, 14,* 595–621.

Weston, D. (2005). Training in infant mental health: Educating the reflective practitioner. *Infants and Young Children, 18*(4), 337–348.

Acknowledgments

This work is the result of many years of clinical experiences, research and reading, teaching, talking and thinking together and with colleagues, and—most important—spending time sitting beside and getting to know young children and their families. We are grateful to the families who let us hear their challenges and see their strengths. You have taught us much about the hard work that parenting can present and why support is so necessary.

We thank our many colleagues dedicated to infant mental health and the development of a competency-based endorsement system through the League of States for their encouragement and feedback. Your efforts to bring awareness to the importance of early experiences, a focus on relationships as key to development and lifelong wellness, and the value of reflection and reflective supervision/consultation in professional development provide a context for our ideas to flourish.

We appreciate the candid feedback from our colleagues and friends who took the time to review our work. Your strong suggestions made our book better and, we hope, more practical and useful to the important work that is done by home visitors and early interventionists.

Projects like this do not happen without the expertise, commitment, and guidance of brilliant editors like Johanna Schmitter from Paul H. Brookes Publishing Co. Thank you for believing in our idea, providing thoughtful feedback that challenged us and improved our thinking, and keeping us on track!

We gratefully acknowledge the steadfast support of our spouses John (Angie) and Jan (Steve), who unselfishly gave up hours of their time with us to make this book a reality. They are our anchor and most ardent supporters in this project and many others.

Finally, we would like to send love and thanks to our own children and grandchildren; having you in our lives gives us the courage and encouragement to do this important work and to turn our passion into reality.

To the children and families in whose care we share:
you inspire us to do the best we can to make things better

Getting Started

It is often acknowledged that the work of home visitors, although very reward-ing and satisfying, can be challenging. Each child and family presents a dif-ferent situation, which must be understood from different perspectives and within the context of one's own values, beliefs, and experiences. To work effec-tively and sensitively, home visitors must find ways to think broadly, remain flexible, consider multiple perspectives, and be prepared with reliable infor-mation and resources that can be shared. Furthermore, because it involves helping families with very young children, is provided in the family's home, and often addresses very personal information, home visiting can be an inti-mate and intense experience. It is not uncommon for home visitors to have many responses and reactions. Altogether, home visitors frequently find that they need more than just information; they also need strategies and supports.

In this book we present the PAUSE (Perceive, Ask, Understand, Strat-egize, and Evaluate) framework, a way of working with families that blends relationship-based practice, reflective skills, and concrete information in a way that home visitors can use in everyday interactions with children and families. Our goal is to take evidence-based strategies and translate them into practical concepts and actions you can use. Using the PAUSE framework to observe, listen, and ask questions, the home visitor can better understand child behavior and development, understand sources of challenging behav-iors, recognize and respond to stressful family situations and needs, and find ways to manage his or her own reactions to this often difficult experience.

Throughout the chapters you will find many vignettes, examples, and worksheets with opportunities to think and try out skills you can use in your everyday practice. The first three chapters provide an overview of relationships and relationship-based practice, reflective practice, and how these two practices can work together. Chapter 4 covers how to understand and address common behavior problems in early childhood: a common reason for which families seek home visiting services. Chapters 5 through 8 explore specific challenging behaviors. These include regulation, aggression, compliance, and anxiety. Chapter 9 focuses on stressful family issues such as parental mental illness and disability. Chapter 10 revisits relationship and reflective practice from the perspective of significant challenges, including the need for home visitors to take care of themselves by setting boundaries and employing reflective supervision or consultation. The chapters end with Tips for Practice and suggestions for further reading and learning.

We hope this book provides a useful set of tools to help you reach your goal of improved practice. Let's get started!

Connecting and Keeping Connected

Relationships Matter

Home visiting is exciting and challenging work. Who else has the opportunity to support young children and their families in such an intimate and meaningful way? When families invite home visitors to support them in meeting their children's needs at such a young age, they have a unique opportunity to engage in relationships that can significantly affect families' lives (Weatherston & Tableman, 2015).

In the field of early intervention, relationships matter and different kinds of relationships are connected. Relationships of all kinds matter because we learn best through them (Guralnick, 2001; Norman-Murch, 1996; Watson, Gatti, Cox, Harrison, & Hennes, 2014). A positive relationship supports learning at any level. Three interrelated relationships must be considered in home visiting and other early intervention fields: parent–infant/toddler, parent–provider, and provider–supervisor.

Because early intervention professionals are acutely aware of the benefits of early relationships, their work is often focused on supporting the parent–child relationship. For many, this work includes specific goals for improving relationships between parents and their young children. Others attend to relationship less formally. Either way, attention to parent–child relationships is critical in early childhood (Jones Harden & Lythcott, 2005). A wealth of evidence stretching back more than 60 years supports the importance of parent–child relationships and makes the following clear:

- A positive relationship between a young child and his or her caregiver is necessary for healthy development (Ainsworth, 1979).

3

- A positive relationship between parent and child can provide long-lasting benefits, including school readiness and better social skills (Thompson, 2008).

- A positive parent–child relationship provides support in the face of challenging environments, such as exposure to traumatic events (Weinfield, Sroufe, Egeland, & Carlson, 2008).

- Problems in the parent–child relationship may exacerbate difficult experiences and can lead to long-term problems such as behavior disorders, unhealthy relationships, and antisocial behaviors.

FIRST RELATIONSHIPS: ATTACHMENT

Attachment, the first relationship a baby forms, is developed over time when parents respond to babies' needs. Through careful studies that document parent and infant behaviors, researchers have come to recognize that babies and parents can form different kinds of attachments depending on the way caregiving is delivered. For the most beneficial attachment to form, usually called a *secure* attachment, it is important for parents to do the following:

Be interested and attentive to the baby's needs and signals for help

Be able to read the baby's signals accurately

Respond to the signals in an appropriate, timely, and reliable way

When babies have the ongoing experience of a parent who is consistently able to identify and fulfill their needs at the right time and the right level, they feel important and safe, and they learn to trust in relationships. Knowing that basic needs will be met helps a baby stay calm or regulated in both an emotional and behavioral sense. In other words, babies come to count on the adults in their lives to help them calm down, and learn to trust that the caregivers are there to help them navigate life's complexities. When babies don't have to worry about these basics, they are free to learn and develop in all skill areas. In this way, the kind of attachment that infants have affect what they learn about themselves, other people, their families, and their cultures. Over time, this knowledge informs a person's ideas about relationships in general, setting expectations about future relationships and even guiding future behavior.

What happens when babies do not receive sensitive caregiving? For many reasons, parents may not provide the kind of caregiving that leads their baby to feel a sense of safety and security, leading to attachments that are described as *insecure*. Insecure attachments occur when the caregiving is insensitive or inconsistent. A range of parental responses are possible, resulting in attachments that vary from mildly maladaptive to those that are highly disturbed or even not present at all (Ainsworth, 1979; Main, 1996). See Table 1.1 for examples of behaviors to attend to.

This book further explores the kinds of parent characteristics and experiences that may interfere with parent and baby relationships. Over the course of this book, we present the PAUSE framework that providers can use to systematically pause, reflect, and form helpful responses to a variety of situations in home visiting. The steps in PAUSE are Perceive, Ask, Understand, Strategize, and Evaluate. Using the PAUSE framework, home visitors can integrate relationship and reflective practices with knowledge of child development and behavior. In chapters 5 through 10, we explore how the PAUSE framework can be applied to a variety of child and family situations that occur in home visiting.

Good or bad, early experiences require the home visitor's attention because they have the potential for lifelong consequences. A good deal of

Table 1.1. Examples of concerning parent behaviors from an attachment perspective

Behavior	Examples
Pulling away from the child	Parent stays far away from baby; parent isolates baby in bouncy seat
	Parent encourages toddler to play alone and ignores bids for attention or comfort
	Parent often leaves child alone in playpen
	Parent does not speak to the child when returning from separation
Parent acts afraid or seems distant	Parent speaks in frightened or uncertain-sounding voice
	Parent interacts, but seems distant or unengaged
	Parent has trouble relaying information about his or her child, such as naming a favorite food or toy
Role confusion	Parent talks to or about the child as though the child is an adult
	Parent defers to the child about decisions; begs the child to comply
	Parent cries when trying to discipline the child or asks the child, "Do you want to make me cry?"
Confusing communication	Expression, tone of voice, and words do not match (e.g., parent says, "Mommy loves you," with a scary-looking facial expression)
	Parent laughs when the child is hurt or looks angry when the child is behaving appropriately
	Child smiles and reaches for the parent; parent looks upset, pushes the child away
Lack of attunement	Parent is intrusive (e.g., keeps trying to get infant eye contact and interaction when the baby is distressed, overstimulated, or tired)
	Parent teases the child by showing, but not giving, a toy or bottle
	Parent rejects the child's request for comfort (e.g., pushes the child away when the child is hurt or afraid)
	Parent has trouble thinking about or talking about what the child's experience might be like

Source: Zeanah, Berlin, and Boris (2011).

important brain development occurs after an infant is born. Researchers have learned that social experiences are a key factor in how babies' brains will develop and work (Bruer & Greenough, 2001; Shonkoff & Phillips, 2000). Simple interactions, including making eye contact, smiling, and talking to a baby, help the baby's brain form pathways that will be used for future learning and functioning. In this way, attachment relationships are integrally important to all aspects of development. Building positive relationships at such a young age actually helps prepare children for later relationships and situations. They develop skills needed for playing with other children, sitting at a desk in school to learn various subjects, working with another person in a job environment, having a relationship with another adult and creating a family, and so forth.

Strategies for Supporting Attachment

Home visitors can take actions to help parents increase their ability to show interest in their infant, build skills needed to recognize infant cues, and act in ways that promote a positive relationship. Home visitors can identify the baby's actions, including when the baby looks at the parent, facial expressions, movements, or other small actions that may be overlooked. When the home visitor highlights the baby's behavior and connects the behavior to a need, parents may be more able to notice and respond at a later time. It can be especially powerful when the home visitor helps the parent see the baby respond to something about the parent. Table 1.2 provides some examples.

Carolyn is a home visitor working with Deidre, a 15-year-old mother and her 14-month-old son, Gage. Gage has many developmental delays and has few ways of showing his needs or interests. Deidre is a vivacious young woman who has many friends and receives what seem like constant text messages during the hour-long visits with Carolyn. She often laughs out loud and frequently asks Carolyn if she would like to see a funny post or message. Carolyn notices that Gage watches his mother and sometimes smiles when she smiles or laughs. The next time this happens, Carolyn says, "Deidre, look how Gage is smiling when you laugh. He really likes to see your smile. Maybe he wants you to talk to him too." Deidre looks surprised. She looks at Gage and smiles. He smiles back and Deidre says, "Well, hello!"

Sometimes the role of the home visitor is to be the voice for the baby. In a gentle way, the home visitor states what the baby can't say. In the case of Deidre and Gage, Carolyn simply noticed how Gage responded to his mother. Carolyn's quiet observation helped Deidre see her son in a way that supports a feeling of connection. Over time, these small moments can be significant in their relationship.

Table 1.2.   Strategies for supporting attachment

Strategy	Examples
Show interest and empathy	Body language: use an open posture, lean in, maintain eye contact.
	Ask and wonder about the parent's experience (e.g., "How has it been for you with Garrett attending the new child care?").
	Recognize and respond to feelings (e.g., "I can see that you are upset that Carter had that big tantrum at the store. That might have been embarrassing for you.").
Clarify and connect	Rephrase and repeat the parent's statements to ensure understanding (e.g., "So would you say the biggest problem you have right now is Susan's sleeping?").
	Comment on the parent's efforts and the baby's responses to ensure recognition (e.g., "Beth is smiling at you. I think she really likes to read with you.").
	Ask for clarification when needed (e.g., "We talked about a lot of ideas today. What do you think is the most important thing for you to work on next?").
Demonstrate consistency and reliability	Follow through with plans and promises (e.g., "I wanted to call and give you the phone number for the housing help that we talked about on Tuesday.").
	Check in about previous events (e.g., "I was remembering last week when we spoke about how worried you are about Promise's weight. Did it work out for you to talk with the doctor?").
	Set and keep boundaries as needed (e.g., "I know you are having a hard time getting out to the store. Our agency won't let me give you a ride. Let's think together about other ways we can get you that help.").

It is important to note that human beings' needs for supportive relationships continue throughout their lives. A supportive relationship is one of the ways that people can learn new ideas and behaviors, even in adulthood. Research on the relationship needs of adults is vast, spanning every possible relationship, including those with romantic partners, friends, co-workers, and even spiritual beings. The next section addresses relationships that can form between parents and home visitors.

PARENT AND PROVIDER RELATIONSHIPS: THE WORKING ALLIANCE

Parenting is hard work. Home visitors know that the ability to respond to a baby in supportive ways does not come naturally to all parents and caregivers all of the time. For many reasons, even the best parents may sometimes struggle to give their babies the emotional supports they need. It is important to recognize that just as young children learn best when supported by positive relationships, parents need supportive relationships themselves to be their best with their babies (Edelman, 2004). As a result, for all professionals who support families with young children, their work includes a responsibility to develop a positive relationship with the parents in addition to a relationship with the child (Gomby, Larson, Lewit, & Behrman, 1993). The term *working alliance* (Bordin, 1979) describes the kind of relationship home visitors hope to form with parents: a collaborative partnership. When providers use their relationship with parents to effect change, it is called *relationship-based practice*. Learning through positive relationships is a pillar of home visitors' and other early intervention providers' work and is considered the best way to achieve changes in both parents and a child (Guralnick, 2001; Norman-Murch, 1996; Watson et al., 2014). At times, this responsibility to form a positive working relationship is an explicit goal of the home visiting program or practice approach. This is often the case for home visitors who work with highly vulnerable families, including those at risk for child abuse and neglect. However, even when an intervention is focused on infant development, the provider–parent relationship is frequently a central piece of the work.

In early intervention practice, it has been established that parents who trust and feel supported by the interventionist are more likely to become engaged and continue in the work needed to make changes for their children (Daro & Harding, 1999). Home visitors who act in ways that are described as empathetic, warm, understanding, and responsive toward parents facilitate positive changes in both parent and child behaviors (Popp & Wilcox, 2012). Furthermore, as Edelman (2004) noted, "the way that expertise is delivered becomes an essential aspect of the work" (p. 5).

Strategies to Support the Parent–Professional Relationship

What home visitor actions help parents feel supported? How do these actions build good relationships with parents? It is helpful to think about the parent behaviors that help a baby feel safe and supported:

Showing interest and attention

Accurately reading signals about needs

Responding to needs in a timely and sensitive way

Consider how these kinds of behaviors can be applied to provider–parent relationships. Paralleling the parent's actions toward babies, home visitors build relationships with parents when they demonstrate an active interest in the parent and the parent's needs. Next, home visitors need to accurately understand what parents are saying and showing with regards to their relationship needs. Finally, home visitors make efforts to respond in consistent and reliable

Table 1.3.   Child action and home visitor response

When the child...	The home visitor might say...
Lights up when the parent enters the room by looking toward the parent, smiling, and cooing	"Your baby really notices you when you come into the room. Look how he smiles and watches for you. He wants to be with you."
Hands the toy over to the parent	"She gave you the toy. How nice that she is learning from you to share and take turns."
Looks away from the parent while sitting in the car seat	"He seems to look away from you now. I wonder if he is telling us he needs a little break from the action. See how he looks back at you after a little while?"
Imitates the facial expressions and sounds of the parent during a simple interaction	"Look how she tries to copy what you say and how you look. You two are so expressive with each other. She likes to play with you."

ways to meet those needs. See Table 1.3 for examples of how a home visitor might respond to a child's actions to promote the parent–child relationship.

At the next visit, Deidre complains that Gage gets into everything now that he has started walking. She shares that he got into her purse and scattered her things all around the house; now she can't find her phone charger. Carolyn considers explaining that curiosity is a good thing and suggesting that Deidre make a plan to keep her purse out of Gage's reach. If Carolyn wants to show interest in Deidre's experience, what could she say instead?

Home visitors may question the emphasis on forming a parent–provider relationship and concern for the parent's experience. After all, we are infant and toddler specialists, so doesn't that mean we need to keep our focus on the babies? The term *parallel process* can help define what happens when home visitors support parents and why these parent–provider relationships are an important part of the work. Parallel process conveys the concept that events and experiences in one relationship may affect another relationship, either in the present or at a later time. This can occur in many ways. Any time you have a hard work day and then are irritable at home with your family, parallel process may be at work. On the other hand, you could feel your mood lightened after talking with a close friend over dinner and find yourself giving your server a big tip! Table 1.4 provides examples of parallel process in action. The concept of parallel process helps home visitors understand how their supportive actions will in turn help parents act in more supportive ways toward their young children. The support parents receive from a home visitor can be

Table 1.4. Parallel process in action

Situation	Relationship A	Relationship B	Parallel process
The parent is upset that the child is very hard to manage in public situations.	Lulu cries when she explains how active and aggressive her toddler Isabel is. She tells the home visitor, Sandra, "I am embarrassed all the time. She just runs and grabs things when we go to the store. I really don't know what to do." Sandra says with sympathy, "Wow, that's tough! I am sorry that things are so hard for you."	Lulu's shoulders relax when Sandra expresses concern for her. When Isabel comes close, Lulu reaches out to her daughter and rubs her back. She says, "I know it's hard for her when I am yelling all the time."	Sandra addressed Lulu's feelings. Lulu was able to think about how the situation was for her daughter once her own feelings were addressed.
The home visitor is frustrated when the family does not follow through with suggestions.	Desiree arrives for her supervision with Karl. She is visibly upset and immediately starts telling Karl about a phone call she just had with a family. "It's so ridiculous! I have given this family a million ideas for how to get their child signed up for child care. And every time, they just don't do it! I don't know why I even bother." Karl thinks to himself that he and Desiree have had this same conversation several times. He wonders why Desiree has not tried any of his suggestions to address the follow-through problem.	Karl says, "We have talked about this a few times. It can be frustrating to feel that your ideas are not being used." Desiree agrees and seems to calm down. "What can I do?" she asks. Karl says, "Maybe it's not about what you do or don't do. Can we think a little about what might be getting in the way for this family?"	The family did not follow through with the suggestions Desiree gave; similarly Desiree has not utilized suggestions that she has received from Karl. Instead of repeating his suggestions, Karl suggests stepping back to examine what might be getting in the way.

Table 1.5. Filling up the family's emotional tank

At the beginning of a visit	Geneel, the home visitor, began the session by saying, "Emma, I was thinking about you this week. I remembered how excited you were last time with Evelyn's progress and her interest in looking at pictures, pretending to eat the food in the pictures. You were going to practice 'reading' to her again this week. Tell me how it went."
During the visit	Bryan works with Evan's father, William, on interacting more with his baby. During a diaper change, William begins to play a game with Evan to keep him distracted. He flips him over from side to side in between caring for Evan. Evan squeals in delight. Bryan notes afterwards, "Evan really likes to play with you and you found a way to help him learn how to roll over at the same time you did a diaper change. That makes changing a diaper a pretty fun activity. Great idea!"
Summarizing the visit	At the end of the home visit, Susan summarizes what was discussed with Carol by saying, "You asked about finding a different place to live today. We talked about the different options and you decided to talk with your current landlord about changing apartments. We practiced what you might say, and you sounded pretty confident about how to ask for what you need. You really know what's best for your family and how to get that in a respectful way."
In between visits	Samantha sees her home visitor, Rebecca, in the hallway at the agency where the home visiting program is co-located with other agencies. Samantha has come for a WIC appointment and is early. She tells Rebecca in a quiet voice that she realized during the last visit that she could take Anthony to the local library to check out some books, since he seemed to have so much fun with the hard-paged picture books they used in the home visit. She had just gone to the library prior to the WIC appointment; she pulled out a canvas bag to show Rebecca the books they found. Rebecca comments, "What a great idea you had to get more books from the library so you and Anthony can read together!"

thought of as energy they can use to fuel their positive actions toward their own children (Webster-Stratton, 2001). Parents should fill up their emotional fuel tanks so they then have the responsive energy for their child's needs. See Table 1.5 for examples of home visitors supporting parents.

REFLECT: RECOGNIZING AND REPAIRING MISSTEPS IN HOME VISITING PRACTICE

Carolyn visits Deidre and Gage again after a few missed sessions. She wonders what led to the canceled sessions and whether she should mention this during the visit. When Deidre answers the door, she is unusually quiet and appears sad. Carolyn notices that Gage is in need of a new diaper and seems fussy. She is unsure if she should start by addressing Deidre's apparent distress, alert her to Gage's immediate need, or ask about the canceled visits.

Despite their best efforts, home visitors and other early intervention professionals may find it very difficult to establish a positive and productive relationship with some families. A block to forming a good relationship can come from the parent, the home visitor, or a combination of both. Barriers for parents (e.g., a mental health problem, competing demands) could cause them to not prioritize this particular relationship. Sometimes parents' own backgrounds and histories include so many relationship challenges that they are unfamiliar with the kind of relationship the home visitor is seeking to form. Box 1.1 lists examples of parent experiences that could block relationships between caregivers and home visitors. In fact, some parents may never have experienced the kind of support home visitors offer and cannot understand or even recognize what is being offered. For these families, the home visitor's

---

BOX 1.1   Parent Experiences that May Block Relationships with Home Visitors

- Home visitor reminds parent of someone in the parent's life that was difficult

- Losses in early childhood (e.g., parent's own parent died or left the family)

- Separation or divorce (e.g., of child's caregivers, grandparents)

- Domestic violence or other trauma

- Medical illness or disability

- Mental illness, including depression, personality disorder, and bipolar disorder

- Criminal histories; incarceration of parent or other family members

- Past or current alcohol and/or drug use or abuse

- Past experience with systems such as child welfare and other social programs

- Current worries about housing, food, health care, education, and other basic life needs

persistence and consistency can help. It may take a long time for the parent to begin to trust the provider and listen to the home visitor's guidance.

When establishing trust is an issue, a home visitor may want to create opportunities for the parent to learn that he or she can be counted on. For example, the home visitor can make plans to bring information or activities to the next session so the parent can see the home visitor follows through. The home visitor can make a point to bring up something that happened during previous sessions to demonstrate attention and memory about the family. A statement indicating the home visitor is thinking about the child and family outside of sessions can be a powerful indicator that the home visitor is holding the parent in mind even when not with the family. In Chapters 5 through 10, we explore these concepts more specifically, using the PAUSE framework to think about parent experiences that may get in the way of forming positive relationships with home visitors, and suggest practical responses and actions.

Carolyn brings a recipe for modeling dough to her visit with Deidre and Gage. She says, "I found this recipe for you. I remembered that you and Gage had a lot of fun with the modeling dough I brought last week, so I thought you might like to make some yourself." Deidre smiles and says, "Thanks! I bet my mom will like this. We used to make modeling dough when I was little." She puts the recipe in a folder on the table and sits with Carolyn to start the session.

Home visitors can also experience blocks in their ability to see or do what the parent needs. Home visitors may find the parent reminds them of another client that was hard to work with or perhaps someone else from their own past. The parent may have behaviors that the home visitor has trouble tolerating (e.g., discipline or housekeeping practices that make the home visitor feel uncomfortable). The home visitor may find it difficult to maintain a balance between attending to the parent's needs and those of the baby. At other times, a home visitor may simply feel worn out from all the families' needs. In some cases, the parent and the home visitor are just not a good match. For whatever reason, the practitioner won't always get it right. When mistakes or mismatches occur, the practitioner should acknowledge them and take steps to repair the relationship. These issues are discussed in greater detail in Chapter 10.

Carolyn is aware that Deidre once again canceled two sessions in a row and she has not returned several phone calls. She sends a text to ask if they can meet the following week, and Deidre agrees to the appointment. However, when Carolyn arrives, the grandmother is at home with

Gage and Deidre is not there. Carolyn wonders what could be happening. She decides to keep trying, and the following week, Deidre is present for the appointment. Carolyn says, "It's been a while since I saw you. I was wondering if everything is okay." Deidre says she is fine, but Carolyn still feels like something is not right. She says, "I am concerned that I might have done something to upset you. Is there anything we should talk about?" Deidre crosses her arms and says, "Well, I am kinda mad at you. You told my mom I am not feeding Gage right." Carolyn is surprised. She doesn't think she said that, but she says, "Wow. I am sorry; I really don't remember saying that. You and I have been talking a lot about how you are enjoying feeding Gage and watching him grow. Maybe we can figure out what happened." Deidre's shoulders relax and she seems calmer. She snuggles a little closer to Gage on the couch and helps him reach for a toy.

SUPPORTS TO HOME VISITORS: MENTORING, COACHING, AND SUPERVISION

One of the best ways for home visitors to gain perspective on their work with families, including their own responses, is to regularly seek support from someone more experienced in the work. This brings us to the third important relationship in home visiting or other early intervention work: the relationship between the home visitor and a supervisor. Whether it is called supervision, mentoring, consultation, facilitation, or coaching, consensus is growing that infant and family workers benefit from ongoing professional development experiences that come from this kind of relationship (Watson et al., 2014). Home visitors who regularly receive this kind of guidance feel supported, recognized, and better able to identify their own strengths and needs (Watson & Gatti, 2012). Supervision that includes reflection has been used for years in many settings, but research on the approach is relatively new (Tomlin, Weatherston, & Pavkov, 2014). There is growing interest in research showing how using reflective supervision will ultimately improve outcomes for parents and children (Watson et al., 2014).

There are many types of supervision and styles of supervisors (Heffron & Murch, 2010). Home visitors who have received unsupportive supervision may be skeptical about how reflective supervision might be different and more helpful. Supervision that follows a reflective model has been described as a relationship for learning (Shahmoon-Shanok, 2006). Just as consistency and reliability build trust in parent–child and parent–provider relationships, these attributes are required in the provider–supervisor relationship as well. Therefore, it is important that reflective supervision occurs regularly. This allows the home visitor to see the supervisor as a consistent source of support.

It is also important in this model that supervisors form a collaborative relationship with the supervisee. One way of demonstrating collaboration is avoiding an "expert" stance (i.e., the supervisor should not just tell the supervisee what to do). Using reflective supervision as a method for building skills, the supervisor guides the supervisee to consider many possibilities and to figure out his or her own solutions. The supervisor will accomplish this goal by using his or her own reflective skills and by promoting reflection by the supervisee. Use of reflective skills that encourage the supervisee to consider his or her own responses to the work is the third hallmark characteristic of this type of supervision. Such consideration will typically include attention to feelings (Fenichel, 1992).

Carolyn keeps thinking about her last few meetings with Deidre and Gage. When she prepares for her supervision time with Toby, she puts talking about Deidre's family at the top of her list. During the session, Carolyn shares the story about Deidre canceling sessions and the discussion they had. She tells Toby, "I know I did not say what Deidre thinks I said!" Toby listens carefully and says, "It's pretty upsetting to have someone say something about you that isn't true." "It sure is!" Carolyn replies. "I think I am doing the best I can with them. Deidre is really hard to read. I am never sure if she is really taking in what I say about Gage. Some days I wonder if I am wasting my time." Toby says, "It's hard to feel successful when you don't get a response or the response you get is negative." They continue to discuss this issue for several minutes. Then Toby says, "I remember you said that Gage is kind of a quiet baby. You mentioned that it's been hard for Deidre and Gage to connect. I wonder what it is like for you to see that struggle." Carolyn responds, "It's frustrating. Last month I even tried to get Deidre's mother to help prompt her a little with him. I asked her to praise Deidre whenever she sees her do something well." Carolyn stops suddenly. She looks thoughtful and says, "I guess that could explain why Deidre thinks I told her mom she wasn't feeding Gage right. She does try very hard, and I guess her being upset was really showing that she does listen and try things we talk about. She must feel bad when she tries but Gage doesn't respond right away."

Although there is less empirical research to support reflective supervision than there is for the other two relationships discussed, there is a good deal of clinical thinking and practical experiences that highlight the value of the practice (Tomlin et al., 2014). It is thought that reflective supervision provides many benefits to agencies, providers, and families. Individuals who participate in reflective supervision report feeling more supported and that they gain the ability to move from knowledge to practice. Agencies benefit when providers benefit. For example, when professionals feel supported, they may be more likely to stay on the job, reducing turnover. Less frequent turnover is a benefit for agencies, because it reduces hiring and training expenses. Participation in reflective supervision can also result in home visitors who can deliver better services, leading to better attainment of family goals and higher family satisfaction with services (Norman-Murch, 2005; Watson & Gatti, 2012; Weatherston, Kaplan-Estrin, & Goldberg, 2009).

WHAT'S NEXT?

In Chapter 2, we talk more about reflective skills, why they are important in early childhood work, and how they can be enhanced in ourselves and families.

TIPS FOR PRACTICE

▶ Attend and respond to parent needs to build relationships and increase parental sensitivity to their children.

▶ Monitor your own feelings about children, parents, and family situations. Awareness of your feelings can provide information about what is happening. Plus, when you are aware of feelings, you can better manage them in order to respond more effectively.

▶ Regularly seek supervision that includes reflection to build skills and to obtain support for the challenging feelings that home visiting brings.

KEY POINTS TO REMEMBER

▶ Early experiences have the potential for lifelong consequences, both positive and negative. Evidence for the long reach of these early experiences includes changes to brain structure and functioning.

▶ Effective home visitation services attend to the formation of positive relationships between parents and their young children (attachments), parents and home visitors (working alliance), and home visitors and supervisors (reflective supervision relationships).

▶ Current and past relationships and experiences within relationships are interconnected and have reciprocal effects through parallel process.

SUGGESTED FURTHER READING

Landy, S., & Menna, R. (2006). *Early intervention with multi-risk families: An integrative approach.* Baltimore, MD: Paul H. Brookes Publishing Co.

Looking Inside

Reflective Practice and Relationships for Learning

Families face multiple challenges—big and small—every day. Family life is incredibly complex, from making small choices such as what to have for dinner to facing major decisions such as what to do when an infant is born prematurely, a military parent is deployed overseas, or an eviction is looming. Home visitors and other early intervention workers often have as part of their duties a responsibility to support families in their coping and decision making. As part of this work, home visitors likely make multiple decisions of their own. Furthermore, home visitors, like anyone else, may have personal concerns and worries to hold in addition to those related to the work. Every day, home visitors too face many decisions. Whose needs are most important right now? What and who can wait? What action would be most helpful? It can be hard to figure out how to find balance between these competing needs.

At 4 p.m. on Friday, Theresa is struggling to complete paperwork due first thing Monday. She is scheduled for a volunteer shift at the high school concession stand at 6 p.m. Her phone rings, and she recognizes that the number belongs to a new family she started working with this week. Theresa realizes this family is just beginning to trust her and recognizes taking the call is a chance to build the relationship. Theresa feels her shoulders tense as she is aware of being pulled three ways: paperwork, volunteer responsibility, and the needs of a client.

For each person reading this scenario, the right answer to Theresa's dilemma may be different. Some may think Theresa should absolutely take the call and figure out the rest later. Others would let the call go to voicemail, continue to complete the paperwork, and then try to get to the high school as scheduled, leaving the needs of the parent to the next scheduled visit. Although it is not possible to identify one solution that is right or perfect for every person and every situation, home visitors can develop skills that improve our thinking and enhance our practices. One important way to develop the kinds of skills that help us feel competent in such situations is to encourage reflection.

REFLECTION AND MINDFULNESS

Reflection is one of many mindfulness skills that allow us to focus on the present and to be truly aware of our own experiences and responses to experiences, as well as those of other people. *Mindfulness* most often refers to giving full attention to what is happening in the moment, including being aware of thoughts, feelings, and sensations. Think about how it would feel to talk with someone who is practicing mindfulness by giving you his or her full attention. Now contrast that with how it might feel to talk with someone who is checking his or her phone, creating a grocery list, or just answering you automatically without thinking. Mindfulness is seen as a pathway to wellness; benefits to being more mindful are noted for health, relationship, and overall well-being (Siegel, 2013).

Taking time to reflect amid the pressures of competing demands can offer many practical benefits to the quality of the work, including better decision making, increased confidence or feelings of effectiveness, and enhanced ability to take in and use new information. In this way, skills in mindfulness benefit the practitioner and those with whom he or she partners. Taking time to reflect may be the most helpful when situations are most complex; paradoxically, this is also often the time when we feel most pressed to act. Home visiting must be counted among the fields in which complex situations are the norm. Each family brings its own set of novel situations, and home visitors must learn to adapt to a high level of uncertainty. Reflective skills can help the home visitor find ways to make sense of the situations that face many families (Weston, 2005). This practice can help the home visitor better integrate and make good use of the often competing emotional and cognitive processes inherent when addressing complex situations (Mann, Gordon, & MacLeod, 2009).

Theresa lets the phone go to voicemail while she organizes her thoughts. She recognizes that she is being pulled in several directions and that the resulting emotions are causing her to have trouble completing any task at all because she cannot concentrate. Theresa considers how her boss, fellow volunteers, and the new family may respond to any decisions she makes to prioritize these tasks. "I would never call someone this late on Friday unless it was an emergency," she thinks worriedly. Suddenly, Theresa realizes that she does not actually know the reason that the family called. The parents are so new to her that she has not yet learned their patterns. Theresa decides to text back to acknowledge she got the call and ask if calling in a few hours would be okay. A few minutes later, Theresa's phone pings with a response. The mother replies she had a quick question and adds it can wait for their meeting next week. Feeling relieved, Theresa continues with her original plan, glad that she did not let her own assumptions get in the way.

Use of reflection to increase self-awareness, improve self-regulation, and promote learning about self and others is not new. For example, from ancient times, many of the world's major religions have promoted forms of reflection, including meditation and prayer. Reflection is also used as a way of improving work in many professional fields, including education, business, health, and mental health (DiStefano, Gino, Pisano, & Staats, 2014; Mann et al., 2009; Watson, Gatti, Cox, Harrison, & Hennes, 2014). Among modern authors, Donald Schön (1983, 1987) is often credited with bringing the concept of reflection to the forefront for practitioners.

To be effective, home visitors need to demonstrate knowing (content knowledge) and doing (practical skills; Schön, 1987). Reflective skills help bridge the gap between knowing and doing, making information we learn in school or continuing education activities concrete and usable (Wesley & Buysse, 2001). We can use reflective skills in the moment when working with families or later when we look back and try to make sense of what happened (Schön, 1987). For example, we use reflection in action when we slow down, observe what is happening, and make purposeful decisions about what to do or say in a given situation during our work. Reflection on action is used when considering multiple aspects of experiences outside of the situation. This may occur during supervision with colleagues or by oneself during informal processing.

When done with others (colleagues or supervisors), reflection reduces provider isolation and increases felt support (Wesley & Buysse, 2001). Reflection supports movement from discussion (presenting and defending one's viewpoint) to dialogue in which individuals suspend their views, carefully listen, and learn about someone else's input (Wesley & Buysse, 2001).

Reflection as a practice contains the idea of reflection as a skill that can be taught, practiced, and honed (Mann et al., 2009). Reflection must occur regularly for one to become comfortable with the practice. Just as practice improves skills in other areas (e.g., music, athletics), time and repetition enhance our ability to reflect. In addition, an appropriate learning environment with mentors of specific skill sets is necessary (Mann et al., 2009). In the next section of this chapter, we will consider how the capacity for reflection develops, its benefits and role in home visiting fields, and how it can be enhanced.

REFLECTIVE FUNCTION OR CAPACITY

Reflection can be thought of as a skill and also as an innate capacity or function of human beings (Slade, 2005). As a social skill, reflection is understood to underlie many behaviors that are critical for smooth social interactions. Reflective functioning is complex and involves many components (Fonagy, Gergely, Jurist, & Target, 2002; Fonagy & Target, 1998):

1. The capacity to consider many different kinds of mental experiences in oneself and others

2. Appreciation that these mental states are connected to behaviors

3. Recognition that people can have mental states different from one's own state

4. Awareness that even if a person shares one's mental state, the behavior that results may or may not be the same (Slade, 2005, 2007)

The interconnected skills that make up reflective functioning allow us to better regulate our own emotions, understand what might be behind our own actions, and make decisions or choices about our future actions. For example, a person who is aware of a bias or attitude that he or she holds may set aside that bias and think about a situation more critically.

One component of reflective capacity is the awareness that one person's responses—including attitudes, beliefs, thoughts, feelings, and behaviors—in a specific situation are not necessarily the same as those of the next person. Awareness that other people have internal states can help explain another person's behaviors and provide information about how they view and respond to someone else. We may make decisions about how to present ourselves based on our predictions about how the person may respond. Overall, being able to think about mental states and behaviors of others increases understanding and informs decisions about potential action (Slade, 2005).

Candy is a home visitor in an early intervention program for infants and toddlers with developmental delays. She is preparing for a first visit with Tony, a 30-month-old with delays in speech and social behavior, and his mother, Sierra. As she drives up to the home, she sees a sign in the yard for a candidate for state senator. Candy knows this candidate is advocating some policies and viewpoints that are different from her own. She wonders what this sign means about the family's beliefs and how this might affect their work together.

Reflective capacity can also promote a better understanding of other people's experiences, making it one of the factors that allows relationships to be formed and kept (Slade, 2007). For someone on the receiving end, the experience of having another person show awareness of one's internal state can be powerful. Consider how it would feel to hear statements like these:

I was thinking about you today.

I got you a copy of this book because I know you like this author.

You must be so proud of your daughter.

I imagine this is a very hard time for you.

The connection between attending to someone's experience and the formation of a relationship may sound familiar. In Chapter 1, we discussed that a big part of how a baby's attachment to his or her caregiver forms is the parent's ability to be aware of and attend to the infant's experience and needs. A special case of reflective function is parental reflective functioning (PRF; Slade, 2005, 2007), which refers to a parent's ability to understand that his or her mental states and behaviors and those of his or her child are connected. PRF underpins the parent's ability to attend to the child's experience, which in turn is part of the prerequisites for the formation of a healthy attachment. PRF also has a role in the child's growth toward self-regulation of emotions and behaviors. Parents with more developed PRF may be better able to recognize that a child's mental states are connected to behavior, resulting in more sensitive responding to and scaffolding of positive child behaviors. Parents who act in ways that show recognition and understanding of a child's internal states help the child gain self-awareness. This can be done with actions and with words. Here are some examples:

Pamela wakes when she hears her 3-month-old daughter crying. Glancing at the clock, she realizes that the baby is probably hungry. As she picks up her daughter and prepares to feed her, she says, "Hello, little one. Mommy is here. Are you ready to eat?"

Gabby, an 18-month-old toddler, is running in the backyard while her father weeds the flower beds. She stumbles, falls, and begins crying loudly. Her father, Gino, sees that she has a skinned knee but is not seriously hurt. "Uh oh! That was scary. You hurt your knee but you will be okay," he says.

At the playground, 30-month-old Danny watches his friend Donita play with a light-up wand. After a couple of minutes, Danny grabs the wand, pulling it away from her. When Donita tries to take it back, Danny hits her. The children's mothers intervene, comforting both children. Danny's mother says, "You really wanted that wand, so you took it from Donita and you hit her." She goes on to explain to Danny that he hurt Donita and talks to him about taking turns.

Reflective skills fall along a continuum (Slade, 2007). For example, parents may have a range of responses when hearing results of early intervention screening that indicate serious delays. One parent might look upset but ask no questions and insist that she is perfectly fine. This parent could be having difficulty recognizing her own feelings. Another parent might yell at the provider, then apologize, saying, "I am sorry. What you said made me afraid and I took it out on you." This parent is able to recognize her own feelings and connect them with behaviors. Another parent may immediately begin to wonder about how to share this news with her spouse. This parent can think not only about her own responses to difficult news, but also about how another person might respond.

When people have higher levels of reflective functioning, they are often able to blend and connect thinking and feeling, which can lead to more functional and adaptive behavior overall (Mann, Gordon, & MacLeod, 2009; Slade, 2007). When people are aware of and able to manage their own thoughts, feelings, beliefs, and behavior, they are better able to think about what might be happening for another person, including their children. Some home visiting programs view increasing parental reflective skills as a way to improve child development and behavior. Often, a parent who has the ability to think about his or her own experience just needs a little help to apply that skill to his or her baby's experience. For these parents, home visitors can help by supporting the parent in accurately recognizing the child's experience and needs. Use of comments and questions that draw the parent's attention to the baby may be enough. See Table 2.1 for examples of the reflective functioning continuum.

Some parents with underdeveloped reflective skills might benefit from psychotherapy to improve recognition of their own internal states and ability to connect these internal states to behaviors. However, even families with high needs and parents with significant risk factors may benefit from non–mental-health providers who adopt methods to support the development of parental reflective skills (Slade, 2007).

Table 2.1. Reflective functioning continuum examples

Little reflective functioning	Some reflective functioning	Skilled reflective functioning
"Susie just turns off that TV to make me mad!"	"When Susie goes to the TV to turn it off, she looks at me first and grins."	"I noticed Susie turned off the TV to get my attention. She likes to read books with me."
"Jose is mean to other kids. He hits them hard."	"Jose hits other kids when he doesn't get his way or to get what he wants."	"Jose seems to use hitting as a form of communicating, but the other kids don't understand him. When I see him getting ready to hit, I ask him what he is feeling and if he needs help."

Source: Slade (2007).

Providers can draw on their own reflective skills to respond to parents in ways that support emotion and behavior regulation. In order to work with parents in this way, the home visitor is encouraged to make an effort to recognize the parents' general level of reflective skills. This does not mean that the home visitor will be doing psychotherapy. Rather, the home visitor can informally gauge how often a parent shows reflective behaviors, such as recognizing feelings and other internal states in others, demonstrating an understanding of links between his or her own mental states and behavior, and, especially, taking an interest in and trying to act in accordance with his or her child's experiences.

Getting a handle on the parent's general skill level can help the home visitor zone in on the best port of entry for a parent, select interventions that are most effective, and avoid beginning at a level that a parent cannot understand or tolerate (Slade, 2007). For example, Mary is a home visitor who assumes that all the parents she serves have high levels of reflective skills and are able to easily consider their babies' feelings and needs. She prides herself on putting needs of babies ahead of adults. Some of Mary's families do well with this approach, but others struggle. One parent, Melissa, finds Mary's talk about babies' emotional needs confusing. Melissa thinks Mary is making things too complicated; she doesn't believe that babies need much more than regular feedings and dry diapers. Another parent, Marcus, starts feeling uncomfortable when Mary talks about what is happening inside his baby. It feels like too much to have to think about! Eventually, Mary may find that the parents like Melissa and Marcus become disengaged or even drop out of the program because they are not relating to Mary's methods (Barak, Spielberger, & Gitlow, 2014). If Mary can more accurately assess Melissa's and Marcus' abilities to be reflective and modify her ways of supporting them, everyone may experience increased success and satisfaction. In fact, by better understanding their abilities to be reflective and starting where they are, there is increased opportunity for Mary to help Melissa and Marcus expand their reflective capacities, which may ultimately enhance their parenting experiences. Box 2.1 summarizes points a home visitor might consider when thinking about a caregiver's reflective functioning capacity.

We have discussed how the home visitor can model a supportive relationship by attending to the parent's experience first and gradually shifting to supporting the parent in attending to the baby's experience. Frequent statements that connect feelings and other mental states with behaviors are helpful (Slade, 2007). For example, the home visitor could say, "She's reaching for your phone. I wonder if she wants to see what you are doing." When a parent has little or very limited reflective skill, the home visitor can often help by modeling or demonstrating reflective behaviors. This can include statements that describe one's own inner states or a statement that shows interest in the parent's inner state. For example, the home visitor might say, "So the baby is not sleeping well. You must be so tired."

Beginning levels of reflective skill may include some recognition that internal states (i.e., thoughts, feelings, attitudes) are connected to behavior. Often, however, the person still needs help to accurately recognize the internal state of him- or herself or others. Home visitors could capitalize on feelings as they occur normally in the course of family life to build parent skills. Many routine parenting activities could lead to negative feelings, such as anger or frustration. Many parents are able to manage those feelings and may even be able to use coping strategies such as humor to attenuate them. For example, virtually every parent has had the experience of changing a baby only to have the baby immediately need changing again; and sometimes the parent then needs changing as well! A parent with well-developed reflective skills is likely to take this in stride, recognizing that it is the sort of thing that a baby cannot

---

BOX 2.1. Parent or Caregiver Reflective Functioning Capacity

- Recognize parent level of reflective functioning.

- Work from that level.

- Model or demonstrate reflective skills.

- Make comments or ask questions that encourage parents to wonder about the child's experiences.

- Make good use of feelings that happen in a real-life situation.

- Demonstrate in concrete ways that the provider is holding the parent in mind.

Source: Slade (2007).

help and viewing it as a minor nuisance. In contrast, parents with less developed reflective skills might view this as the baby doing something on purpose to upset them. A parent with a low level of awareness of his or her own inner state might handle the baby roughly without recognizing his or her own feelings of frustration. A home visitor could name the parent's possible feelings, help set them into context as normal, and support the parent in coping. In this example, the home visitor could say, "Oh dear, after you just got her cleaned up, she spit up on the new outfit! That can be so frustrating." Statements like these not only support reflection but may also lead to deeper conversation between the parent and home visitor.

WHAT'S NEXT?

In Chapter 3, we describe the PAUSE approach, which uses both relationship-based practice and other reflective methods to build a foundation of skills. These skills can be used to address the common difficult challenges in home visiting and other early intervention work with families with very young children.

TIPS FOR PRACTICE

▶ Learn to pay attention to inner experiences such as beliefs, attitudes, and emotions—the baby's, the parents', and your own.

▶ When you feel strong emotions, such as anger or worry, give yourself time, slow down, and take a breath. Try to avoid pushing for a solution or forcing an action.

▶ Be an example of how to recognize and respond to emotions. Talk about your response to what a parent said and what you imagine the parent or baby might be experiencing.

KEY POINTS TO REMEMBER

▶ Reflective capacity or functioning is the ability to think about mental states or inner experiences in oneself and others, including one's children, and how those mental states are connected to behaviors.

▶ Reflection is a mindfulness skill that allows one to pause, slow down, and consider situations from many angles before acting; integrate thinking and feeling in a way that is regulating; develop new insights and ideas; and evaluate actions once taken.

▶ Both reflective capacity or functioning and reflection can be developed and enhanced through supportive relationships and practice.

SUGGESTED FURTHER READING

Siegel, D., & Hartzell, M. (2014). *Parenting from the inside out: How a deeper self-understanding can help you raise children who thrive* (10th anniversary ed.). New York, NY: Penguin.

PAUSE—
A Problem-Solving Framework
Blending Relationship and Reflective Skills

Carmen arrives for a scheduled home visit with Charley, a 15-month-old girl with developmental delays and multiple medical issues connected to prematurity. Her mother, Frances, is near tears. She tells Carmen that Charley has been "cranky" and no one is getting any sleep. Furthermore, Charley is so irritable that she has started hitting her mother when she tries to do anything with her. On cue, Charley smacks Frances and they both burst into tears.

Working with families of young children is complex and can be messy. Every family and child is different, and methods that worked perfectly with one family may be ineffective or even an utter disaster with the next. Furthermore, every home visit, even with a family that one knows well, is different from the last. Many families struggle with serious issues, including poverty, domestic violence, and serious health needs of their children. These concerns can and may draw home visitors' attention away from our role or purpose with a family (Bernstein & Edwards, 2012).

How do we stay focused on our work when families come with so many challenges? Although there are no "tried and true" recipes guaranteed to work in all situations, there are some ways of thinking and acting that set the stage for flexible partnering and effective problem solving. In the first two chapters, we have separately discussed the benefits of using relationship-based and reflective practice approaches when working with very young children and

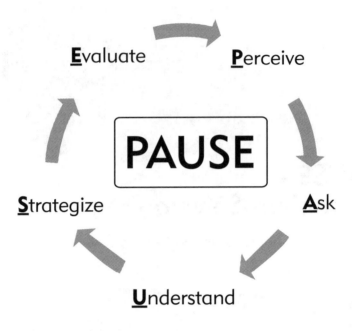

Figure 3.1. The PAUSE framework overview.

their families. Next, we discuss how these two methods can be integrated. In this chapter, we explain the PAUSE method to explore a way of thinking about work with families that is grounded in relationship and that encourages reflection on the part of the provider and the parents. *PAUSE* is an acronym for a cycle of five steps: Perceive, Ask, Understand, Strategize, and Evaluate (see Figure 3.1).

As discussed in previous chapters, relationship-based practices and reflective skills complement each other and are critical to forming and maintaining all kinds of relationships. Reflective and relationship-based skills are also used in a specific type of professional development called *reflective supervision* (Watson et al., 2014). Use of reflective practice methods within a supportive supervisory relationship can help home visitors avoid getting lost in the weeds of complicated family life, thus increasing the home visitor's ability to focus on building the parent–child relationship (Bernstein & Edwards, 2012). This chapter discusses how to blend these approaches through a process providers can use to work with families about their concerns. The process organizes thinking about the behavior or issue, helps providers respond appropriately and effectively, and uses reflection to assess the experience. The five main components of the PAUSE process are as follows:

1. *Perceive:* observe and listen.

2. *Ask* questions to learn more about what is happening.

3. *Understand* each participant's experience or viewpoint.

4. *Strategize:* select and take actions.

5. *Evaluate* the outcomes using reflective processes.

The PAUSE Worksheet provides a way for the home visitor to document his or her thoughts about the child and family in order to work through challenging situations and discuss them with a supervisor. A blank copy of the PAUSE Worksheet can be found in Appendix 3A. This and following chapters include vignettes and sample completed PAUSE Worksheets. These materials illustrate how to use the PAUSE Worksheet in a variety of situations home visitors may face. First, let's explore each of the PAUSE components in more detail.

PERCEIVE: OBSERVE AND LISTEN

Carmen can see that Frances is overwhelmed with Charley's difficult behavior. She is aware that these issues have been happening for a while, and she has already formed some ideas about what might help. Carmen thinks how easy it would be to just take Charley herself and model an age-appropriate time-out. After that, she could sit down with Frances and teach her how to implement a better sleep schedule.

The PAUSE process begins with learning more about the situation by observing, listening, and asking questions. As home visitors slow down and learn more, they may see things are not as they appear at first. Observing and listening are not passive behaviors, and they are not as easy as they may seem. Giving full attention is a skill that takes time and practice. Consider how the response "I'm fine" could sound in these two situations:

Situation 1: Betty slightly trips when going upstairs to work. When her co-worker walking behind her asks if she is okay, Betty laughs and says, "I'm fine; it's just Monday."

Situation 2: Mark comes home from work later than expected; he wasn't able to call because his phone died. As he apologizes for not being home to help get their children to bed, his wife, Kayla, interrupts him, saying, "I'm fine."

Clearly the person in the first situation actually seems to be just fine, but the person in the second scenario may not be. The appropriate response to each situation is likely to be very different. For example, in the first scenario, joining Betty in laughing about the situation would be acceptable. Laughing in the second situation, however, is most likely unwise. Listening includes attention to what is said and how it is said (Weatherston, 2000). Slowing down and listening with care also lets one notice and wonder what is *not* said. For example, in some cases, the speaker may avoid a seemingly critical topic. The home visitor may be left to wonder about that topic and its absence from the conversation. Consider the following two examples:

Kara, a developmental specialist in an early intervention program, meets with a family for an evaluation. The other team members described their concerns for the child's "behavior" and the child's mother describes him as "anxious." Kara notices immediately that the child has very repetitive speech, makes brief eye contact, and walks on his toes. She knows these are characteristics of autism, but because that wasn't in her paperwork, she is not sure if she should mention this.

Beatrice arrives for a home visit with Juliette and her infant son, Alexander. She notices that Juliette has a cast and asks, "Are you okay?" Juliette says she is okay and begins to tell Beatrice a story about Alexander taking steps. Beatrice feels concerned but does not feel comfortable pressing for more information.

Observation is a great partner to listening. Much can be learned by what is seen. For example, eye contact, facial expressions, and body language may add a good deal of information about the emotional state of the speaker. Incongruence between body language and words should prompt the observer to wonder. Consider how the home visitor might respond to this mother if she listened only to her words rather than attending to both the words and how they were said:

Katarina held her newborn baby, Heidi, loosely across her lap. The home visitor expressed excitement about seeing the baby for the first time and asked if Katarina was enjoying motherhood. Katarina looked away and sighed. After a long moment, she said, "It's pretty great, I guess."

ASK QUESTIONS TO LEARN MORE ABOUT WHAT IS HAPPENING

In addition to careful listening and observation, information gathering includes asking the right questions (Heffron & Murch, 2010). Different questions are useful at different times. It is often productive to begin with open questions that are conveyed in a simple and supportive manner. Once the provider has the big picture or a general direction, more specific questions can be asked to clarify the situation. It takes practice, but providers can learn to respond and ask questions that open up a discussion instead of narrowing it too soon. Examples of these types of questions or statements include those that express interest or concern, encourage the responder to think about his or her own or other's experiences, and include an offer to explore an issue together. Here are a few examples of responses that both acknowledge how a person might be feeling and invite more discussion:

I imagine that was difficult for you.

Wow, that must have been an amazing experience!

How is it for you when Jan has trouble sleeping?

I wonder what it was like for your daughter when your family moved.

Questions that start a discussion can be paired with more specific follow-up questions (Green & Palfrey, 2000). Using an answer as a springboard is a great way to continue to expand the conversation while encouraging the person to give additional information or think about the issue in more detail. In addition, by repeating all or part of the conversational partner's comment, understanding can be confirmed and interest demonstrated:

I was a little confused about the therapy Clara is receiving. How often is that happening?

Could you tell me more about your work schedule?

You mentioned you have been concerned about Jon's coughing. What things have been tried so far to help him?

I was thinking about how tired you said you feel. It made me wonder if you have seen your doctor.

Questions that curtail discussion should be used sparingly or avoided (Heffron & Murch, 2010; Sattler, 1998). Often, these types of questions are not really questions at all. For example, a forced-choice question limits the answers that a person can give. The options offered may not be an answer the parent wants to give. Questions that can be answered with "yes" or "no" can be useful for gathering specific information, but they may feel judgmental and leave out the opportunity for expanded information. Some statements can also shut off discussion or indicate that the provider has made an assumption that the family member may not feel comfortable correcting. Examples of questions or responses to avoid include the following:

Forced choice

Do you think the problem with Emmanuel's sleep is your work schedule or the bedtime routine?

Are you using time out or redirection for discipline?

Yes-or-no questions

> Are you giving Abdul enough sleep time? (Compare: How has Abdul been sleeping?)
>
> Are you following your physical therapist's recommendations? (Compare: What suggestions has the physical therapist offered that you think could help?)

Presumptive statements

> I am sure you are getting Cassidy's shots on schedule.
>
> No one is playing violent video games when the children are around, right?

UNDERSTAND EACH PARTICIPANT'S EXPERIENCE OR VIEWPOINT

We have emphasized the importance of relationships as a core underpinning of work with families. In order for relationships to function smoothly, each person's experience or perspective should be considered. It is important to recognize that the parent, the baby, and the home visitor may each view the situation differently. Therefore, one of the responsibilities of a provider taking this approach is to monitor and ensure that all voices are represented (Pawl, 2000), including the baby, the parents, and the provider. The home visitor should encourage the parent to tell the story from his or her perspective, gently prompt attention to the baby's experience, and share his or her own observations with care. The skills reviewed earlier, including observing, listening, and asking helpful questions, can be applied to the quest to learn about the perspectives of all the participants, including the babies. Spending this time gathering information assists the home visitor to better understand not only the situation at hand, but also how that situation is being received or experienced by each participant. This additional information, in turn, leads to a decision about the most effective port of entry, or best starting point, for intervention at that moment. In the following examples, briefly consider each participant:

Home Visitor: Thinking about one's own perspective may seem redundant or even out of place in this discussion. However, because each person brings biases, beliefs, attitudes, and preferences to every situation, it is necessary to consider the provider's perspective along with those of family members. The home visitor should recognize that his or her own past experiences and perspectives affect each new experience; what is seen and heard, how the behaviors of others are interpreted, and what choices are made about how to respond. It is not possible or even desirable to have no personal history or to never have opinions! Home visitors have their own set of attitudes or beliefs and must attend to their effect on their work with families (Heffron, Ivins, & Weston, 2005).

Parent: A central facet of home visiting work is attending to the parent's needs as a way of developing the parent's skills (Bernstein & Edwards, 2012). Even when the focus of the home visit is the baby's safety or development, gaining the parent's buy-in is needed; therefore, a good deal of home visiting involves forming a relationship with parents and encouraging change (Weatherston, 2005). For example, the home visitor might be tasked with instructing parents on child development, implementing a specific therapy technique, or supporting the parents in the completion of court required tasks. In order for the home visitor to implement this part of the work effectively, he or she must be able to read and respond to the parent's reactions to his or her suggestions and efforts. These efforts on the part of the provider lead to "synchrony" in the parent and home visitor relationship, which in turn is connected to parental feelings of competence and increased responsiveness to the child (Popp & Wilcox, 2012).

Baby: Although all three parties are important, it may be most critical to avoid losing sight of the baby's experience. Because babies are unable to speak for themselves, their voices can easily be ignored or drowned out by the needs of adults. Therefore, remembering to ask "what about the baby?" (Weatherston, 2001, 2005) is an important responsibility of the home visitor and a critical part of making real progress with families. The provider's ability to keep the baby in mind will help in many ways, both directly and indirectly. Babies are helped directly when their needs are seen and attended to. Babies are helped indirectly when the home visitor provides a good model for the parent of how to consider the infant's experience.

Poised to gather up Charley and demonstrate a time out, Carmen suddenly stops. Trusting her observations, she realizes that this might not be a good time for teaching, given that both mother and daughter are tired and upset. Furthermore, as Carmen reflects that Frances identified lack of sleep as a primary problem, she questions her initial impulse to solve the problem with a behavior technique. Instead of springing into action, Carmen starts with sympathy and a demonstration that she is listening, saying, "You poor guys! What a hard time you are both having. What can I do to help?"

Later in the visit, when both Frances and Charley are calmer, Carmen is able to ask a few questions. She discovers that Frances has recently increased her work hours, resulting in a corresponding increase in the amount of time that Charley spends in child care. Carmen wonders if this change is the source of both Charley's difficult behavior and Frances' weariness. At the same time, Carmen knows this is a resilient family, so she is confident that they will adjust in time. When Frances admits that she is tired, Carmen says, "I wonder if Charley is a little tired too." Frances snuggles Charley close and says, "I guess we both need a little more time to adjust to the new schedule." Carmen has been successful in two ways: supporting Frances and Charley directly and helping Frances consider Charley's experience. These two interventions may be enough to help this family.

STRATEGIZE: SELECT AND TAKE ACTIONS

In the first three steps of the PAUSE method, information that increases one's understanding of the situation or problem is gathered. As part of this understanding, multiple perspectives should be considered. As the home visitor observes, listens, and asks questions in dialogue with the parent, a variety of possible action steps will emerge. Together with the parent, the home visitor will choose some steps to try. As next steps are negotiated, consider together what results would be satisfactory.

Now let's explore the PAUSE Worksheet, which can be used to pull together thoughts, feelings, and actions as reflection on interactions takes place (see Appendix 3A). The PAUSE Worksheet is intended to allow the home visitor to organize the information that has been gathered and to capture what is happening from both the parent or caregiver and the home visitor perspective. In the first section of the worksheet, the home visitor reflects on the parent's question or issue and considers how both the parent and the home visitor him- or herself view the identified concern. Next, the home visitor is encouraged to clarify what is happening. In this second section, the home visitor reflects on questions he or she could ask to gather more information. In the third section, the home visitor considers possible reasons why the behavior or situation is occurring, again from the parent or caregiver and home visitor perspectives, but also from the child's perspective. This encourages the home visitor to reflect on all of the potential relationship dynamics we have discussed. Finally, the home visitor is encouraged to identify some possible responses or solutions with criteria to evaluate progress and success.

Consider how Carmen could use the PAUSE Worksheet format to capture her experience with Charley and Frances. For example, as Carmen later uses this information in reflective supervision, she may notice her own reactions and her urges to "fix" the problem. She may also note any changes in the behaviors of Frances and Charley when she was more reflective and patient, compared to when she was direct. This information can help Carmen to have a better understanding of the needs that Frances and Charley each present. Carmen would be able to use the PAUSE Worksheet to document any plans that she and Frances co-create to address the issues as they have identified them. Similarly, the worksheet can help Carmen and Frances discuss the effectiveness of the strategies they tried. A sample completed PAUSE

Worksheet illustrating Carmen's experience with this family can be found in Figure 3.2.

A second form, the Provider Reflection Worksheet (Appendix 3B), is intended for use in reflection on action or after the interaction with the family is complete. The goal of this set of questions is to help the home visitor consider actions to improve skills as well as to identify potential issues to discuss in reflective supervision. This is a key part of the process, as the home visitor will gain great insights, both from the self-reflection component of completing this process and from discussing it with a supervisor. Figure 3.3 illustrates Carmen's self-reflection of her work with Charley and Frances and how she might plan for future sessions with this family.

EVALUATE THE OUTCOMES USING REFLECTIVE PROCESSES

Because family life is often complex and sometimes stressful, it is not unusual for workers who support families to feel the stress themselves. Reflecting on the choices made in the work provides a way for the home visitor to gain support, evaluate efforts, and engage in continuous learning and growth. Being able to step back and reflect on the work is valuable, whether done on one's own or, preferably, within a supervision or consulting relationship. Therefore, part of taking action is reflecting back on that action in an evaluative way. In the vignettes, Carmen provided support and empathy to Frances and Charley. She was later able to successfully direct Frances' attention to Charley's experience of absence from her mother while in child care. However, things could have gone differently. Imagine the following variation in the vignette.

Frances responds to Carmen's question about her new work schedule by snapping, "It's fine. I have to do it." Undeterred, Carmen pursues her concern for the child by asking, "I wonder how it's been for Charley to be at child care longer hours?" Frances, now clearly irritated, replies, "Well, we are both stuck, aren't we?" The visit ends shortly after this exchange.

In this version, Carmen missed Frances' tone and pursued her own agenda of highlighting Charley's experience. Later, Carmen may reflect that the sympathy and empathy offered at the beginning were more effective and that she jumped too quickly from that strategy, resulting in an ineffective and unsatisfying end to the session. She may plan to stay longer with Frances' perspective next time.

So far, we have discussed how a provider can form an initial or on-the-spot response and then evaluate the effectiveness of that effort in reflection

PAUSE WORKSHEET ━━━━━━━━━ pause

Child: Charley _____ Date: 1/20/15 _____

Parent: Frances _____ Provider: Carmen _____

PERCEIVE—Explore what is happening.

Parent/caregiver perspective:	*Provider perspective:*
Charley is misbehaving/hitting. Frances is frustrated with Charley's behavior. No one is getting sleep.	Charley is tired, probably overtired. Frances is struggling with what action to take. Maybe a time-out is needed? Develop a sleep schedule?

ASK—Clarify what is happening.

Starting with the parent/caregiver's priorities and concerns, ask more detailed/specific questions to clarify what is happening.

Ask Frances about changes in family's routine.

Ask when behavior changed and what was happening with Charley.

What strategies have been tried to help the family get more sleep?

UNDERSTAND—Explore why it is happening.

With the parent/caregiver, explore explanations for what is happening. Consider possible explanations that include the environment, the child, and the parent. Listen and observe closely as you explore the situation in conversation with the family.

Parent/caregiver perspective:	*Provider perspective:*	*Child's perspective:*
Frances changed her work schedule to include more hours. Charley is in child care longer hours each day.	I want to support this mom to deal with Charley's behavior. My first instinct is to take over and model a time-out. When I step back a	Charley is likely adjusting to a new schedule. Her sleep patterns have been disrupted. She is trying to tell her mom this

(continued)

Figure 3.2. Carmen's PAUSE Worksheet for Charley and Frances.

Figure 3.2.   *(continued)*

PAUSE WORKSHEET *(continued)*

UNDERSTAND *(continued)*

Parent/caregiver perspective:	Provider perspective:	Child's perspective:
Frances feels frustrated at not having as much time with Charley and certainly does not like this behavior.	moment, I wonder what might be behind this new behavior and ask some questions. Maybe this mom's change in schedule is more disruptive than I realized and they need some time to adjust.	through her behavior. Since she can't say, "I'm tired and I miss you at the end of a long day," she instead is irritable and sometimes hits. She wants some mommy time and to rest.

STRATEGIZE and **EVALUATE**—Identify possible responses/solutions.

1. Solution/action to try:	How will we know if it works?
Hold off on giving problem solving/ giving advice. Instead, respond to the parent's emotion about the situation.	Frances may seem calm or report feeling less frustrated. Frances may be more attentive to Charley. Charley's behavior will improve.
	When will we evaluate if it works?
	Monitor Frances' attentiveness and Charley's behaviors during the next session.

2. Solution/action to try:	How will we know if it works?
Acknowledge the change in the family schedule and suggest everyone needs some time to adjust. If the situation does not improve, suggest exploring a sleep schedule to help everyone get better rest.	A family report of improved sleep will indicate success.
	When will we evaluate if it works?
	We'll evaluate this at each session.

PROVIDER REFLECTION WORKSHEET

Child: Charley   Date: 1-20-15

Parent: Frances

Provider: Carmen

1. How did I follow the parent's lead to learn what is most pressing or important to the family?	I was able to stop myself from just stepping in and taking over the situation. But it was so challenging, and I could see it was bothering Frances. Yet I was able to understand her main concern was getting back to "normal" and getting some much-needed rest.
2. How did I ask clarifying questions to help me understand the problem better?	After realizing Frances was exhausted, I said "You poor guys! What a hard time you are both having. What can I do to help?"
3. How did I provide information that may help the family better understand the child's behavior?	I think I was able to help Frances see that, given the change in the family's schedule, they needed some time to adjust and Charley's behavior might be a reflection of the stress the family is experiencing.

(continued)

Figure 3.3. Carmen's Provider Reflection Worksheet for Charley and Frances.

Figure 3.3. *(continued)*

PROVIDER REFLECTION WORKSHEET *(continued)*

4. *How did I engage the family to develop a response that may include a strategy to try, a resource to use, or more information to increase understanding?*	I decided to wait to offer strategies about sleep schedules or behavior management, in order to see whether, with a little time, they might adjust to the new schedule.
5. *How did I provide support and emotional containment if needed?*	I think my acknowledgment of how hard this is helped Frances see the issue was about being tired and not something more serious. I noticed they both snuggled together a bit when Frances calmed down.
6. *How do I plan to follow up on promised actions to maintain trust?*	I will explore some sleep schedule resources in case they are still struggling, and I have some behavior management techniques in mind if needed.
7. *What do I want to discuss in reflective supervision to improve my practice and outcomes with this child and family?*	I am curious why I was so quick to want to just take control and model a time-out instead of really listening to this mother. How can I slow myself down in these situations?

later. Sometimes, that simple strategy will be enough to resolve the issue. In some cases, the provider may realize that a longer term solution is needed to resolve the problem. This could mean many things, ranging from helping the family obtain additional concrete resources to identifying others that can help. In the vignettes, Carmen's strategy of supporting Frances to consider Charley's perspective may be enough. Other simple solutions could include problem solving with Frances to identify someone who can watch Charley while she gets some rest or checking with the child care provider to look for solutions to improve Charley's adjustment.

Considering the scenario with Carmen and all of the possible variations, it seems clear that home visitors will benefit from taking time to wonder and reflect about what might be happening with a family. Regardless of practitioners' best intentions and efforts, they will encounter some situations or events that are beyond their scope of practice. Part of reflection may need to include reframing one's understanding of the child, family, or situation. In the vignettes, Carmen knows that Frances has increased her work hours and assumes that this was her choice. However, suppose that she does not know that Frances needed more income because her partner, Thomas, has left her and Charley and the family is on the verge of being evicted. If she had this additional information, Carmen might have a very different perspective and response. The questions she asks, information she needs to gather, and other helpers and resources that may be needed may change dramatically.

COMMON CHALLENGING ISSUES

Next, we address a few of the more common but challenging issues that home visitors might encounter with families and suggest helpful responses. In all of the scenarios presented so far, the home visitor and the family have a relationship that includes willingness to engage and work together. However, as with any approach, there will be times when it does not work smoothly. For example, there may be times when a parent does not respond or seems unwilling to participate in the dialogue. Possible explanations are virtually infinite, but might include: it's too soon in the relationship for the discussion, the parent is preoccupied with something else, or the parent does not think the home visitor will be able to help. No matter the reason, resist the urge to keep pushing a perspective! Stay patient, remain available but not intrusive, and continue to build the relationship (Beeber & Canuso, 2012).

Other times, the home visitor may find that his or her sympathetic ear has unleashed a torrent of emotions or words. Although a parent may benefit from venting emotions, the home visitor may find this to be overwhelming and may worry that it is unproductive. It would be understandable for the home visitor to try to set limits, including ignoring the emotional flood and trying to turn the conversation to a more concrete level. However, setting a limit alone is unlikely to have the desired response. If this is an infrequent occurrence, it may be fine to allow the venting to proceed. However, if the emotional flood continues, the home visitor may need to address it directly. Ask the parent if it would be okay to step back and revisit the home visitor's role and function with the family. Directly discuss the parent's apparent need to vent emotions and ask who else is able to provide this role and support.

Another common problem for the home visitor is a parent who does not follow through with any plan that is made. Sometimes this is obvious from the beginning, as the parent greets every suggestion with "yes, but" or informs the provider that his or her ideas will not work. Other parents appear to agree with all suggestions but never actually try them. Again, the issue may be timing, so patience and persistence may be appropriate. If the situation continues, a direct approach may be needed. The home visitor can identify what he or she observes and ask the parent to talk about what is happening. Presenting the issue as something to be discussed and better understood can prevent the parent from feeling accused. Instead, the home visitor conveys the sense of interest and collaborative problem solving.

We have discussed the importance of trying to understand how the family sees various issues or concerns. Understanding a parent's perspective is useful because it informs strategies that may be helpful. Also, from a parallel process perspective, the provider's efforts to understand the parent's experience are likely to help the parent's ability to take his or her child's perspective. There are likely times when it is extremely difficult to come to a shared understanding of the situation. Some parents may have very strong beliefs about children in general or about a specific child. Acknowledging the difference of opinion and asking the parent to share more about his or her views can be useful and set the stage for gently challenging the parent's view. By asking the parent to explain his or her views and ideas, the home visitor can better understand the source of the beliefs and then carefully offer other perspectives. Helping the parent to name his or her own beliefs and begin to understand how these views connect to behavior is an important reflective skill that allows perspective taking. Consider how Bob, a physical therapist, uses this strategy in a home visit.

Bob, a physical therapist in an early intervention home program, is completing paperwork at the end of a session with Tom and his daughter, Cristy. Suddenly, Cristy pulls over a large plant, spilling dirt everywhere. Tom begins shouting, grabs Cristy, and threatens to spank her. Bob is aware that Tom believes in spanking, but he has never witnessed him doing it and they have never spoken about it in detail. Bob freezes and considers his options: gather his things quickly and leave or address what is happening. Tom, noticing Bob's expression, says, "I know you all think I should not spank her. But just look what she does!" Bob answers carefully, "I see this is a big mess and that you are pretty upset. And it's true I am not in favor of spanking. But I would be willing to hear how you think spanking would help."

There is a long pause. Finally, Tom says, "My dad spanked me and I turned out just fine. I want Cristy to learn that there are some things that aren't allowed, like making a big mess." Bob says, "Yes, I agree that kids need some limits and they need parents to teach them what they should and should not do. I wonder what Cristy learns from spankings?"

In this example, the PT showed respect by asking to learn more about the parent's beliefs and parenting practices. This method ultimately challenged the parent's beliefs indirectly, by helping the father to think about his ideas about parenting more critically. Next steps in this discussion could include talking about what Cristy might have been trying to do with the plant and what other ways there could be to teach her not to make a mess.

REFLECTING ON REFLECTION

When faced with a family that is struggling, a provider may often feel a "press" (pressure) to offer a solution or fix the problem quickly (Heffron et al., 2005). It is hard to maintain the discipline needed to think broadly when the situation seems to call for action. Although it may not be appropriate or possible to solve every problem or alleviate every difficult situation, we often can provide some relief through listening, offering empathy, or asking a question that opens up discussion.

In Chapter 2, we discussed a variety of concepts related to reflective practice. Using reflection in our partnerships with young children and families sounds simple, but it takes a good deal of practice to be able to apply these skills in the moment. Performing skills such as observing, listening, and asking questions also takes time; it can be hard to remain patient and refrain from taking what may feel like needed steps to solve a problem. This may be especially likely for early childhood professionals who are often action-oriented people: those who are more comfortable with doing than talking about doing. They may feel proud of their ability to "get 'er done" or may have been praised for a "take charge" attitude. Parents, used to professionals working from other frameworks, may seem to want professionals to take over. At other times, a situation may seem so concerning that the home visitor feels strong internal pressure to take action based on his or her perception of the family's needs or own need to resolve a situation that feels intolerable (Heffron et al., 2005). This "press," though normal to feel, can be extremely hard to resist!

Although it is true that there are times when being able to solve problems and "just do it" is called for, there are many other times when a different approach may be more effective in the long run. One important outcome of taking time to slow down and deepen one's thinking is that it may prevent conclusions that lead to hurtful actions. With a wondering stance, many possible explanations for what is happening are allowed and time for considering many possibilities emerges. Multiple alternatives can be considered and judgment can be suspended until more information has been gathered. As Jeree Pawl once said, "Don't just do something, stand there and pay attention!" (Pawl & St. John, 1998, p. 7). Because the action needed may be different than it originally appeared, slowing down and asking questions can result in a more accurate picture, leading to better solutions.

In some situations, there is no action that is appropriate for the home visitor to take, regardless of how much information is collected. Perhaps the appropriate action may be to seek help from professionals other than the home visitor, such as a mental health or child welfare worker. At other times, instead of taking direct action or enlisting action from others, the home visitor may be most helpful when providing support for the parent to explore and understand the situation him- or herself. Sensitive supports such as this allow parents to develop better problem-solving skills of their own that they can use when the home visitor is not there. This support may or may not lead to a decision or action by the parent. Finally, it is important to recognize that there are some situations for which there is no adequate solution; it may be that accepting the situation "as is" is really all that can be done. Examples might include sudden tragic situations such as the loss of a family member or chronic problems such as living in extreme poverty. In all of these situations, the message is that the most appropriate step is to better understand the issue before considering any action.

WHAT'S NEXT?

Next, it is time to translate the relationship-based and reflective skills we have reviewed into practice. We will begin by thinking about behavior challenges and how to gather information to help us partner with families to address these concerns. Then we will explore some common issues home visitors encounter in their daily work in the following several chapters. These chapters are intended to serve as reference material for you when discussing similar problems with families. The chapters will not give you simple answers for every family, but they will provide context for starting the conversation and problem-solving process.

TIPS FOR PRACTICE

❱ Be prepared for sessions as planned, and be open and flexible for unexpected changes to the plan.

▶ Remember to PAUSE—slow down, wonder, and consider multiple perspectives—before taking any action steps.

▶ At times, an action is not necessary. Simply sitting with a parent, hearing his or her concerns, and connecting to emotions may be best. This strategy can help a parent calm down and allow him or her to have better thinking, leading to the chance that a solution might emerge.

KEY POINTS TO REMEMBER

▶ Combining relationship-based and reflective practice strategies—including observing, listening, and asking questions—can result in better understanding of situations in home visiting work and thus lead to more effective responses.

▶ It is important to consider the perspective of all participants (i.e., child, parent, home visitor) when working to understand what may be happening and what will be helpful.

▶ Recognition of role boundaries is necessary. There may be times when the home visitor should not take action or responsibility; rather, the home visitor would be most helpful when supporting the parent to reflect or by encouraging the parent to seek help from others.

▶ PAUSE is an acronym for a cycle of five steps: Perceive, Ask, Understand, Strategize, and Evaluate. The process organizes thinking about the behavior or issue, helps providers respond appropriately and effectively, supports relationship-based practices, and uses reflection to assess the experience (see Figure 3.4).

SUGGESTED FURTHER READINGS

Foley, G., & Hochman, J. (Eds.). (2006). *Mental health in early intervention: A unity of principles and practice.* San Francisco, CA: Jossey-Bass.

Weatherston, D., & Tableman, B. (2015). *Infant mental health home visiting: Supporting competencies/reducing risks.* Southgate, MI: Michigan Association for Infant Mental Health.

Evaluate
- Evaluate the outcomes using reflective processes.

Perceive
- Observe and listen.

PAUSE

Strategize
- Select and take actions.

Ask
- Ask questions to learn more about what is happening.

Understand
- Understand each participant's experience or viewpoint.

Figure 3.4. The PAUSE framework in detail.

PAUSE WORKSHEET

pause

Child: _____ Date: _____

Parent: _____ Provider: _____

PERCEIVE—Explore what is happening.

Parent/caregiver perspective:	Provider perspective:

ASK—Clarify what is happening.

Starting with the parent/caregiver's priorities and concerns, ask more detailed/specific questions to clarify what is happening.

UNDERSTAND—Explore why it is happening.

With the parent/caregiver, explore explanations for what is happening. Consider possible explanations that include the environment, the child, and the parent. Listen and observe closely as you explore the situation in conversation with the family.

Parent/caregiver perspective:	Provider perspective:	Child's perspective:

(continued)

UNDERSTAND *(continued)*

Parent/caregiver perspective:	Provider perspective:	Child's perspective:

STRATEGIZE and **EVALUATE**—Identify possible responses/solutions.

1. Solution/action to try:

How will we know if it works?

When will we evaluate if it works?

2. Solution/action to try:

How will we know if it works?

When will we evaluate if it works?

PROVIDER REFLECTION WORKSHEET

Child: _____ Date: _____

Parent: _____

Provider: _____

1. How did I follow the parent's lead to learn what is most pressing or important to the family?	
2. How did I ask clarifying questions to help me understand the problem better?	
3. How did I provide information that may help the family better understand the child's behavior?	

(continued)

4. How did I engage the family to develop a response that may include a strategy to try, a resource to use, or more information to increase understanding?	
5. How did I provide support and emotional containment if needed?	
6. How do I plan to follow up on promised actions to maintain trust?	
7. What do I want to discuss in reflective supervision to improve my practice and outcomes with this child and family?	

What's Going on in There?

Understanding Causes of Behavior

Problem behavior can be counted as one of the primary reasons for which parents seek help from any kind of professional, because virtually every young child displays challenging behavior at some point. However, the fact that it is a common problem is not likely to be comforting for parents, who often just want to know how to stop hard-to-manage behavior. Furthermore, many of the parents with whom home visitors work have trouble tolerating even "normal" challenging behaviors, often due to their own vulnerabilities. Parents are not alone in wanting to eliminate challenging behaviors, such as aggression or noncompliance. The home visitor, child care provider, or other adult working with a family may also have trouble tolerating a specific behavior and may feel highly motivated to reduce or eliminate it. All in all, when challenging behavior is present, the "press" that we discussed in Chapter 3 can seem relentless (Heffron et al., 2005).

Behavior health or social-emotional issues are now recognized as among the most frequent conditions that cause functional impairment in children (Slomski, 2012). The problems are so prevalent that the American Academy of Pediatrics released guidelines in 2015 for routine screening for childhood behavior and emotional concerns (Weitzman & Wegner, 2015). Because they work closely with families, home visitors also commonly observe challenging behaviors directly or hear concerns from parents and caregivers about behavior and social-emotional issues and want to be able to address them. Situations that challenge families are varied, and there are no "one size fits all" solutions to difficult behaviors. For some problems, limited immediate support can be all that is needed to help the family and parents cope. In other cases, a long-term solution may require a good deal more work and, at times, involvement of other people or systems.

In the previous chapters, we considered the work of a home visitor from a perspective that combines relationship-based and reflective practice strategies in order to gather information, gain a better sense of the issues, and begin to consider the perspective of all participants. In this chapter, we weave in a third piece: knowledge about what leads to and maintains, and what reduces, challenging behaviors. Taken together, relationship, reflective practice skills, and knowledge of behavior form a strong foundation that allows providers to respond effectively to the needs of families with very young children. The reflective stance and questioning methods discussed in Chapters 1 through 3 will be helpful when applied to understanding behavior concerns that parents bring to the home visitor.

Let's consider an example. Miranda, 20 months old, often pinches and scratches her mother, Linda, when she tries to stop her from doing something. Linda and the developmental therapist, Jason, have discussed this problem several times in the last couple of months. When Linda brings up the problem again, Jason says, "I am sorry that this is still happening. I know we have talked it about it a few other times. Maybe we can step back and you can let me know what you have been doing." Linda agrees and reports that she has been using time-out. Jason has many questions about what time-out means to Linda. He wonders if Linda has tried other strategies that he has suggested, such as redirection or helping Miranda show frustration in other ways. He also wonders how Linda is implementing time-out, because he knows that in the past she would typically tell Miranda "time-out" but did not actually enforce it.

In this instance, Jason considers what he knows about Linda and Miranda and reviews their earlier discussions about behavior. Jason will ask questions and problem-solve with Linda as he learns more. Maybe Linda is not implementing a strategy correctly, or maybe she stopped using it before it could start to work. Perhaps Miranda has gained some skills and the method is no longer appropriate. From this discussion, Jason and Linda may learn what will guide their next steps. They may retry something discussed in the past, rule out strategies that were ineffective or inappropriate, or develop new ideas. At times, the discussion will need to continue, going deeper in order to achieve better understanding and generate a plan. For example, maybe Linda and Jason will discuss a new stressor that the family encountered and discover that Miranda was reacting to that event. In this case, behavior methods are likely to fall flat and support to the parent is appropriate. In the next section, we present some additional frames that the home visitor and the family can use to consider the behaviors of young children from different angles.

SHIFT THE FRAME—THINK ABOUT THE BEHAVIOR DIFFERENTLY

One reflective strategy that can be applied to challenging behavior is to shift the frame, which means thinking about behavior in a different way. Many reframes are possible. Some of the more likely and useful reframes in early childhood include the following:

- Considering the behavior as a sign of something intrinsic to the child, such as developmental level or temperament style (e.g., separation problems in a child between 8 and 12 months old at the height of stranger anxiety)

- Recognizing the behavior as a form of communication (e.g., a child who has not yet learned to use words screaming in protest)

- Identifying the behavior as a response to something in the environment that could be changed (e.g., running off when in large stores as a reaction to the wide spaces; Denno, Carr, & Bell, 2010).

Each of these possibilities brings different ways of understanding the meaning of the behavior as well as potential responses on the part of adults. We discuss each of these frames briefly in the following subsections.

Behavior as a Sign of Development or Temperament Style

Knowledge of typical development is useful for helping parents have appropriate expectations for young children's behavior. At times, both parents and home visitors may need reminders to consider typical development as a source for difficult behavior. Parents may feel frustrated that a child "won't" do something, when the truth is that he or she is not yet able to perform the task independently. Providers who are working to help a child gain skills or meet outcomes can also sometimes lose sight of development as a source of challenging behaviors and should consider this factor in any planning. When working with a child who is struggling with a skill, for example, a home visitor might think about dropping back to earlier skills to allow the child to regroup and gain confidence. This strategy helps ensure the child is ready for the skills that will be taught. From this stronger position, the home visitor, parent, and child can restart with more success.

Understanding of typical development can also help parents and home visitors anticipate challenging behavior that occurs as a result of a new developmental phase the child has entered. Attainment of new developmental skills is a cause for celebration; however, the new skill may very often result in challenging behavior, particularly around natural needs for independence or the frustration that results when the child wants to perform a skill that he or she is not developmentally able to perform. Typical examples include a young child insisting on feeding him- or herself even though his or her fine motor skills are not quite sufficient, or the all-too-common "no" phase. The possibility that a difficult behavior is actually a sign of developmental progress is especially important to consider when a behavior is new.

When using the frame of development as a driver for challenging behavior, keep in mind that the child's chronological and functioning ages may differ. This situation may often be the case for home visitors who are partnering with families whose young children have or are at risk for developmental delays due to prematurity or other reasons. For young children with delays, a challenging behavior may be out of step with chronological age but perfectly acceptable for the developmental age of the child.

A second intrinsic child factor that may result in behavior viewed as difficult by adults is temperament (Denno et al., 2010). Although a full discussion of temperament is beyond the scope of this book, we discuss it briefly here and return to it in Chapter 5 through Chapter 8. Perspectives on temperament have changed a good deal since the Chess and Thomas (1996) approach that many are familiar with. In this pioneering model, temperament is understood as being composed of a set of inborn traits that influence behavior and can be organized into three types: easy, difficult, and slow to warm. Current descriptions of temperament retain the idea that it is an inborn tendency but focus on the person's positive and negative emotional reactions along with how those reactions are regulated over time (Rothbart & Bates, 2006; Ursache, Blair, Stifter, & Voegtline, 2013). Research suggests reactivity and regulation work together and parent support is required for babies to develop the ability to manage emotions and behavior in the long term (Ursache et al., 2013).

Temperament-related behaviors that most challenge parents include those associated with negative emotions in combination with tendencies to approach novelty that are too high (impulsivity) or too low (fearfulness). Specific examples of difficult behaviors that have been associated with various temperament styles include high activity, extreme persistence, and resisting changes and transitions. Furthermore, the temperament style or personality of the adult, parent, or home visitor may conflict with the style of the child; as can be expected, some fits between adult and child style are better than others. For example, some children with an active or "feisty" temperament may be perceived as very atypical when living with parents who are more "laid back," leading to more friction in the family. Other children who are very sensitive and have their feelings hurt easily and who live with parents who are risk takers and active might also experience some challenges. Overall, it is helpful to consider the personality and temperament of both the child and caregiver when gathering information about behavior challenges that are reported. Some home visitors simply ask the caregiver(s) to share three words to describe the child and then three words to describe themselves to both gather information and begin a discussion about how temperament and personality affect behavior and relationship. Another way to approach this discussion is to ask whether the child reminds the parent of someone or whether the child is like anyone in the family.

Behavior as Communication

Behavior always has a meaning, purpose, or function. It is useful to realize that very young children have limited ways to communicate needs, feelings, or wishes. Therefore, instead of thinking about difficult behavior as something to get rid of, a more fruitful frame is wondering what the child gets from the behavior or what the behavior is communicating about the child's needs. Often, just figuring out the answer to that question makes the behavior more palatable, if not more understandable. Furthermore, knowing the purpose of the behavior will help later when plans are made to change it.

The communicative functioning of behavior is clearly recognized in very young babies, who use crying to communicate a variety of needs such as hunger, fatigue, and pain. Older babies and toddlers have more skills, especially when compared to younger babies. However, their range of skills is still relatively small and they may not be able to apply their skills in all situations. For example, tantrum behavior is very common in toddlers and likely to occur at least once per day. Frequent reasons for toddlers' tantrums include frustration from inability to clearly communicate, challenge in performing a task, or being prevented from doing something by an adult. Knowing what is behind the tantrum can help the adult be more sympathetic and plan an appropriate and effective response. In the vignette presented in Chapter 3, Charley hit her mother. If Carmen did not recognize the aggression as stemming from fatigue, she might have proceeded to teach time-out. Instead, she provided support that helped Frances to understand the behavior as a result of a family schedule change. Getting beyond the surface behavior created additional knowledge that changed how Frances saw Charley's behavior and changed Frances' reactions.

Behavior as a Response to Changes

Another helpful reframe of difficult behavior is to see it as sparked by a change in the child, family, or environment. Remember to consider changes that seem positive as well as those that are not as positive. We have already mentioned developmental changes in the child as a likely source for changes in behaviors. Other common changes for young families include moving, changing jobs, or the addition of a new sibling. Bear in mind that even small changes that might not be troubling to an adult could have an impact on a child. For example, a minor change in the parent's work schedule, moving to a different bed or sleeping arrangement, or an older sibling adding a sport that shifts the family's dinner time could be the reason for a change in the child's behavior.

When the behavioral change is more intense or extreme, the potential for trauma exposure must be addressed. A good way to introduce this issue is to ask if the child has had any experiences the child thought was frightening. Give examples, such as medical procedures, weather-related events, car or other accidents, or seeing or hearing serious arguments between adults. Again, consider the interaction between the child's current development and the child's experience of an event or situation. Something that has never bothered a child in the past may be troublesome when experienced at an older age. A common example is a toddler who suddenly becomes fearful of the bath. Child or parent temperament can also play a role in how well the family copes with new events and situations. The topic of fears and anxiety is explored in Chapter 8.

Summary

So far, our problem-solving approach has been extended to consider some of the more likely root sources for challenging behaviors in very young children. These include developmental levels, temperament styles, a need to communicate, and a response to changes. After thinking about difficult behaviors from these varying perspectives, we may understand them better, but we still may wish to find a way to change them! Next, we review some basics about behavior that can form a foundation for developing a plan to change difficult behaviors.

BEHAVIOR 101

Very young babies enter the world with an extremely limited set of skills. Within a few years, they have learned an amazing amount. A typically developing child goes from crying to using sentences, needing full physical support to running, and having uncontrollable impulses to following directions and participating in a group. How does new behavior get started and what makes it keep happening? Basic behavior theory explains that anything that is going on in the environment before a behavior happens and anything that happens after a behavior may each play a role in determining when a behavior might occur and whether it will keep happening (Murphy & Lupfer, 2014). Often this is summarized as the ABC model or three-term contingency model. *A* is the antecedent of the behavior. This can be events, situations, and actions of others that occur just prior to the targeted behavior. *B* is the behavior that needs to be changed. It can be a difficult behavior that needs to be decreased or a positive behavior that should be taught or increased. Finally, *C* is the consequence, or what happens after the behavior. Although practitioners are often focused on the behavior itself, one must step back and consider all three—A, B, and C—to be successful.

A.   Antecedent

     Events, situations, actions of others that happen before the behavior

B.   Behavior

     Positive behavior to be increased, such as cooperation

     Negative behavior to be decreased, such as aggression

C.   Consequence

     What happens immediately after the behavior occurs

     When rewarding, consequences may increase a behavior (e.g., praise, getting what you want)

     When undesired, consequences may decrease a behavior (e.g., ignoring the behavior, loss of something preferred such as a toy or privilege)

MAKE A CHANGE TO THE ENVIRONMENT, THE OUTCOME, OR THE RESPONSE OF OTHER PEOPLE

When a behavior is followed by something positive, that behavior is said to be reinforced and can be expected to continue to occur. If the behavior does not result in a desired response or event, it is unlikely to keep happening. In a common scenario, a young child asks for a toy or candy in a store. When the parent says "no," the child has a tantrum. If the parent continues to hold firm and does not purchase the toy or candy, the tantrum behavior is not rewarded and is less likely to occur in the future. On the other hand, if the parent does make the purchase, the child may learn that a tantrum is the way to get a treat. This simple example explains how parents and other caregivers shape the behaviors of young children by their responses to the children's actions. For very young children, the most powerful type of reinforcement is the response of a caregiving adult. When a very young child hits his or her parent, for example, any strong emotional response (crying, laughing, yelling) may interest the child and actually encourage him or her to repeat the action. Changing our response following the behavior is one way to stop or increase it. Consider these two similar situations:

Version 1: Braxton went up to the television, stopped, turned, and looked at his father and smiled. He then pushed the off button. William said, "No turning off the TV, Braxton!" Braxton walked away and then a few seconds later repeated the behavior. Again his father yelled. "No, Braxton! What did I just tell you?"

Version 2: Braxton went up to the television, stopped, turned, and looked at his father and smiled. He then pushed the off button. William said, "Wow!

Look at this truck over here. How cool is this!" Braxton immediately turned his attention to the toy truck and made a zooming noise. Without saying a word about the television, William turned it back on and lowered the volume so he could still see the game but help William keep his attention on the toy truck.

In the first example, the "attention" was placed on the errant behavior, which inadvertently had the effect of reinforcing it rather than stopping it. William's telling Braxton not to turn off the television seemed to teach Braxton that he could engage his father by "pushing the button" and turning if off. In the second example, Braxton's father used redirection with positive attention for a different, desirable behavior. Braxton's attention was directed to a toy he liked, and what he learned was that his father will give him attention when he plays with toys. This helped Braxton learn to both leave the television alone and how to interact with his father in a positive way.

Notice that we have not mentioned use of punishment as a way to reduce a challenging behavior. Although it is true that withdrawal of rewards is a form of punishment, we have chosen to use the term "consequence," because many people think of methods such as spanking when they hear the term *punishment*. Applying a negative, such as spanking, is also a form of punishment. However, this type of punishment is not recommended, as it does not teach alternatives, plus it provides an aggressive model and may actually increase challenging behaviors. We talk more about this issue in Chapter 5.

Young children also learn by watching what others do, as described in social learning theory (Bandura, 1977). Children do not automatically know what is expected in all situations and settings. Instead, they learn over time by imitating others. Babies watch the response of their parents to decide if interacting with a new person is safe. Similarly, young children copy other children to learn how to play with toys or on playground equipment. Over time, humans learn to do different things with different people and in different places. For example, people may dress, act, and speak differently at home compared to work, school, church, stores, or the gym. When looking for the origins of difficult behaviors, it is important to recognize that young children may imitate the full range of behaviors of their parents and caregivers, both desirable and undesirable. Parents and other adults who model good regulation behavior are helping children learn these skills (McClelland & Tominey, 2014). Another way that people learn socially is by attending to what happens after another person acts. If a child sees another person receive a reward after doing something, the child may be more likely to perform that behavior himself or herself later. Parents can praise an older child who is demonstrating a skill that they would like to see their toddler develop, such as waiting a turn.

The physical environment itself also can affect our behaviors, often interacting with personal characteristics. Certain types of environments lend themselves to certain responses. For example, wide-open spaces—not only those found in parks, but also in malls and office buildings—invite young children to run. Tempting objects placed at low levels may as well have Lewis-Carroll-like tags stating "Touch me!" Young children need appropriate environments where they can safely play and be themselves. Home visitors are in a good position to help parents consider how well the home environment supports the child to explore and learn safely. They can suggest environmental changes that will reduce friction between parents and young children. Parents are typically comfortable with the idea of child-proofing their home for safety reasons; expand this notion to include environmental changes that prevent behavior problems. Some examples of environmental changes might include the following:

- For a young child who has just learned to climb, parents might change their furniture around to limit climbing for a time or provide safe toys that allow climbing.

- Parents can be encouraged to keep special, fragile, or valuable objects out of sight—or at least out of reach—if their child is at an age to explore these objects.

- Parents and other extended family members may want to designate special areas for young children and have a small selection of age-appropriate toys and games in that place.

- Child safety locks on doors, cabinets, and drawers as well as on electrical sockets can reduce access to dangerous items and prevent exit from rooms or the home.

Home visitors can also help parents plan to be successful when exposing children to environments outside of the home so that they can be supported to develop behaviors that suit these settings. As part of this discussion, parents should be supported to consider the child's typical routine and how it may be affected by the new environment or experience. For example, parents may wish to take their child out to a family dinner in a restaurant. Encourage the parent to reflect on this experience from the child's perspective; so many things are different! The young child may be distracted by all of the new people and things to see and hear, making it hard to settle down and eat. There may be a wait for a table and the meal may take longer than usual, meaning that the child may be hungry or confused when his or her expectations about eating are violated.

This discussion can naturally lead to planning prevention for potential problems. For example, once the parent recognizes how challenging it might be for a child to wait in a noisy, stimulating place, he or she could bring a favorite book, small toy, crayons and paper, or other items so the child has something to do while practicing waiting. Alternatively, a parent may choose a more child-friendly restaurant or to go out to lunch instead of dinner, when the restaurant is likely to be less crowded and the wait shorter. The family might also decide to go to a restaurant designed especially for young children and that has activities and child-friendly foods.

TEACH A DIFFERENT BEHAVIOR

Often, home visitors and parents are so focused on getting "rid" of a problem behavior, they don't think about what might take its place. For example, Marsha notices that Betsy cries in her highchair when she is finished eating to signal she wants down. Marsha finds this behavior annoying. She remembers that ignoring a behavior is sometimes effective, so she tries to turn away when Betsy cries. As Betsy cries louder, Marsha continues to ignore her. Suddenly, Betsy throws her plate on the floor. Marsha realizes that Betsy has changed her response, but unfortunately Betsy's replacement behavior is worse than the original behavior Marsha sought to eliminate. This undesirable outcome explains why it is important to pair efforts to decrease one behavior with simultaneously teaching a desirable replacement behavior.

The basic information on understanding and framing behavior can help guide how to determine an appropriate replacement behavior. Adults need to know the function the child's behavior serves so they can choose an alternate that serves the same purpose. Some of the more common reasons for a behavior are that it is enjoyable, it results in getting something that is desired, it results in avoiding or escaping something that is not desired, and it fills a sensory need. In the recently described example, Betsy wanted out of the highchair. If Marsha misread the crying as requesting more food, she would likely end up with a bigger mess! Recall that in the first three chapters we talked about attending to the child's inner experiences as part of increasing reflective functioning and building relationship; here we explain the usefulness of thinking about this from a behavioral perspective.

Adults also need to consider the child's developmental level so that they can select a behavior that the child is able to perform or can learn to perform. In the example, Marsha recognized crying as a signal that Betsy was finished eating and would like to get down from her highchair, but she found the crying annoying and wanted it to stop. Marsha might be successful if she chose to teach Betsy that she will be reinforced for doing an alternate behavior that she already can do, such as saying or signing "all done." If Betsy does not have a suitable alternative behavior in her repertoire, then Marsha would need to teach one. Again, considering Betsy's developmental level is necessary for success. Marsha may hope that one day Betsy would ask to get down using a full sentence, but that may be unrealistic at this time. Teaching a single word or sign could be an appropriate next step.

PULLING IT TOGETHER

Sometimes understanding challenging behavior requires a bit of sleuthing to get the whole picture. Aspects of the child, the environment, and the parent must be considered when helping families address challenging behaviors. This kind of dialogue works best within a positive relationship and can benefit from use of reflective methods.

In the example introduced earlier in this chapter, Jason asked Linda to explain more about how she was giving a time-out. Linda explained that she told Miranda to take a time-out, but Miranda never did it. "She knows where her time-out chair is," Linda said, "but she just won't stay." Jason knew that they had talked about the scratching and pinching several times. He felt frustrated that Linda was still not giving a time-out correctly. Linda also mentioned that another provider had shown her how to use a "holding technique," but Jason remembered restraints have a lot of disadvantages. Jason thought about reteaching time-out but instead decided it would be better to hear more about what might be happening when Miranda pinched and scratched.

Linda at first said that the behavior happened "all the time." Jason said, "I bet it feels like it is constant! But maybe we can think a little more and figure out exactly when it happens." With this support, Linda was able to identify that Miranda usually scratched or pinched when Linda tried to stop her from doing something by picking her up. Jason said, "Miranda is getting to be a big girl. She wants to do things on her own. I wonder how she feels when you pick her up like that." After some discussion, Linda was able to see that picking up Miranda was a trigger, because Miranda did not like to feel confined. Plus, by breaking down the order of what happened when, Jason helped Linda recognize that she would often let Miranda go back to doing what she wanted to do after she pinched or scratched. At this point, Jason and Linda recognized that time-out or a "hold" might have actually made Miranda's behavior worse, and they were able to see that some other options, such as redirection, might be more effective. Figure 4.1 provides examples of questions to ask and perspectives to maintain when addressing behavior challenges using the PAUSE framework. See Appendix 4A for a blank reproducible version.

WHAT'S NEXT?

Chapter 5 through Chapter 8 explore some specific challenging child behaviors in detail, show how to apply the PAUSE framework through use of scenarios, and review some concrete strategies home visitors can use to support families.

EXPLORING CHALLENGING BEHAVIORS— PULLING IT TOGETHER WORKSHEET

Child: Miranda   Date: 7/13/15

Parent: Linda

Provider: Jason

TARGET BEHAVIOR—Help the parent or caregiver to specifically describe the child's challenging behavior.

Miranda pinches and scratches her mother, Linda, when she tries to stop her from doing something.

Areas to Explore About the Child and Family

What is the child's current developmental level?	Miranda has some emerging language skills with more understandable words.
What is the child's temperament style?	Miranda is impulsive and very active. She requires a lot of attention. She also shows a desire to do things on her own.
What is the parent(s) temperament style?	Linda seems to be pretty laid back, yet she is easily angered by Miranda's behavior.

(continued)

Figure 4.1. Sample Exploring Challenging Behaviors—Pulling It Together Worksheet.

Figure 4.1. *(continued)*

EXPLORING CHALLENGING BEHAVIORS—PULLING IT TOGETHER WORKSHEET
(continued)

Describe the family culture and environment.	Linda is a single parent who shares that she wants to do the best job she can to help Miranda learn to behave so she is better prepared for preschool next year.
Describe the family's parenting practices.	Linda is open to trying new ideas. She asks all of the providers for ideas on handling behavior.

Questions to Ask the Parent

How has this situation or behavior been for you?	Linda feels frustrated and like she has already tried many ideas that don't work. Maybe she feels embarrassed that her parenting techniques have not stopped the pinching/scratching.
Who is helping you?	Linda asks for help from all the other providers. Her family has been critical of her parenting. She may be getting some conflicting advice.
Is the concern new or ongoing?	This behavior has been going on for several months.
Have there been any changes in the family?	The family recently moved into a new apartment because Linda got a new job.

(continued)

Figure 4.1. *(continued)*

EXPLORING CHALLENGING BEHAVIORS—PULLING IT TOGETHER WORKSHEET *(continued)*

How often and how long has this behavior or situation been happening? How long does the behavior last?	It seems the scratching and pinching started a few months ago and has gotten progressively more problematic. It happens most often when Linda tries to pick up Miranda to get her to stop doing something. When Linda puts her down, she calms somewhat.
When, where, and with whom does it happen?	Linda is not aware of Miranda behaving this way with others. It seems to happen most often at home in the evening.
What usually happens after the behavior? What happens before the behavior?	Miranda scratches and pinches as soon as Linda starts to pick her up to stop a behavior. Linda will often put her down when she is pinched or scratched. Miranda often wants to be alone for a few minutes after this happens.
What happens to "end" the behavior (e.g., does the child just give up, does the parent give in, does the child get distracted)?	The pinching seems to stop when Linda lets Miranda go. If they have been struggling for a while, sometimes Miranda runs to her room to be alone and sometimes falls asleep.
What might be the purpose of the behavior or what need does it fill for the child? What is the child trying to "tell" you?	When Miranda pinches or scratches, Linda lets her get down, so the behavior results in escape from restraint and sometimes in being able to do something forbidden. I also wonder if part of Miranda's struggle is with communicating her needs and wants. Or maybe she gets tired and less able to regulate herself.
What would you like your child to do instead?	Linda would like Miranda to use words or signs to tell her when she wants something and for her to listen when she tells her to stop doing something.

(continued)

Figure 4.1. *(continued)*

EXPLORING CHALLENGING BEHAVIORS—PULLING IT TOGETHER WORKSHEET
(continued)

Does he or she know how to perform the new behavior, or will we need to teach it?	Miranda is behind in her communication skills. She may need help with using words to make requests and to follow some commands.
What have you tried already? How did that work?	Linda has tried time-out and holding in addition to telling Miranda to stop whatever behavior is disliked. Miranda "does not stay" in the time-out place. Redirection has been suggested but may not have been tried.

Summarizing the Plan

What changes to the environment, routine, or adult reactions will we try?	I can encourage Linda to use redirection and to avoid picking up Miranda. Linda may need to moderate her reactions or responses to the pinching and scratching. Miranda might benefit from fewer toys that are out for play. Linda might benefit from creating a more consistent schedule so Miranda gets sufficient sleep.
What steps will we take to teach a new behavior?	We might work on requesting and refusing skills (words and signs). We can try some games that include following directions. It will be important to stress that this will take some time to change, as Miranda will try her old and currently successful ways to get what she wants before learning the new way.
What will we see if the strategy works?	Miranda will be calmer, will stop doing something when asked, and will use words or signs instead of pinching and scratching.

(continued)

Figure 4.1. *(continued)*

EXPLORING CHALLENGING BEHAVIORS—PULLING IT TOGETHER WORKSHEET *(continued)*

What does the family need to do in order to stick it out and be consistent with the plan? Are there others in the family who can help?	Linda will need regular affirmation of progress, as she is a single parent. She might benefit from someone to call when she is frustrated, just for some moral support. She has mentioned her mother and sister could also help and might be useful to give her breaks as needed.
How long will we try the strategy before checking in again?	I really would like for Linda to try any new behavior method consistently for at least 2 to 3 weeks so Miranda successfully learns a new way.

Self-Reflective Questions

Is this issue within my scope of practice?	Yes, I can help Linda learn this behavior management approach.
How can I be most helpful in this situation?	Because we are already meeting weekly for therapy, I can make this topic a regular part of our work to help Linda stay consistent with the plan. I can check in to see if Linda has enough support to continue.
What reactions am I having to this behavior or situation?	I feel somewhat frustrated because I feel like we have discussed these strategies before with little success. I'm not sure how to redirect my frustration.

TIPS FOR PRACTICE

▶ Acknowledge that challenging child behavior is one of the most common issues presented and reassure families there are steps to take to make things better.

▶ Encourage parents to consider the behaviors from many different frames and perspectives.

▶ Consider development and temperament, the context of the behavior—including the environment and adult expectations and responses—and how behaviors are started and what makes a behavior stop.

KEY POINTS TO REMEMBER

▶ Families are increasingly seeking help from all professionals, including home visitors, for difficult behaviors in young children. Home visitors can help parents reframe their response to some behaviors to understand them as a reflection of typical or delayed development, related to temperament style, or as a response to factors in the environment.

▶ Developing an effective plan to address challenging behavior in young children requires considering the behavior from multiple frames; having realistic expectations related to child development; gathering detailed information about the meaning, purpose, and overall context of the behavior; and supporting families to develop and implement plans.

SUGGESTED FURTHER READING

Clark, L. (2005). *SOS for parents: A practical guide for handling common everyday behavior problems* (3rd ed.). Bowling Green, KY: SOS Programs and Parent Press.

EXPLORING CHALLENGING BEHAVIORS— PULLING IT TOGETHER WORKSHEET

Child: _____ Date: _____

Parent: _____

Provider: _____

TARGET BEHAVIOR—Help the parent or caregiver to specifically describe the child's challenging behavior.

Areas to Explore About the Child and Family

What is the child's current developmental level?	
What is the child's temperament style?	
What is the parent(s) temperament style?	

(continued)

Describe the family culture and environment.	
Describe the family's parenting practices.	

Questions to Ask the Parent

How has this situation or behavior been for you?	
Who is helping you?	
Is the concern new or ongoing?	
Have there been any changes in the family?	

(continued)

How often and how long has this behavior or situation been happening? How long does the behavior last?	
When, where, and with whom does it happen?	
What usually happens after the behavior? What happens before the behavior?	
What happens to "end" the behavior (e.g., does the child just give up, does the parent give in, does the child get distracted)?	
What might be the purpose of the behavior or what need does it fill for the child? What is the child trying to "tell" you?	
What would you like your child to do instead?	

(continued)

Does he or she know how to perform the new behavior, or will we need to teach it?	
What have you tried already? How did that work?	

Summarizing the Plan

What changes to the environment, routine, or adult reactions will we try?	
What steps will we take to teach a new behavior?	
What will we see if the strategy works?	

(continued)

What does the family need to do in order to stick it out and be consistent with the plan? Are there others in the family who can help?	
How long will we try the strategy before checking in again?	

Self-Reflective Questions

Is this issue within my scope of practice?	
How can I be most helpful in this situation?	
What reactions am I having to this behavior or situation?	

When Parents Say...
Calm Down!

Early Regulation: Sleeping, Eating, and Soothing

Darlene arrives for her scheduled early intervention visit with Katarina and Phil, parents of 10-month-old Jasmine. Although she has been working with the family for a few months and comes at the same afternoon time each week, Darlene notices that the family is never ready for her visits. Often the family is not yet dressed, and she frequently arrives in the middle of a meal. On this day, Jasmine is smiling and interactive as usual, although she appears to have just recently woken up. She is sitting with her mother on the couch. Katarina is watching a news program and trying to get Jasmine interested in a bottle with a red-colored liquid. Darlene hopes that it is juice and not a soda, as she has often seen Katarina give Jasmine sips from her own beverages.

"Are you guys ready to start or do you need a minute?" Darlene asks. Katarina says, "You can work with her for a while. Phil went out to get us some lunch 'cause we just got up after going to bed late last night." Just then, Phil arrives bearing bags of fast food. The two sit on the couch and pull out the sandwiches, large bags of fries, "super-sized" drinks, and several desserts. Darlene sits on the floor with Jasmine, unsure of what to do, feeling awkward and a little annoyed that her session is interrupted again. She feels even more uncomfortable as Phil leans down to give Jasmine a fry to chew on. Phil says, "Look at this! Jasmine is figuring out how to eat by herself."

As Darlene finishes up her paperwork, she reminds Katarina of the next appointment. "I think it would be good to talk about your schedule for bed and eating next time. What do you think?" she asks Katarina. Phil laughs and leaves the room. Katarina says "We can talk about that. It's hard to get a schedule here when things at Phil's work are so crazy. We never know when he will have to go in or stay late. I want him to be able to spend time with us when he can." Darlene realizes that there may be more to this situation than she knew.

Earlier chapters reviewed how important it is for a baby's mother and father to learn to read their young child's cues and respond appropriately to meet their needs. Gradually, as the child gains in skills, the parent can allow more and more opportunities for the child to do things for him- or herself. In addition to supporting a positive attachment between parent and child, this complex set of parent and child interactions is one of the ways that the young child gains self-regulation skills (Brown, Pridham, & Brown, 2014).

For all infants, the very beginning of self-regulation can be seen in a triad of skills that develop in the first few months of life: sleeping, eating, and the ability to be calmed or soothed. When these skills are slower to develop or develop atypically, the baby feels bad—and so does everyone else in the house. As infants change to toddlers, these daily behaviors may become battle grounds related to independence. Throughout the period of early development, parents and other caregivers facilitate a baby's growing self-regulation in many ways, including providing a supportive relationship, setting up structure through routines, and providing good models for behavior and healthy practices (McClelland & Tominey, 2014). This chapter discusses how a typically developing baby can attain these skills with the support of sensitive caregivers and how home visitors can identify common problems related to learning these skills, and suggests ways that home visitors can help families struggling in these areas.

SELF-REGULATION IN INFANCY

Self-regulation is a term used to describe a person's ability to manage or control his or her own behavior, emotions, and thinking. It is also described as the ability to think and plan before taking action (McClelland & Tominey, 2014). Self-regulation is used throughout the lifespan. Consider this situation: You arrive home after working overtime and are looking forward to taking a shower and relaxing for the evening. Instead, you find that family members have dropped in unexpectedly. They have brought food and planned to eat dinner and visit for the evening. What thoughts, feelings, and ultimately actions or behaviors would occur? Whether one is a child, teen, or adult, it is highly adaptive to be able to maintain composure, choose appropriate and effective behavioral responses, and think clearly when in an upsetting or exciting situation. In this example, a person with low self-regulation could blow up, angrily asking why the family members did not call ahead. The person could also break into tears of frustration that his or her plan was destroyed. Or, a person with better self-regulation might be able tell him- or herself to think about this change in plans as an opportunity to have fun with seldom-seen family members and be able to revise plans to relax for another day. In the long term, self-regulation skills are associated with positive outcomes such as getting along better with others and success in school and work (McClelland & Tominey, 2014). Poor self-regulation, not surprisingly, is associated with mental health problems including depression, anxiety, and conduct problems (Bridgett, Oddi, Laake, Murdock, & Bachman, 2013).

Temperament, a topic briefly introduced in Chapter 4, is a set of inborn tendencies that may relate to regulation (McClelland & Tominey, 2014; Rothbart & Bates, 2006). For example, a baby's ability to self-soothe or accept soothing from caregivers when afraid, hungry, or tired is a temperament feature that relates to regulation. Similarly, the way that individuals respond to new situations, people, and events is also part of their temperament style. People whose temperament style lets them manage new experiences may also be more skilled in emotional and cognitive regulation. Babies who are less reactive to changes in routine or new people often are also calmer in general.

Researchers usually connect the concept of regulation with a set of specific thinking skills called *executive function*. Executive function is the overall term used to talk about ways that we manage or control thinking processes. Three different but related skills are involved in executive functioning: attentional flexibility, working memory, and inhibitory control (Garon, Bryson, & Smith, 2008). See Table 5.1 for explanations and examples of executive function skills.

Table 5.1. Executive functioning: How we manage or control thinking processes using a specific set of thinking skills

Thinking skills	Description	Examples
Attentional flexibility	Ability to attend to tasks without either becoming too distracted by non-essentials or getting so consumed by the activity that transitions are difficult	Continuing to play with a shape sorter while a big brother is loudly pretending to be "Spectacular Spiderman"
Working memory	Ability to keep information in mind long enough to act on it	Remembering and following a rule or set of directions to go to another room, retrieve a pair of shoes, and come back to the door to leave
Inhibitory control	Refraining from enacting one response or action in favor of a more appropriate one	"Using your words" instead of hitting when things do not go your way

Source: McClelland and Tominey (2014).

It is typical for infants and very young children to need adult supports to manage their behavior, emotions, and thoughts. At first, almost all the burden of regulation is on the adult, making the relationship between caregiver and infant the vehicle through which regulation occurs and is learned. Even though it is expected that adult supports will continue to be needed throughout the early childhood period, some of the skills that underlie self-regulation begin to appear as early as 12 months (Bridgett et al., 2013). Sometime between 18 and 24 months, young children have beginning skills needed to manage their emotions, such as distracting themselves from upsetting events. Even very tiny babies may break off eye contact and look away to calm down when overexcited. This is one of the reasons that redirection is such an effective behavioral strategy for children this age.

Because very young children are not able to regulate on their own, parents need to pay attention to their babies' behavior; make informed guesses about what the child wants, needs, or is reacting to; and then respond in consistent ways. The goal is for the parent to do just enough so babies have room to build self-regulation skills gradually without being overwhelmed. Over time, the child begins to practice more and more self-regulation with less parental support. Recent studies show self-regulation depends on a combination of the young child's emotional reactivity and parenting behaviors. In one study, babies who were emotionally reactive and who had good abilities to regulate their emotions tended to have sensitive parents. Babies with high emotional reactivity but low regulation had less supportive parenting. In a follow up at age 4 years, reactive children, who had positive parenting and better regulations, developed better executive functioning skills needed for school success than those who had lower regulation and less positive parenting (Ursache et al., 2013). Studies like this one help explain how important it is for babies to receive and accept support from caregivers. These early experiences in regulating behavior and emotion eventually build executive functioning skills needed for better behavior at school age.

FIRST STEPS IN DISCUSSING
ISSUES IN REGULATION WITH FAMILIES

Later in this chapter, we discuss detailed background and recommended supports for specific problem areas in self-regulation. Before we get to those specifics, let's start with some important general principles related to sleep, feeding, and self-soothing. Home visitors need to find ways to ask about these three areas of family life and then be prepared to share information about how to develop healthy routines. Fortunately, home visitors are in a great position to observe both successful family practices and potential struggles in all aspects of parenting, and will typically have many good opportunities to ask specifically about sleeping, feeding, and soothing as they are occurring.

Being able to talk about a parenting practice in the moment is likely to be more meaningful for parents. Some parents may ask a direct question about how to resolve a perceived problem with sleep, feeding, or soothing. At other times, the home visitor may be the one to initiate the conversation. This means the provider must be alert for opportunities to ask and wonder about a child's behavior when observed and be ready to share recommendations when parents ask for help. See Table 5.2 for questions to ask about sleeping, feeding, and soothing.

As we have discussed, the first step to helping with a concerning issue is to learn more about it and how the family views the situation. At times, problems with regulation could occur along with a medical concern. Therefore, it is often a good idea to ask if the family has consulted a pediatrician or other primary care provider before giving behavioral suggestions. As always, it is best to ask more about how the family thinks about these areas of child behavior and what their beliefs are around caregiving in general. If the family is from a culture that is different from the home visitor's, he or she may want to specifically inquire about practices related to sleeping, eating, and behavior to ensure that any recommendations are acceptable. Finally, finding out who the family can call on for help is smart, particularly when families are struggling with regulation issues. Hungry or overtired children combined with hungry or overtired parents may lead to a lot of frustration! Ask if there is anyone who can give the parent a break.

Table 5.2. Questions to ask regarding sleeping, feeding, and soothing

Sleeping	How is your baby sleeping? What time does he go to bed? What time does he wake up in the morning? Does he sleep through the night?
	How often is she waking at night? What happens when she wakes up? What do you do?
	When does he nap? How long does he nap?
	What concerns or questions do you have about your child's sleep?
Feeding	How do you know when your child is hungry?
	How do you know when your child is full?
	What does your child like to eat and drink?
	What does meal time look like? Where do you feed your child? What is happening while he is eating?
Soothing	How would you describe your baby? What three words would you use to describe her?
	What startles or scares him? How do you know when he is scared?
	When she is upset, what do you do to help her calm down? How long does it take for her to get calm?
	Who is able to calm him down when he gets upset?
	How do you know when she is going to become upset? What do you do to avoid upsetting situations?

PREVENTING PROBLEMS IN REGULATION THROUGH ROUTINES

Putting to sleep, feeding, and calming are activities that parents perform multiple times every day with their young children. Preventing problems in these three areas can be effective (American Academy of Sleep Medicine, 2006) and is very important, given that babies with low self-regulation may have difficult behaviors by the time they are toddlers.

For example, across many different studies, behavioral interventions have been shown to be effective in improving sleep for young children. There is limited evidence for effectiveness of behavioral interventions on improving sleep for older children, underscoring the importance of developing good sleep patterns early in life (Meltzer & Mindell, 2014). Similarly, behavioral and sensory-based interventions can help with feeding concerns. For high-risk families, teaching parents the importance of the baby learning to self-soothe may be particularly helpful in avoiding later problems (Sheridan et al., 2013).

One of the more important ways the home visitor can help prevent behavioral problems stemming from self-regulation issues is to help families set up basic routines (St. James-Roberts, Sleep, Morris, Owen, & Gillham, 2001). In order to set up effective routines, parents need information about typical development. Home visitors can share information about typical child development that helps parents to view feeding, sleeping, and calming as skills developed over time. Similarly, the home visitor can teach parents to recognize that their children's needs for support related to sleep and skills in feeding and self-regulation will change over time. What works for an infant may not work as the child approaches 3 years. As discussed in Chapter 4, helping parents have appropriate expectations and anticipate challenges in these areas related to typical development may be beneficial.

As part of these discussions, home visitors should emphasize the effect that parents' own behaviors in sleep, eating, and emotional regulation have on their children. Some parents may wish that their children would grow up to have better habits than they themselves have, but they are unaware of how much their children learn from watching them. The home visitor can point out times when he or she sees a child copy something that a parent says or does to help support the general idea that parental modeling is an important way that children learn (McClelland & Tominey, 2014). When parents bring up concerns about sleep or feeding, the home visitor should ask about the habits of other family members. For example, parents may ask about how to get their child to eat more vegetables but admit they rarely eat anything green themselves. Asking the parents to imagine what the child will learn from watching their routines can be a good way to start them thinking about these issues. For some families, asking parents to remember how eating, sleeping, and managing emotions were handled when they were growing up can help them see how modeling works. A list of questions that explore family routines is shown in Box 5.1. The home visitor can document answers to these questions in any

---

BOX 5.1.　Exploring the Family's Daily Routines

Tell me about a typical day.

What time do family members wake up?

What happens after waking?

How do you handle meals and snacks?

What happens in between meals and snacks?

Does your child take naps? What time?

What happens after nap time?

What are the child's activities? What does the child like to do?

What time do family members go to bed?

What happens before bedtime (e.g., bath, reading)?

How does everyone sleep?

Where does everyone sleep?

Do the child's caregivers work outside the home? What is the schedule?

If the caregiver(s) work, who takes care of the child? Where?

Are there other children in the home? What are their schedules?

---

format that makes the most sense for the family's daily routines. Some may structure a day by morning, noon, and night. Others might draw a circle to represent a 24-hour period.

At times, a home visitor, like Darlene in the example, may have a concern about how the parent is handling these basic activities but is unsure how to bring up this worry. The parents may be satisfied with their current practices, whereas the home visitor, aware of the potential for problems down the road, is concerned. In this situation, the home visitor could step back to consider the pros and cons of bringing up the concern, attending to the seriousness of the observed concern, the likelihood of success in changing the behavior, and the danger of a relationship rupture.

Darlene continues to work with Jasmine and her parents but finds herself thinking about the parenting practices Phil and Katarina use. In her mind, she checks off the many ways she would like this family to change: get on a sleep schedule, eat healthier foods, and stop watching so much television, to start. As she drives to her next visit, Darlene thinks about how to share information about these topics with the family, and she imagines giving Katarina a set of handouts related to these areas. Darlene laughs to herself as she considers how being handed a bunch of papers about something she is not worried about would seem to Katarina. She wonders how to share ideas in a way that is respectful.

Darlene shares her experience with Jasmine's family with her supervisor. In the discussion, Darlene is helped to recognize that although she might wish the family made some different choices, nothing truly dangerous is happening. With the supervisor's help, Darlene is able to recognize that she missed some opportunities to bring up topics in the last visit. For example, when Katarina indicated that Darlene should start the session with Jasmine, Darlene could have said, "You are an important part of this visit, too. Is there a way that we can plan to meet when you can participate?" A statement like this could lead to a discussion related to schedules and allow space to talk about the value of regularity in eating and sleeping.

NAVIGATING PROBLEMS IN SELF-REGULATION

Ideally, all families would develop and use strategies such as consistent routines and modeling healthy practices that prevent problems for babies and toddlers. However, many families who use home visiting services have behaviors that are established and need more intensive support. In the following subsections, we provide some practical ideas and approaches to help address problems with sleeping, feeding, and soothing.

Sleep

Many parents are unaware of typical infant sleep patterns when they have a new baby, and this lack of knowledge may lead to fatigue and frustration. At first, many newborns do not adhere to the daily sleep cycle that most adults follow. Often, a new parent will complain that the baby has his or her "days and nights mixed up." However, it is routine for typically developing young babies to have fairly short periods of sleep and wakefulness that alternate throughout the day and night. Over the first year of life, parents can expect babies to gradually increase the length of their periods of sleep and wakefulness so that there are both longer sleep and wakeful times. This process is often discussed as *sleep consolidation*. In addition to the advantages of longer sleep periods, there is also a benefit of longer periods of wakefulness to allow for more social interactions and learning opportunities.

In order for a baby to be ready to learn to sleep for longer periods, he or she must be developmentally ready for lengthier sleep times and must know how to fall asleep on his or her own. This is because longer periods of sleep include very brief times of wakefulness; no one actually stays fully asleep all through the night. We all wake up a little and must use self-soothing to fall back into sleep (Henderson, France, Owens, & Blampied, 2010). Sleep is known to contribute to children's psychological and physical health (Bonuck, Hyden, Ury, Barnett, Ashkinaze, & Briggs, 2011). Problems in sleep can lead to long-term difficulties ranging from behavior problems to increased irritability, delays in cognition, and even slowed growth (Bonuck et al., 2011; Magee, Gordon, & Caputi, 2014). Children who continue to sleep shorter amounts through age 6 or 7 are more likely to have physical, emotional, and social issues than those whose sleep was typical from infancy or those whose sleep improved over time (Magee et al., 2014). Table 5.3 provides a summary of helpful information about sleep.

Child and parent sleep affect each other. For example, when babies and toddlers have poor sleep, it is likely their parents do, too. Both fathers and mothers report feeling more stressed when their young child does not sleep well and may have health problems and poorer overall daily functioning as a result (Goodlin-Jones, Sitnick, Tang, Liu, & Anders, 2008). Similarly, poor parental sleep is connected to problems with child sleep, supporting the idea that sleep is a whole family issue.

Table 5.3. Recommended sleep patterns

Age of child	Optimal hours of sleep per 24 hours	Tips and milestones
Newborn	14–17 hours	Watch for signs of sleepiness and put babies to bed drowsy but not asleep so they learn to fall asleep on their own. Many babies can sleep through the night (from midnight to 5 a.m.) by about 2–3 months.
4–11 months	12–15 hours	Use routines for nap and bedtime and a good sleep environment that is quiet and dark with no video or computer screens. More than half of babies sleep between 10 p.m. and 6 a.m. by 6 months, paralleling many parents' sleep patterns.
1–2 years	11–14 hours	Expect to reduce to one nap by 18 months. Encourage a security object to help promote self-soothing.
3–5 years	10–13 hours	Preschool children often still wake during the night, often with night terrors. A relaxing bedtime routine is recommended.
6–13 years	9–10 hours	Continue to avoid video or computer screens near bedtime. Avoid caffeine and begin to teach about good sleep habits.

Sources: Henderson, France, Owens, and Blampied (2010); Hirshkowitz et al. (2015).

Sleep is also connected to family characteristics. Problem sleep is more likely in families with high risk compared to low risk (e.g., psychosocial stressors and low socio-economic status; Sheridan et al., 2013). Babies from high-risk families start out with similar sleep habits compared with their low-risk peers. By 18 months, however, babies in high-risk families already show differences in sleep (i.e., problems settling to sleep, night waking, inconsistent bedtimes, sleep length) suggesting that family issues rather than infant characteristics lead to the sleep problems (Sheridan et al., 2013). Other studies showed that children with sleep problems may be more likely to live in families with financial hardships and have mothers who work full time. Home visitors in programs that support high-risk families may, therefore, frequently encounter problems with sleep.

Parenting behaviors can promote or inhibit sleep. Consistent with the idea that young children need to learn to self-regulate, it has been shown that children who learn to sleep on their own with little parental assistance may be the best sleepers. Paradoxically, active maternal strategies intended to help a baby settle to sleep were found in families in which babies were the poorest sleepers. Active settling includes methods such as walking the baby, touching for comfort, and staying with the child to get him to sleep. These strategies were associated with poor sleep, and the families continued to struggle when the child was 5 years old (Sheridan et al., 2013). Helping children learn to self-soothe and fall asleep on their own is needed, as research has shown that children fall asleep more easily and sleep longer when the parent is not present as they fall asleep (Touchette et al., 2005).

Other parenting behaviors that are not directly part of a sleep routine can also affect child sleep. In a longitudinal study, aggressive parental actions, including hitting and slapping, were associated with problems such as staying asleep (sleep continuity; Kelly, Marks, & El-Sheikh, 2014). In this study and others, sleep problems were connected to later child emotional and behavioral symptoms. Taken together, these studies suggest that child sleep can be disrupted by a myriad of issues including challenges with schedules and routine (Magee et al., 2014) and family conflict or parenting practices that lead to feelings of threat and vigilance (Sheridan et al., 2013), none of which promote good sleep.

How Common Are Sleep Problems?   Sleep problems are among the most common problems brought to pediatricians and other primary care providers (Goodlin-Jones et al., 2008). There are several different ways of categorizing sleep problems, which may include behavioral issues and sleep difficulty related to snoring (Bonuck et al., 2011). According to the American Academy of Sleep Medicine (2006), the following are the most common behavioral sleep problems: resisting bedtime, problems falling asleep, not sleeping long enough, waking during the night, and fears or anxiety about sleep. Behavioral sleep problems and sleep problems associated with breathing are most common in infants and young children (Bonuck et al., 2011). Disorders of sleep can be diagnosed accurately in young children, although usually not until after 1 year (ZERO TO THREE, 2005).

Estimates of sleep problems in young children range from 20% to 40%. Children with neurodevelopmental disorders, including autism and developmental delays, are likely to have more problems with sleep than their typically developing peers, with estimates between 40% and 75% in those populations (Bonuck et al., 2011; Goodlin-Jones et al., 2008; Wiggs, 2001). Although common in young children, sleep problems tend to decline with age. Young children are likely to be more dependent on their parents for sleep; therefore, parents are more involved with and concerned about sleep problems of young children (Goodlin-Jones et al., 2008). In one longitudinal study, parents reported that about 85% of children will have a typical sleep pattern by 4 years, so home visitors can reassure parents that sleep will almost always improve.

Co-sleeping Many parents co-sleep with their infants, for many different reasons, including parenting beliefs, reluctance to be apart from the baby, and cultural practices. Some families may co-sleep due to practical reasons, such as not having the money for a separate bed for the infant or young child or enough funds to heat or cool the whole house. In other situations, the child is unable to fall asleep or stay asleep on his own, so one parent stays with the child so that the entire family is able to get some sleep. Most U.S. medical providers caution against co-sleeping in the same bed, citing an association with sudden infant death syndrome (SIDS) and fears about smothering the baby accidentally in sleep (American Academy of Pediatrics [AAP], 2011). Others have argued vehemently that co-sleeping has an evolutionary basis and that Western concepts of solitary infant sleep and infant sleep training are far from universal (McKenna & McDade, 2005). These and other experts, including the AAP (2011), now also note that having an infant sleep in the same room but in a separate bed and following "back to sleep" positioning is not only the safest arrangement, but may also enhance breast feeding and provide protective advantages in terms of reduced likelihood of suffocation and SIDS. It is important to note that co-sleeping in chairs or couches has been reported to be more dangerous than planned co-sleeping in a bed in studies from the United Kingdom and Ireland (Fleming & Blair, 2015). Other risk factors that increase the risk of co-sleeping were reported, including parental smoking, use of alcohol or drugs, and infant vulnerability due to younger age (less than 4 months), prematurity, or low birth weight (AAP, 2011; Fleming & Blair, 2015). Overall, it is suggested that a more individualized approach that takes into account other risk factors such as poverty, parental smoking and drug use, and infant characteristics (e.g., low birth weight, prematurity) is needed when advising parents about sleeping arrangements (Fleming & Blair, 2015; McKenna & McDade, 2005).

How Is the Whole Family Sleeping?   Because sleep is so important and sleep issues are so common, it is critical to ask about overall family sleep, not only when the issue is specifically brought up, but also when parents express concern about development and behavior or when parents themselves are irritable and fatigued (Bonuck et al., 2011). Providers cannot count on typical developmental assessment tools used in early childhood programs to gather this information, as most either do not discuss sleep or may ask only one question (Bonuck et al., 2011). A helpful mnemonic, BEARS, was developed by Owens and Dalzell (2005) to guide discussion about sleep:

*B*edtime issues

*E*xcessive daytime sleepiness

Night *A*wakenings

*R*egularity and duration of sleep

*S*noring

Responding to Sleep Concerns   Once the home visitor has information about how, when, and where the baby or toddler sleeps and the overall family sleep habits, he or she can work with the parent to identify some strategies to help with identified concerns. Box 5.2 provides a useful checklist for working on improving sleep issues with families.

Feeding

Feeding skills also progress across the first few years of life. Healthy newborn babies with typical development are able to coordinate their sucking, swallowing, and breathing in order to successfully nurse or take formula from a bottle. By about 4 to 6 months of age, a baby should have enough tongue movement to be able to manage soft solid foods, but the ability to bite and chew solids well will not occur until closer to 18 months. Independence in feeding also occurs gradually, beginning with the ability to hold a bottle around 6 months, some self-feeding as early as 12 months, and demonstration of food preferences or pickiness starting between 18 and 24 months (Bruns & Thompson, 2010). Being able to feed a baby or young child is important to a parent's feelings of competence and confidence (Bruns & Thompson, 2010). When feeding interactions are not "synchronous and positive" (Bruns & Thompson, 2010), the parent and baby may be frustrated and their relationship can suffer. Problems with feeding directly affect the child on a nutritional basis and may have an impact on growth at times. In addition, feeding problems may be connected with problems in language, social-emotional, and motor development (Bruns & Thompson, 2010). Finally, sleep and feeding can be related. Young children who have digestive problems such as reflux and those who do not

BOX 5.2. Checklist for Responding to Sleep Concerns

- Make sure the sleep goals make sense from a developmental perspective.

- Ensure that there are no medical problems that relate to sleep.

- Teach and support the family to use an appropriate daytime schedule and sleep routine including following the "back to sleep" rule.

- Arrange for playtime in a well-lit or sunny room to help a child establish a day and night cycle.

- Identify the child's skills in self-soothing and teach additional self-soothing skills as needed.

- Encourage parents to put the baby down for naps and bedtime when he or she is sleepy but not asleep so the baby can learn to fall asleep on his or her own.

- Recognize that some babies will prefer to fall asleep on their own and may not like being rocked or held.

- Discourage hovering or frequent checking in on the baby, as this may disrupt sleep.

- If the baby or toddler wakes at night, encourage parents to wait briefly (e.g., several minutes) to see if the child can fall asleep on his or her own but not to wait so long that the child becomes significantly upset or distressed.

- Encourage parents to resettle the child, if needed, while keeping a quiet and calm manner.

take in enough food can have associated sleep issues, often waking due to discomfort or hunger, for example.

Food choices and feeding practices as early as 4 months of age may connect to later obesity (Ong, Emmett, Noble, Ness, & Dunger, 2006). As parents fully control the foods available to young children, their own eating preferences must be considered, as they are likely to inform the choices they make for their children. In one study, babies as young as 7 months had diets that were very similar to those of their mothers, the majority of whom were reported to be overweight. In the same study, mothers engaged in many inappropriate feeding practices with their babies under 12 months (Karp & Lutenbacher, 2011). Overfeeding; providing a diet that included insufficient fruits and vegetables; substituting water or juice for formula or breast milk;

mixing formula incorrectly; being unaware of potentially dangerous foods such as eggs, peanut butter, or honey; giving young babies foods like french fries; and feeding babies while watching television were common.

Although many feeding problems are behavioral, such as food refusal, others are related to medical or developmental issues. For example, a child with a cleft lip or cleft palate may require special equipment and even surgeries in order to successfully feed. Children with autism spectrum and other neurodevelopmental disorders may struggle with the sensory aspects of eating. Consulting with the child's physician to make sure that there are no medical barriers to feeding is important.

Home visitors will often have a chance to observe feeding early on and can use this opportunity to promote good habits. For very young children, suggestions including use of supportive positioning and a quiet voice, feeding in a low-traffic area with soft lighting, and gentle patting or caressing can be helpful. In contrast, behaviors that discourage positive feeding habits might include using loud or harsh voices, rough touch and strong movements such as rocking, prodding the baby with the nipple, pushing the baby's chin or cheeks while feeding, and feeding in loud or overly bright environments (Brown et al., 2014). As children get older, attention to the types of foods and drinks offered and a focus on gradually increasing independence with feeding is often appropriate, although family preferences, values, and beliefs around feeding may vary. Encourage parents to both offer and model eating healthy foods. This can be hard for some families who may have limited access to healthy foods in their neighborhoods. For some families, concrete supports may be needed to encourage healthy eating practices. For example, families may need referrals to places to obtain healthy food when needed, including Special Supplemental Nutrition Program for Women, Infants, and Children (WIC) and food pantries. A summary of expected feeding milestones with strategies for promoting healthy eating habits is given in Table 5.4.

Crying, Calming, and Soothing

Infant crying is considered normal, especially for very young babies! However, crying is also quite common throughout the first year of life (Evanoo, 2007; Gilkerson & Gray, 2014). Across cultures, most babies' crying increases over the first 6 weeks, and most of that crying happens during the night. Over the next couple of months, crying will usually decrease but continue at this lower level until about 1 year (Evanoo, 2007; Gilkerson & Gray, 2014). Although no one knows for sure why babies cry, this pattern has led to guesses that crying is innate or related to maturation. Because the amount and intensity of crying varies widely from baby to baby, may vary each day in individual babies, and likely is influenced by the environment, including parenting practices, there is not really a "normal" amount of crying, however.

Table 5.4. Encouraging healthy eating habits

Age	Skills and milestones	Reading the baby's independence signs	Strategies and supports	Avoid
Newborn	Baby can coordinate sucking, breathing, and swallowing. Breast-fed babies eat more often than babies who take formula.	Baby turns the head, fidgets, or closes the mouth to signify that he or she has had enough.	Use supportive positioning. Arrange a quiet environment.	Do not try to force the bottle. Do not squeeze the baby's cheeks. Offer only formula or breast milk in the bottle. Babies do not need water or other beverages.
4–6 months	Feeding may begin with solids. Breast-fed babies do not need other foods until 6 months.	Signs of baby's readiness for foods include holding head up and showing interest in foods. Baby opens mouth to take a spoon.	Introduce foods in any order: cereal, fruit, or vegetable. Introduce one food at a time and watch for allergic reactions. Go back to formula or breast milk if the baby does not take food.	Follow the baby's lead. Do not overfeed the baby. Do not prod the baby with the bottle or spoon. Do not prop the bottle.
6–12 months	Baby may learn to drink from a cup. Encourage breast feeding through the first year.	Baby may hold a bottle around 6 months. When the baby can sit well and brings hands to mouth, try soft finger foods that do not require chewing.	Caregiver can let the baby hold a spoon while he or she feeds with another spoon. Mashed-up foods like bananas can be offered.	If parents make their own baby foods, they should avoid food high in nitrates such as spinach or green beans. Juice should be avoided until at least 6–9 months and preferably until toddlerhood. Juice drinks with added sugar should also be avoided.

(continued)

Table 5.4. *(continued)*

Age	Skills and milestones	Reading the baby's independence signs	Strategies and supports	Avoid
12–18 months	Baby may eat some table foods. Weaning from the bottle is recommended by 15 months. Weaning from the breast can occur when mother and baby are ready; parents should talk to the baby's doctor.	Continue to encourage self-feeding (finger foods) by offering small pieces of soft foods.	Provide a good model as an adult healthy eater. Encourage family meals.	Avoid processed foods or adult foods with added salt and other unhealthy additives. Do not put the baby to bed with the bottle.
18–24 months	The child can bite and chew. The child eats small amounts at a time, so offer three meals and healthy snacks in between meals.	The child may show food preferences and pickiness. Offer new foods multiple times.	Offer a variety of foods and textures. Provide a good model as an adult healthy eater. Give water or milk to drink.	Do not make feeding a battle. Offer a variety of foods, but do not force the child to eat. Avoid sugary drinks, including juices.

Sources: Brown, Pridham, and Brown (2014); Bruns and Thompson (2010).

Most people find it hard to tolerate a baby's cry and typically seek to reduce the crying by attempting to soothe the infant. An infant's ability to calm on his or her own or to be soothed by others may be part of his or her temperament style and is also considered an early self-regulation skill (McClelland & Tominey, 2014). Babies between 1 and 4 months who cry with greater frequency and cannot be calmed may be said to have colic. Published research on colic goes back at least 50 years; however, there is still no good agreement about the definition, etiology, and treatment of colic (Kaley, Reid, & Flynn, 2011). For the most part, "colic" is crying that is described as having a sudden onset, being intense, and resulting in parents feeling that they cannot cope. Although there are many definitions of colic, the best agreed upon is the "rule of threes"; a baby who cries 3 hours per day, 3 days per week, for 3 weeks in a row (Wessel, Cobb, Jackson, Harris, & Detwiler, 1954).

Colic may occur in as many as 28% of babies (Evanoo, 2007). Although common, colic has been associated with undesirable outcomes for babies and for their families (Gilkerson et al., 2012; Maxted et al., 2005). Children with histories of prolonged crying past 6 months, or beyond the colic period, have been reported to have an increased risk for externalizing disorder at later ages, for example. Other concerns included the potential risk for child abuse (specifically, shaking), overall family stressors, and parental depression (Gilkerson & Gray, 2014).

Once parents get to know their baby, they can usually identify the need that crying or fussing signifies, such as for food, comfort, sleep, or a diaper change (Evanoo, 2007). Parents will typically learn to guess correctly and, if not, can always go through a process of checking the most likely reasons for tears. Home visitors can encourage parents to respond to their infant's needs in a timely manner. A small baby cannot be spoiled, so there is little to be gained by making a baby wait. In fact, many parents are surprised to hear that research has shown that babies who are attended to quickly actually end up crying less in the long run. Babies who are responded to learn that their needs will be met. When this experience occurs regularly, the pathways in the brain create patterns that help build the ability to self-soothe as the baby develops.

For very young babies, less than 8 weeks, swaddling is often effective (Evanoo, 2007). It is helpful to model and suggest that parents use a low and calm voice when trying to settle the baby. Higher-register tones may signal play time to babies; unfortunately, some people's voices get higher when they are anxious, which may happen when a tired parent feels unsuccessful in soothing his or her infant. Encourage caregivers to monitor their voices so that their tone matches their goal: drop the voice lower to help down regulate (calm) and raise higher to up regulate (alert). Other simple strategies that are likely to help include making a change in the environment to either provide more or less excitement (e.g., change the light, sounds, activity level), massage techniques, providing movement by walking or rocking, or offering soothing sounds including music and "white noise." Every baby is different, so home visitors can encourage parents to try different types of soothing strategies to figure out what their baby likes. See Appendix 5A for some tips for calming a baby.

There will inevitably be times when the baby does not respond to soothing efforts, and this may be the case for babies with colic. Unfortunately, there is no definitive treatment for colic, a fact that may lead to even more frustration for parents who cannot be sure of how to help their babies (Kaley, Reid, & Flynn, 2011). Although it is unlikely that excessive crying has a medical source, parents should be encouraged to check with a physician if there are physical symptoms such as vomiting or diarrhea or if the baby seems to be in pain, indicated by high-pitched cries (Gilkerson & Gray, 2104). In general, methods for soothing babies with colic are the same as for babies with lower levels of crying. Home visitors can help by normalizing crying and assuring parents that the higher levels of crying are unlikely to last past 4 months. Again, encouraging parents to engage in self-care and to have sufficient support is useful when given with sensitivity and support. Some parents have suggested that they tire of hearing suggestions about what to do, so make sure that the parent wants advice before giving it!

Darlene arrives for a visit with Jasmine and her parents at noon. Phil answers the door with Jasmine, who is crying very loudly. Darlene sees that Jasmine is rubbing her eyes and she immediately wonders if the baby is sleepy. Phil says, "You're here! Please take this grumpy baby." Darlene replies, "She does seem out of sorts. I see her rubbing her eyes. Could she be sleepy?" Phil says, "Well, I'm sleepy! She woke up at 7 a.m., so I did not get any sleep." Darlene resists her urge to explain about sleep schedules of infants. Instead she empathizes with Phil and then asks more questions about Jasmine's sleep pattern. As they talk, Darlene notices that Phil seems interested in figuring out how everyone can get more sleep. Darlene says, "I have some ideas about how you could all get better sleep. Is that something that we could talk about together?" Phil says he will talk to Katarina about this idea and agrees to let Darlene know what they decide at the next visit.

WHAT TO DO WHEN ROUTINES
AND PARENT EDUCATION ARE NOT ENOUGH

Despite their best efforts, some families will experience difficulties in these basic areas, requiring more direct interventions by behavioral or medical professionals. Examples include babies with genetic conditions that affect their eating, babies who have been exposed to drugs in utero and are experiencing withdrawal, and young children with exposure to significant trauma leading to difficult-to-manage emotional and behavioral reactions.

When the behaviors related to problems in regulation do not resolve, home visitors may determine that the issue is outside of their expertise. In these situations, the home visitor can help support families to gain access to other needed resources, including work with medical or behavioral health professionals. Specialized programs may be available in some locations. For example, the Fussy Baby Network (Gilkerson et al., 2012), a program that provides both practical and emotional supports to families, is available in many states. Through this program, parents can receive immediate support by phone within 2 days of the initial contact, followed by additional contacts that are individualized to family needs (Gilkerson & Gray, 2014).

Many health professionals would value detailed information about the frequency, duration, and intensity of the concerning behavior and about what has been tried. Therefore, the home visitor should encourage the parents to share information with the next provider that the home visitor and the family have gathered together to support their own efforts to address a behavior. When appropriate, the home visitor may need to talk directly with other team members to better serve families. In this way, the home visitor can play an important role in supporting a family while staying within his or her scope of practice and expertise. More details about coordinating with other professionals can be found in Chapter 10.

Darlene returns to the home of Phil, Katarina, and Jasmine regularly for visits over the next several months. The family is happy with the progress Jasmine has made with sleep. They now have a simple routine that includes regular bedtimes and naps. Jasmine, at age 17 months, is sleeping better, and her parents also have more rest. However, Darlene notices that Jasmine is making little progress in self-feeding and that she is still primarily taking a bottle with formula or juice. She realizes during one visit that she has not seen anyone offer Jasmine food for a while, even a french fry! She decides to ask about her eating during the next visit.

Darlene says, "Jasmine does really well with the bottle, doesn't she?" Katarina replies, "Yes, she really likes the bottle." Darlene continues, asking, "Does she ever seem interested in trying solid foods?" Katarina explains that the doctor said she could have a few things, like Cheerios, a while ago, but it did not go well so she stopped trying. "She kind of choked when I gave her bites from my plate, so I got scared and quit trying that!" Darlene wonders if Jasmine just needs practice with eating or if there could be another problem. She decides to suggest that Katarina check again with the doctor, because the 18 month checkup should happen soon. She helps Katarina organize what to ask the doctor and offers to help with introducing foods if the doctor still recommends it.

USING THE PAUSE FRAMEWORK

Using the vignette in the previous section and Figures 5.1 and 5.2, review how Darlene thinks through her experiences with Jasmine and her family.

WHAT'S NEXT?

In Chapters 6–9, we discuss several specific types of challenging behaviors. Next in Chapter 6, we apply the PAUSE framework to addressing aggression and tantrums.

TIPS FOR PRACTICE

▶ Share with caregivers the expected milestones or phases in early regulation to sort out typical challenges from more complicated problems.

▶ Emphasize prevention methods such as healthy routines and good models for sleep, feeding, and self-soothing.

▶ Support and assist families to reach out to health and behavioral health providers in specialized programs, sleep clinics, and feeding teams when basic strategies are insufficient.

KEY POINTS TO REMEMBER

▶ Self-regulation is a set of skills that allows a person to consciously control his or her thoughts, feelings, and behaviors so that he or she can think before acting.

▶ Although some self-regulation skills are present in infancy, it is best to understand these skills as something that develops over time with sensitive adult scaffolding and caregiving.

▶ Home visitors can help families support their young children to develop self-regulation in many ways. These include helping parents understand typical development so they have reasonable expectations and provide good routines that build their child's skills and supporting families to use other resources when needed.

PAUSE WORKSHEET pause

Child: Jasmine   Date: February 2, 2015

Parent: Katarina and Phil   Provider: Darlene

PERCEIVE—Explore what is happening.

Parent/caregiver perspective:	Provider perspective:
Jasmine is sleeping better. She has trouble eating solid foods.	We have made progress with the sleep routines, but now I am wondering about Jasmine's feeding habits.

ASK—Clarify what is happening.

Starting with the parent/caregiver's priorities and concerns, ask more detailed/specific questions to clarify what is happening.

Ask more questions about what foods were tried and what happened with Jasmine.

What did the doctor recommend? What questions should the family ask the doctor next time?

What would Katarina like to see Jasmine eat?

What is the family's typical eating practice?

UNDERSTAND—Explore why it is happening.

With the parent/caregiver, explore explanations for what is happening. Consider possible explanations that include the environment, the child, and the parent. Listen and observe closely as you explore the situation in conversation with the family.

Parent/caregiver perspective:	Provider perspective:	Child's perspective:
Katarina shares she became scared to try more solid foods when Jasmine "choked" on some table food.	I wonder what ideas Katarina has about the kinds of foods young children eat, where she is getting that information,	It appears Jasmine is eager and ready to try solid foods. She may also need more than milk to grow and develop.

(continued)

Figure 5.1. Darlene's PAUSE Worksheet for Katarina, Phil, and Jasmine.

Figure 5.1. *(continued)*

PAUSE WORKSHEET *(continued)*

UNDERSTAND *(continued)*

Parent/caregiver perspective:	*Provider perspective:*	*Child's perspective:*
	and who she might trust to learn more about this.	What ways is she showing Katarina that she is ready for foods?

STRATEGIZE and **EVALUATE**—Identify possible responses/solutions.

1. *Solution/action to try:*	*How will we know if it works?*
Ask Katarina to ask Jasmine's doctor about this and share the information with me.	Katarina will share the information she receives from the doctor.
	When will we evaluate if it works? When we have our next appointment after the doctor visit

2. *Solution/action to try:*	*How will we know if it works?*
Depending on the doctor visit outcome, we might try some new foods together or pursue other assessment or nutrition information.	We will develop this aspect after the appointment.
	When will we evaluate if it works?

PROVIDER REFLECTION WORKSHEET

Child: Jasmine   Date: February 2, 2015

Parent: Katarina and Phil

Provider: Darlene

1. How did I follow the parent's lead to learn what is most pressing or important to the family?	I have been successful in following this family's lead better. Our success in exploring some sleep practices has helped me with my relationship with both parents. I think I carefully brought up my concern about Jasmine's eating with a good result.
2. How did I ask clarifying questions to help me understand the problem better?	I did get some better information by acknowledging Jasmine's success with a bottle and wondering whether she might be ready to try solid foods.
3. How did I provide information that may help the family better understand the child's behavior?	I helped Katarina come up with some possible questions for the pediatrician and agreed to help implement any ideas they agreed on.

(continued)

Figure 5.2.   Darlene's Provider Reflection Worksheet for Katarina, Phil, and Jasmine.

Figure 5.2. *(continued)*

PROVIDER REFLECTION WORKSHEET *(continued)*

4. *How did I engage the family to develop a response that may include a strategy to try, a resource to use, or more information to increase understanding?*	Katarina committed to asking Jasmine's pediatrician about this issue.
5. *How did I provide support and emotional containment if needed?*	I was able to suggest that Katarina should ask Jasmine's doctor about the choking and develop a plan to get more information. I am worried about Jasmine's eating and will need to come up with another plan if Katarina is not able to bring back ideas from the doctor.
6. *How do I plan to follow up on promised actions to maintain trust?*	I will ask about the pediatrician visit and again offer to help implement any suggestions. I am prepared to find more information or perhaps a referral to a nutrition specialist to help Katarina in any way possible.
7. *What do I want to discuss in reflective supervision to improve my practice and outcomes with this child and family?*	I am still worried about this family and want to know that I am doing everything possible to help Jasmine reach her developmental goals. It's hard for me to follow this family's lead and capitalize on opportunities to address issues when they are ready.

SUGGESTED FURTHER READINGS

Chatoor, I. (2012). *When your child won't eat or eats too much: A parent's guide for the prevention and treatment of feeding problems in young children.* Bloomington, IN: iUniverse.

Lester, B., & Grace, C.O. (2005). *Why is my baby crying? The parent's survival guide for coping with crying problems and colic.* New York, NY: Harper Collins.

Mindell, J. (2005). *Sleeping through the night* (Rev. ed.). New York, NY: Harper Collins.

Tips for Calming Your Baby

- Respond to your young baby's cry! Your baby will cry less when you do.

- For young babies, try swaddling by wrapping the baby "burrito style" in a blanket.

- Keep your voice low to calm the baby down; remember, a high voice is exciting and tells your baby it is time to play.

- Change something—your location, lights, sounds, or activity level.

- Provide movement—walk or rock.

- Lightly tap or rub the baby's back.

- Add soothing sounds like soft music or "white noise" such as a fan.

- Quietly sing a lullaby or favorite song.

- Remember that sometimes babies need to be alone to calm down and may not want to be held or touched.

- Keep track of what your baby likes and what works to calm him or her down.

- Walk away if you become angry or upset. Call a friend or family member to give you a break.

6

When Parents Say...
Stop That!

Biting, Hitting, Throwing, and Meltdowns

Laurie and Vince decide to take advantage of a pretty fall day to take their three young children, ages 10 months to 5 years, to a nearby park. Their early intervention provider, Debbie, suggested they spend more time outside, and the couple feel proud that they are trying to follow her advice. It takes longer than they expect to get ready, so it is almost nap time when they have the stroller loaded up and ready to go. Two-year-old Theresa is rubbing her eyes and fussing, but they decide to go anyway because they are all ready. Once at the park, Vince follows Theresa, who runs and seems to be having a good time. Laurie pushes the oldest child in a swing and the baby naps in the stroller. Theresa goes to the sand box, where another toddler is digging with a small shovel. She grabs at the shovel and begins to wail when the other child protests. Vince shouts, "No, no!" but Theresa continues to cry and pull at the shovel. When the child does not let go, Theresa hits him.

Virtually all parents have been embarrassed when their young child misbehaves in public settings. Examples of this kind of behavior abound, including hitting or biting another child on the playground or an epic "meltdown" when denied a toy in a store. In some cases, the behavior reaches a level where child care providers or other families complain, leading to worry that the toddler who bites, hits, or has tantrums will have problems getting along with peers or will be kicked out of school. In the vast majority of young children, aggressive behaviors are not predictive of serious future problems. Even those with difficult temperament styles may eventually learn to modulate these behaviors, given proper supports. However, in some cases, aggressive behaviors in early childhood may be intense and persistent, and they may predict many adverse outcomes into teen and adult years (Ramchandani et al., 2013). Whether a challenging behavior is part of a temperament style, a transient developmental phase, or a sign of serious problems, it must be addressed.

Although physical aggression is, to a certain extent, part of typical development, or as discussed in Chapter 5, connected to temperament, it is also one of the most common complaints of parents with young children and requires attention. For many reasons, including their own caregiving histories, parents struggle to address these kinds of challenging behaviors. This chapter discusses family- and child-specific correlates of challenging behavior, explains how to tell when difficult behaviors are typical or age appropriate and when they may signal a bigger problem, and discusses how to use the PAUSE problem-solving framework to support families in building skills needed to address aggression in effective ways.

WHEN TO WORRY—WHAT IS TOO MUCH AGGRESSION?

When are aggressive behaviors normal and when should parents worry? Determining when difficult behavior, such as aggression or tantrums, is a sign of a bigger problem versus an age-appropriate phase can be tricky. Researchers point to the frequency, intensity, and persistence of the difficult behavior as indicators of a larger concern rather than a phase that will pass in time (Ramchandani et al., 2013). Recognizing the expected levels of physical aggression in the first 3 years of life can help parents and providers to sort out typical difficult behaviors from those that should give them pause. Table 6.1 shows how aggression changes from infancy to preschool age.

In general, both oppositional behaviors and aggression, such as hitting and biting, are fairly frequent between ages 1 and 3 years. Parents can expect to first see aggressive actions around their child's first birthday, with a steep rise into the second year (Alink et al., 2006; Tremblay et al., 2004). It is reassuring to know that most difficult behaviors should reach their maximum at the end of the second year, with much improvement typically seen after age 3 or sometimes 4 years. It is likely that aggression most often occurs as a result of parental efforts to limit young children's behavior, clashing with the child's interest in autonomy and independence that is so characteristic of this age range (Alink et al., 2006). At the other end of this process, the reduction in aggression after age 3 years is understood to occur because children have better language and cognitive skills and have internalized some social and moral expectations. So in both cases, rising and de-escalating aggression, changes in behavior are due to changes in developmental skills.

Table 6.1. Expected aggressive behavior by child age

	1 Year	2 Years	3 Years
Expected aggression level patterns	Onset of aggression around first birthday	Aggression increases steeply in second year	Aggression should decrease through ages 3 to 4 years
Common reasons for aggression	Tired or does not feel well	Independence needs	Developmental delays
	Limited language and communication skills	High energy; low impulse control	Difficulty matching behavioral expectations to differing situations (e.g., playground versus library)
			Exposure to aggressive models

Sources: Alink et al. (2006); Ramchandani, Domoney, Sethna, Psychogiou, Vlachos, and Murray (2013); Tremblay et al. (2004).

Tantrums or toddler meltdowns are also fairly frequent in children between the ages of about 18 months and nearly 4 years, especially when a child is tired, hungry, or distressed (Potegal, Kosorok, & Davidson, 2003). A tantrum about once per day is not unusual in a child younger than 4 years. To get a picture of typical tantrums, researchers asked a large sample of parents to provide a written description of one of their child's tantrums. From these descriptions, the researchers found that the most common tantrum lasted 30–60 seconds and that 75% of tantrums are less than 5 minutes (Potegal et al., 2003).

Tantrum behavior often happens when a young child has strong emotions and has not yet learned ways to control these feelings and subsequent behaviors. Parents may most often associate tantrums with anger, but they can also occur when a child is very sad, disappointed, or even scared. In the study by Potegal and colleagues (2003), if a child showed physical signs of anger early in the tantrum, such as stomping his or her feet or falling to the floor, the meltdown was likely to be short and parents did not report a need to intervene. Showing other angry behaviors such as screaming, kicking, hitting, and stiffening the body was associated with more intense tantrums. Many children moved quickly from anger behavior to distress, indicated by crying or wanting to be comforted. Parents in the study described their children as initially angry when they couldn't get what they wanted, and sadness followed when the child began to see the tantrum would not result in getting his or her way (Potegal et al., 2003).

Physically aggressive behaviors can be associated with other challenging behaviors. Typical toddlers also have a relatively high activity level, may have problems taking turns, and are likely to have a limited ability to sustain attention (Danis, Hill, & Wakschlag, 2009, as cited in Schellinger & Talmi, 2013). In one study, parents were asked to describe the "hyperactive" behavior of their 17-month-old children by rating the frequency of behaviors such as not being able to sit still, fidgeting, having difficulty waiting turns, and not being able to settle for a task for more than a few minutes (Romano, Baillargeon, & Cao, 2013). Almost a third of the toddlers were described as showing frequent hyperactive behavior, and 70% showed hyperactivity at least sometimes (Romano et al., 2013). In the same sample, oppositional and aggressive behaviors frequently co-occurred in children reported to have higher levels of hyperactivity. In a commentary, Schellinger and Talmi (2013) reinterpret the data from Romano and colleagues as indicating that hyperactivity, but not highly aggressive behaviors, is typical in toddlers.

Earlier, we discussed that normal limitations in language are connected to aggression. For home visitors working with young children with developmental delays, problems with communication may also be a factor in this kind of difficult behavior. Boys, who are more likely to have delayed communication, are also more likely to show physical aggression between age 2 and 3 years compared with girls (Alink et al., 2006). Girls may use other forms of aggression instead of physical aggression. Gender matters in reporting as well. Mothers report more aggression in children 2 to 3 years than do fathers; in the Alink and colleagues' (2006) study, the mothers were more likely to be the primary caregivers. As a result, the difference in reporting may relate to the amount of time that each parent spent with the children, with mothers having more opportunities to interact with children compared with fathers (Alink et al., 2006). Home visitors should consider the gender of the child and the gender of the parent when evaluating the level of difficulty aggressive behavior may be causing for a family.

Although some aggression, noncompliance, and tantrum behaviors are expected in the early years, these types of challenging behaviors should be trending down as the child approaches 3 years of age and language skills improve. One study by Belden, Thompson, and Luby (2008) investigated tantrums in the preschool period (3 to 6 years) and found that a typical tantrum in this age range lasted about 3 minutes, with a range between 90 seconds and 5 minutes. Those authors reported that children who had more than expected tantrums, had more intense tantrums that involved physical aggression toward others and self, and had a hard time calming after a tantrum were at risk for mental health concerns. More than five tantrums in one day or 10 to 20 tantrums within a month, tantrums that lasted longer than about 25 minutes, aggression toward caregivers or self, and destroying things during the tantrum were associated with clinical diagnoses of depression and disruptive behaviors in this study (Belden et al., 2008). In summary, difficult behavior is not unusual in the first 3 years and may even continue, to an extent, past this age. If the behavior usually has a clear trigger, the child can be calmed, and overall the child seems to be gaining skills in self-regulation, parents and providers do not likely have to worry about long-term problems. Table 6.2 provides an overview of tantrum behavior.

Table 6.2. Toddler tantrum behaviors

Typical pattern	Possible problem
One tantrum per day	Five or more tantrums per day or 10–20 in a week
Tantrum lasts up to 5 minutes	Tantrum lasts longer than 25 minutes
Reason for tantrum is clear (e.g., being told no or prevented from doing something)	Child cannot be calmed or self-soothe
	Child hurts self, others, or destroys things
Child can calm relatively quickly	

Sources: Belden, Thompson, and Luby (2008); Potegal, Kosorok, and Davidson (2003).

FAMILY RISK FACTORS AND MAINTENANCE OF AGGRESSION

So far, we have discussed that most difficult behavior is a common part of early childhood. In fact, Weitzman, Edmonds, Davagnino, and Briggs-Gowan (2014) stated that the prevalence of "clinically significant socioemotional/ behavior problems" in children 0–5 has been reported in a range from 7% to 26%. This range is considered similar to rates of older children and adults (Egger & Angold, 2006), which leads to concerns about connections between early problem behaviors continuing into later childhood and even adult years. What are the factors that lead some young children to have physical aggression and tantrums that are more intense, frequent, and longer lasting than others? Family risk factors, parental risk factors, and problematic parent–child interactions are all possible sources behind persistent challenging behaviors.

When young children grow up in families at risk, they are more likely to show both behavioral and social-emotional effects (Weitzman et al., 2014). The risk factors that are most salient include those related to parent status, including parental medical or mental health issues such as depression, anxiety, personality disorders, parental disengagement, and extreme parent distress (Ramchandani et al., 2013; Weitzman et al., 2014). When families face these and other stressors, aggressive behavior can be part of the child's response.

When home visitors see aggressive child behavior, they may be quick to suggest behavior management methods. However, they would be wise to observe the parents' discipline methods to learn if they may be a part of the issue. Both harsh, overreactive parenting and inconsistent or lax discipline have been connected to early-onset behavior problems, including developmentally unexpected levels of defiance and aggression (Mence et al., 2014). Home visitors can watch for parents who are struggling to manage their own responses to stressful situations, including challenging child behaviors. These parents may be so overstressed that they have limited resources to respond appropriately to difficult child behavior. This could range from parents who appear to do nothing to help reduce challenging behavior to those who use harsh punishments, providing an aggressive model. The home visitor can help the parent find a balanced and effective approach to difficult toddler behavior that combines firmness with warmth.

Most research has considered the effects of harsh and overreactive parenting. We have already discussed how common negative behavior is in early childhood. Parents who use a lot of verbal or physical force are more likely to notice this kind of difficult child behavior and less likely to see positive behavior (Mence et al., 2014; Patterson, 1982). These parents may believe that the child is displaying the undesirable behavior on purpose or even to hurt them. As a result, these parent–child interactions are predominantly negative and there are relatively few times that parents and children enjoy fun or even neutral interactions. Researcher Gerard Patterson (1982) explained that both parents and children in these families have learned to use "aversive control tactics," described as escalating cycles of behaviors such as whining, nagging, shouting, and hitting. Because both parties are inconsistent, both parents and children are sometimes rewarded for their responses, maintaining the patterns of behavior. These negative interaction patterns are in place by age 2 years but escalate over time, with the parent's hostile behavior getting more frequent and intense as the child gets older. Even within each episode, the negative behavior on both sides escalates until the episode is ended by the parent doing something like hitting or yelling. Table 6.3 provides examples of common aggressive patterns in families with suggested responses.

Many home visiting programs, such as those that include families involved in child welfare, support parents who are at high risk for negative parenting practices due to their own low self-regulation. It is helpful to recognize that often these families include parents who received negative caregiving in their own childhoods and who may be replicating the hostile, harsh, or overreactive caregiving that they received. Parents who did not have a chance to develop good self-regulation may experience difficulty tolerating their child's negative emotions. Parents perceive their child's angry, scared, or other negative emotions as unexpected and unprovoked. As a result, the parent subsequently feels "emotionally flooded," which can be described as feeling overwhelmed and disorganized (Gottman, 1991). In this overwhelmed state, the parent has trouble thinking in a way that allows him or her to read the child's intentions and needs accurately. Furthermore, the parent's dysregulated emotions and disorganized thinking may result in choosing old discipline strategies that rely on aggression and coercion and decrease the likelihood that the parent will use a strategy that helps the child calm down and feel soothed (Mence et al., 2014).

The home visitor can ask parents what it is like for them when their child demonstrates challenging behaviors. Through discussion, the home visitor can help the parent notice and describe feelings in order to make connections between their own feelings and their responses to challenging child behavior. For example, a parent may realize that he or she feels embarrassment when the child hits another person, prompting the parent to use rough methods in the

Table 6.3. Helpful responses to common aggressive patterns in families

What you might see	How you might respond
The parent has trouble seeing positive child behavior.	Point out positive behaviors the child displays.
	Help the parent provide simple commands the child can follow to give experiences of competence.
The parent thinks the child is displaying negative behavior to annoy him or her.	Sympathize with the parent that it often feels that the child is doing things on purpose.
	Encourage wondering about what a child might get from his or her behavior to promote a more realistic view.
Parent and child interactions involve escalating cycles of negative behaviors by both parties.	Encourage the parent to use a low voice and calm expression.
	Encourage plans for both the parent and child to take breaks to avoid escalation that includes physical aggression.
The parent and child are inconsistent, leading to rewards for poor behavior by both.	Help the parent learn to pick his or her battles.
	Help the parent consistently enforce limits he or she chooses to set.
Parent–child interactions are almost always negative. There is little room for shared positive experiences.	Ask the parent to think of times when he or she had fun or experienced any positive emotion with the child. Encourage the parent to think about how that was for the child, too.
	Set up some simple, age-appropriate activities and coach the parent through them, ending on a positive note.

Sources: Mence et al. (2014); Patterson (1982).

hope of stopping the behavior quickly. Another parent might come to understand that seeing his or her child feel afraid brings on his or her own feelings of fear, and soon they are both paralyzed. Parents can also learn some self-regulation methods, such as reframing the difficult behavior as part of typical development, taking breaks when needed, and being able to ask for help. As the parent gets better at identifying his or her own feelings and learns more methods to manage upset feelings, the parent will be better able to consider the child's perspective.

Vince says, "That's not our shovel. You can't just take things!"
Theresa ignores Vince and keeps crying. He feels embarrassed and wonders what the other parents think. Frustrated, he picks up Theresa and gives her a swat on the diaper. She yells louder and Vince feels worse. He carries her back to the stroller and digs around in the diaper bag for a toy, but Theresa keeps crying. Laurie is angry at Vince for hitting Theresa. "We said we weren't going to use hitting anymore," she reminds him. "No, you

said that. I got whipped as a kid and I turned out fine," Vince retorts. After some time, Laurie finally calms Theresa by letting her play with a cell phone. They leave the park feeling discouraged.

Although less studied, a detached parenting style is also associated with child behavior concerns. Detached parenting (Ryan, Martin, & Brookes-Gunn, 2006) is characterized by inconsistent discipline and low involvement with the child. Parents with a detached parenting style may rarely interact with their child, often due to parental preoccupation with their own interests and activities (e.g., the parent is often observed looking at his or her phone while the child plays alone). In addition, parents with a detached style may fail to respond to their children's bids for interaction or requests for help with frustrating situations. Failure to attend to child needs and to support in upsetting or frustrating situations means the parent misses many opportunities to provide regulation or to scaffold the child's self-regulation (Jones Harden, Denmark, Holmes, & Duchene, 2014). Detached parenting, like harsh parenting, is associated with parent stress, which has been directly associated with child behavior problems in children under age 3 years (Jones Harden et al., 2014). Strategies that help the parent notice child bids for attention, such as speaking for the baby, may be helpful. For example, speaking in the baby's voice, the home visitor could say, "I see what you are eating and want to try some." Home visitors can coach parents through interactions, narrating out loud the positive responses that the child is demonstrating. For example, sitting together with the infant and parent, the home visitor could say, "He is smiling at you. I wonder if he is telling you he is ready to play." At times, the home visitor may find that these parents are hard to engage. In these situations, consider dropping back to spend time noticing and responding to parent needs.

Home visitors observe and hear about a wide variety of difficult behaviors in young children. Although parents and caregivers often expect home visitors to have ideas and suggestions to immediately fix unwanted behaviors in children, this may be impossible, as things may not be as they seem. Use the PAUSE framework to help consider examples of challenging behaviors provided in the following short case studies. As a reminder, the steps to PAUSE include Perceive, Ask, Understand, Strategize, and Evaluate. Here are some questions to consider:

What attitudes or experiences may be related to the behaviors of the parents in the following examples?

What interaction patterns between parent and child might be in play?

How might the child be responding to parent behaviors?

How would it feel to witness these events?

What responses could address the needs of the parent and the child?

How would you know if your responses were effective?

Dylan (age 20 months) was playing with his blocks on the floor at the end of the session with Mary, the home visitor. His father, Robert, joined the play, making a tall tower of blocks and then knocking it down with a big punch. As Dylan squealed in laughter, Robert scattered the blocks again, making a "kaboom" sound. He grabbed Dylan and tickled him while throwing him in the air, yelling "kaboom." After a few minutes, Robert noticed the time and realized they needed to say goodbye to Mary and then get ready to go pick up Dylan's brother at kindergarten. He quickly put Dylan down and started to pick up the blocks. Dylan tried to continue the play, laughing and squealing. Robert shouted to Dylan that play time was over, but Dylan ran around throwing blocks and yelling "kaboom." Robert grabbed Dylan roughly and said, "Hey, no throwing blocks! You can hurt someone!" Mary noticed that Dylan quieted and looked a little scared.

Elizabeth was talking with the home visitor about the next appointment. During the interaction, her daughter, Lydia (age 2 years), tried to ask her for a snack. Elizabeth ignored Lydia's attempts to get her attention. Finally, Lydia kicked her mother in the leg and yelled, "I hungry!" Elizabeth responded angrily by hitting Lydia's hand and saying, "I am talking. You are a bad girl for interrupting me!"

Abby and her son, Carson (age 30 months), are meeting with Jill, a home visitor in a prevention program. Carson is driving his toy cars on a mat on the floor while they talk. When Jill asks how things are going, Abby explains that her ex-boyfriend contacted her over the weekend, even though a restraining order is in place. He wanted to come over to see Carson; Abby did not want to allow it, but she was afraid to refuse. As Abby explained that the visit escalated into an argument, she began to cry. Carson continued to play with his cars, but began throwing them against the walls. Abby shouted at him to stop, and Carson ran over and hit her in the stomach. Abby looked shocked and pulled back from Carson, who then cried and tried to get in her lap. Abby pushed him away while Jill tried to figure out a way to help both parent and child calm down.

The home visitor brought some different toys with her to the session to see how Billy (age 35 months) might respond. She let him choose a toy from her bag. He pulled out a baby doll and grabbed it by the throat and said, "Shut up. I told you shut up." He then punched the doll on the face and threw it on the floor. Next, he picked up a toy truck and started driving it, making horn sounds.

Susanna (age 15 months) was just learning to sit at the table. She struggled to reach her drink. When she reached, she made a squished-up face and made a grunting sound. Her grandmother laughed at this face. Susanna grinned and made the face again while her grandmother laughed. This little fun game continued for several minutes. After snack time, Susanna was playing with her mother on the floor and made the face and noise. Her mother corrected her, saying she should not make a rude face because she might get in trouble at preschool. Susanna appeared confused that her mother did not know the game she had played with her grandmother.

After a long morning and no nap in the afternoon, Ryan (age 27 months) played in the family living room while his mother, Gloria, folded laundry and watched television. Ryan moved from activity to activity quickly. Finding a pile of toys in the corner, Ryan tossed some stuffed animals in the air briefly before he found a toy truck and drove it around in circles, making a honking sound. When he drove over some crayons, Ryan picked one up and started drawing on the truck. His mother yelled at him to stop coloring on the truck and to calm down. He looked at her, turned, and jumped into the pile of toys and hit his head on the corner of the toy box. "That's what happens when you act wild!" Gloria yelled.

Nancy was sitting on the floor getting ready to start the home visiting session with Natalie (age 14 months). She was talking with Natalie's mother, Grace, about the past week. While Grace and Nancy chatted about Natalie's progress, Natalie grabbed Nancy's glasses off of her face and bent the frame before letting go of them. Grace looked embarrassed, shouted at Natalie, and then started to cry. Natalie joined in.

These narratives and other examples of difficult child behaviors and unskilled parent responses to such behavior may be very familiar to home visitors. Parents may describe a behavior that occurred, seeking sympathy and help. Other times, a home visitor may witness the difficult exchange between parent and child. Still other times, the child may display difficult behavior toward the home visitor. In any case, the home visitor is often in a position to wonder about the best response to challenging behaviors. What are some strategies to consider when supporting a parent or caregiver to respond effectively to challenging behaviors? Also, what are some effective and sensitive ways to share these ideas? We first discuss prevention methods, followed by helpful immediate responses when the difficult behavior is witnessed and strategies to cover later when everyone is calmer.

To begin, it is helpful to consider ways to prevent behavior problems before they happen. Because children's behaviors are often predictable, preventing misbehavior is actually possible. Helping parents to plan ahead, consider development, and make use of their knowledge of their child's rhythms related to sleep and routines can help avoid putting children into situations where problem behavior is likely to occur. Let's revisit the vignette to see how the home visitor begins to help Vince and Laurie consider these factors.

A week later, Vince and Laurie talk to the early intervention provider, Debbie, about their experience at the park. Vince is angry that the outing went so poorly. He tells Debbie, "Theresa was so bad. She does that stuff on purpose to make me mad. I know she knows better." Laurie adds, "I can tell you we won't be trying to take all of them out any time soon. It is just not worth it." Debbie is nearly as discouraged as Vince and Laurie. She had been encouraging them to try new things for weeks and now when they finally did, it was a disaster. She thinks about the many things she would like to address, including the use of spanking, trying the trip when the kids were tired, Vince's lack of understanding of Theresa's perspective, and explaining the behavior from a developmental perspective. However, she is unsure where to start.

Debbie says, "I am so sorry the trip did not work out. Was there any part that did go okay?" Vince and Laurie admit that it was nice at the beginning. Debbie asks them to think about what happened before Theresa hit the other child. As they discuss the events, Debbie is able to gently direct their attention to how Theresa might have been feeling: perhaps tired, frustrated because she wanted the toy, and then upset when Vince spanked her. She asks Vince and Laurie to talk about what they might do differently if they tried this again. "Maybe we could leave earlier so Theresa doesn't miss her nap," Laurie suggests.

Prevention through planning ahead will not always work. Parents will still need to have some strategies to address difficult behaviors that are a normal part of child development and responses to strong emotions. Home visitors can help parents learn how to identify triggers for difficult behaviors and to understand how their own reactions and other outcomes might increase difficult behaviors, as discussed in Chapter 4. Use of distraction techniques, such as redirecting the child to another activity, can be helpful if done prior to a tantrum. For this to work, parents must become good observers and notice the lead-up to their child's difficult responses.

Remember that the redirection will be most successful if it matches the child's interest and need. If the child is playing in a way that is too active or too loud for the setting, trying to redirect to a quiet activity right away may not work. Instead, having them go to a place where active play is allowed or modifying what they are doing to fit where you are will probably work better. In another example, Suzy is busily emptying out her drawers and tossing clothing everywhere. Her mother sees that she is interested in taking things out of containers, so she provides her with some plastic containers and small toys. She shows her how to put the toys in and dumps them back out. Other strategies that may fend off a tantrum include offers of help, subtle scaffolding, and encouraging a child to take a break from a frustrating activity.

When children are already upset and having a meltdown, a calm adult is a must. Encourage the parents to stay calm, speak in a low voice, and remain available to the upset young children. Use of simple language to explain what is happening at the child's level, especially when paired with feeling words, may be helpful (McClelland & Tominey, 2014). Remember, many tantrums start as anger when the child is not able to have what he or she wants, but sadness may frequently follow. Trying to redirect, explain, or teach will probably not work at that moment. Parents may have to set limits on aggressive or oppositional behavior at times. Letting the child know with simple words that you will not let them hurt you, others, or themselves can be effective when done with closeness and redirection.

Many parents believe that retribution for aggression, such as hitting a child or "biting them back," is an effective form of punishment. However, this method or any corporal punishment is typically ineffective. One concern is that physical punishment provides an aggressive model (Durrant & Ensom, 2012). In addition, corporal punishment does not help the child understand what behavior is expected. It is also important to note that holding children against their will in an effort to help them calm down is not recommended for very young children. This method also sends the message that using force is the way to solve problems and may actually frighten a young child (Dunlap, Ostryn, & Fox, 2011). Similarly, restraining an upset child in a car seat or other device is also not recommended. Car seats are not designed to be used in this way, and there have been instances of young children being severely injured when this method was used (Bull, 2014).

As Debbie and Laurie finish making plans to try another outing when Theresa is not tired, Vince suddenly says, "I still think I was right to spank her." The home visitor, Debbie, asks what Vince is hoping Theresa will learn from spanking. Vince says, "To be nice and share." Debbie agrees that these are important things to learn. She tells Vince she is interested in hearing more about his thoughts and asks if he would also hear her ideas. Vince, with Laurie's urging, agrees that they can talk more about this. "Nobody else ever said they would listen to my side. I guess I can at least listen to yours," Vince says.

SUPPORTING POSITIVE BEHAVIORS THROUGH TEACHING AND REFLECTION

There are several other strategies home visitors can share with parents to help when young children show aggression. As discussed in Chapter 4, parents can identify a behavior they would like the child to display instead of the aggressive behavior and provide reinforcement for that behavior. The behavior might be one the child already knows how to do or one that is taught. The home visitor can support the parents to think of an appropriate substitute behavior and help them understand the best ways to reinforce it. Chapter 7 describes how to use praise effectively as part of this method.

It can be helpful to encourage parents to recognize how they are responding to their child's behavior. A nice starting point is to ask, "How is it for you when your child is hitting?" This type of question provides an opening to discuss the parent's own reactions. Often, parents are having a hard time tolerating their children's upset feelings or behaviors but are not aware of their own experience. This may be related to their own childhood experiences or simply a result of current stresses. Some parents may feel mildly stressed by their child's behavior, whereas others may be totally overwhelmed. Regardless, the home visitor may support parents to think about ways they can calm themselves at these times. Some quick ways parents can feel calmer include reminding themselves that their child will not be this age forever, taking three long breaths, and using humor to lift their own mood.

When the parent stays calm, he or she will be better able to think about an effective response to the child's distress. If parents are too stressed on a routine basis, asking them to identify who else can help, so that they can take a break, may also be helpful (Mence et al., 2014). When there is no one who can help quickly, parents can be coached to give the child an age-appropriate time-out or to give themselves a time-out. Either of these breaks can help stop escalating high emotions of the parent and child (Mence et al., 2014).

Overall, providers should encourage parents to engage with their young children in warm and supportive ways. This may be even more important to emphasize when young children are having challenging behavior than at other times. Warm and engaged parenting is related to children learning how to self-regulate emotions and manage their behavior in difficult situations (DeKlyen, Biernbaum, Speltz, & Greenberg, 1998). When home visitors show warmth and develop positive relationships with parents, it is more likely that parents will develop and demonstrate similar skills with their young children. For a summary of timely tips for tolerating challenging behaviors, see Appendix 6A.

EXPLORING THE PROVIDER'S FEELINGS AND REACTIONS

It is not unusual or wrong for home visitors to have many feelings, both positive and negative, related to their work with families. Furthermore, just like parents, home visitors can have personal responses to challenging child behaviors, such as aggression, or to the choices parents make regarding discipline methods. Some reactions might relate to the home visitor's beliefs about families, how parents and children should be with each other, or parenting or other household practices. At times, these responses may even relate to the home visitor's own personal history with relationships, including being parented or parenting his or her own children. The ways that family members respond to a home visitor personally and his or her recommendations or ideas may lead to positive or negative feelings. Home visitors might find it hard to accept if a child acts aggressively toward them, for example. They may really enjoy working with some families and feel frustrated when other families are not receptive to their recommendations.

When home visitors see parenting practices that evoke negative feelings or reactions, it is helpful to try to learn more about how the parent is seeing the child, what the parent is hoping the child will learn from use of punishment, or other strategy, and how the parent learned about parenting. As we have discussed, the home visitor is in the best position to learn these pieces of information when he or she has a positive relationship with the parents. Using the PAUSE Worksheet (Appendix 3A) will be helpful in gathering this kind of information.

Stopping to reflect and connect with personal feelings about the situation can help the home visitor slow down and form some good questions that engage the parent in a dialogue. Developing reflective skills can also help home visitors be aware of their own responses and reactions and may improve their ability to consider experiences of parents and children. The Provider Reflection Worksheet (found in Appendix 3B) provides a structured way of thinking about personal responses and reactions. Discussing these types of responses with a supervisor or supportive colleague can be beneficial. When appropriate, the home visitor may also want to discuss his or her own response with parents as part of their collaborative problem solving.

USING THE PAUSE FRAMEWORK

Using the vignettes in this chapter, consider how Debbie could think through her experiences with Theresa and her parents, Vince and Laurie. See Figures 6.1 and 6.2 for examples of how this might look.

PAUSE WORKSHEET pa**u**se

Child: Theresa   Date: March 17, 2015

Parent: Laurie and Vince   Provider: Debbie

PERCEIVE—Explore what is happening.

Parent/caregiver perspective:	Provider perspective:
Theresa purposefully behaves in ways to make them mad. My ideas and suggestions failed. They will never be able to go out to the park or to a restaurant.	The parents are struggling with understanding Theresa's needs and the way she communicates. They tried these activities when the children were tired, a set-up for failure. They feel the strategies we discussed won't work.

ASK—Clarify what is happening.

Starting with the parent/caregiver's priorities and concerns, ask more detailed/specific questions to clarify what is happening.

Ask more about what led up to the event they described to try to understand what might have contributed to the problems.

Ask about what went well to build on the successes.

Ask Vince to talk more about how he knows that Theresa is purposefully misbehaving.

UNDERSTAND—Explore why it is happening.

With the parent/caregiver, explore explanations for what is happening. Consider possible explanations that include the environment, the child, and the parent. Listen and observe closely as you explore the situation in conversation with the family.

Parent/caregiver perspective:	Provider perspective:	Child's perspective:
What is behind Vince's anger and frustration? How can I help him see this in a different way?	How can I remain calm during this discussion? This raised my own red flags about spanking	Theresa is little, was tired, and just wanted to play with a toy.

(continued)

Figure 6.1. Debbie's PAUSE Worksheet for Laurie, Vince, and Theresa.

Figure 6.1. *(continued)*

PAUSE WORKSHEET *(continued)*

UNDERSTAND *(continued)*

Parent/caregiver perspective:	Provider perspective:	Child's perspective:
	and misunderstanding Theresa's viewpoint. No one stands up for her. How can I build their relationships through activities where they have fun together?	

STRATEGIZE and **EVALUATE**—Identify possible responses/solutions.

1. Solution/action to try:	How will we know if it works?
Discover activities to use at home to help build the relationship between the parents and Theresa.	Vince and Laurie identify positive aspects of their relationship with Theresa.
	When will we evaluate if it works?
	Evaluate after 2 months.

2. Solution/action to try:	How will we know if it works?
Practice "going out" by doing it at home, but as a play activity, to simulate what might happen and practice.	Vince and Laurie can identify the parts of the planning process that might ensure a successful outing.
	When will we evaluate if it works?
	Evaluate after two trials of a pretend outing.

PROVIDER REFLECTION WORKSHEET

Child: Theresa   Date: March 17, 2015

Parent: Laurie and Vince

Provider: Debbie

1. How did I follow the parent's lead to learn what is most pressing or important to the family?	I thought the family was ready to try an outing, but I missed something, as they didn't seem to plan well and then felt like they failed. How can I find the positive in what happened? What could I do differently next time?
2. How did I ask clarifying questions to help me understand the problem better?	What was the preparation phase like? How did it feel when Theresa acted out? How did the other parents react? The other children? What would it take to try this again?
3. How did I provide information that may help the family better understand the child's behavior?	I need to figure out how to discuss this from Theresa's perspective. She was tired, so she was not at her best to try something that we know is hard. Theresa is also learning about sharing and how to be with other children her age. How can I help explain this phase of development?

(continued)

Figure 6.2. Debbie's Provider Reflection Worksheet for Laurie, Vince, and Theresa.

Figure 6.2. *(continued)*

PROVIDER REFLECTION WORKSHEET *(continued)*

4. *How did I engage the family to develop a response that may include a strategy to try, a resource to use, or more information to increase understanding?*	I wonder if we might explore everyone's temperament as a way to better understand each person's perspective. How would I do this?
5. *How did I provide support and emotional containment if needed?*	Vince's anger is surprising for me and almost scary. I'm not sure why, or how I can be helpful in containing that, but I know this is important in our work. I am glad he is willing to hear my ideas after I offered to understand his viewpoint.
6. *How do I plan to follow up on promised actions to maintain trust?*	I am worried this family might not trust me with future ideas since this activity seemed to backfire in their minds. How do I repair this?
7. *What do I want to discuss in reflective supervision to improve my practice and outcomes with this child and family?*	I want to discuss my strong reaction to the idea of spanking and my worry that this family seems to be missing Theresa's perspective. I want help to be better able to acknowledge the parents' frustration and their worry about Theresa's behaviors.

WHAT'S NEXT?

In Chapter 7, we apply the PAUSE problem-solving approach to look at another type of common but difficult behavior, noncompliance.

TIPS FOR PRACTICE

▶ Recognize and help caregivers understand that aggression and tantrum behaviors are very common in children between ages 1 and 3 years.

▶ Be aware of caregiver experiences that may contribute to harsh parenting practices.

▶ Help caregivers connect to their feelings to build their own capacity for self-regulation to more effectively manage challenging child behaviors.

KEY POINTS TO REMEMBER

▶ Difficult behaviors, including verbal and physical aggression, are fairly common in children between 1 and 3 years of age. With the growth of self-regulation and communication skills, improvements should gradually be seen as the child is closer to age 3.

▶ Short tantrums about once a day are not unusual for young children. Tantrums in this age range are frequently related to the child's frustration over not getting what he or she wants. Tantrums may start as anger and shift into sadness. Recognizing the triggers for tantrums can help parents prevent them and respond in better ways.

▶ Some parenting practices and family characteristics may increase the chances that aggressive behaviors persist. In contrast, consistent and warm responses from parents may help scaffold children, leading to less aggression as more appropriate coping skills are developed.

SUGGESTED FURTHER READINGS

Webster-Stratton, C. (2005). *The incredible years: A trouble-shooting guide for parents of children aged 2–8 years.* Seattle, WA: Incredible Years.

Webster-Stratton, C. (2011). *Incredible toddlers: A guide and journal of your toddler's discoveries.* Seattle, WA: Incredible Years.

Timely Tips for Tolerating Challenging Behaviors

Prevention

- Provide structure and routine.

- Know your child's rhythms and schedules.

- Maintain realistic expectations! Do not take young children places where they might get overwhelmed or take them out when they are feeling bad or tired.

Immediate Adult Responses that Help

- Stay calm, shown by a low voice and neutral facial expression.

- Provide containment and safety, such as removing the child from a situation to calm down.

- Comfort the child and help the child express negative emotions appropriately: stay close, use physical comfort and a soothing voice.

Follow-Up Responses

- Remember to follow up when everyone is calm and well rested.

- Talk about what happened; make a plan to do better next time.

- Teach a substitute behavior to replace a behavior that is undesirable.

- Teach, coach, and reinforce prosocial behaviors.

Caregiver Self-Care

- Take a break or ask for some help.

- Maintain perspective—remember the child will not be this age forever, and look for the humor in the situation.

- Use a calming strategy such as taking three long, deep breaths.

When Parents Say...
Why Won't You Listen?

Cooperating and Following Directions

Colleen arranges to meet Jeanette and 20-month-old Paul, a family on her caseload, at a local library. Paul is an active boy who lives with both parents in a small apartment. He likes to run and be loud, like many boys his age. Jeanette worries that the neighbors will be angry when he is so loud. Colleen has been trying to get Jeanette to bring Paul out more often. She has chosen the library for several reasons, including that it is located on a convenient bus route and has a good children's section. Colleen plans to introduce the young family to the library, help them check out some books, and encourage Jeanette to participate in the library's programs for children.

About 10 minutes past the scheduled meeting time, Colleen hears the family arrive before she can see them. Jeanette can be heard loudly whispering for Paul to stay quiet, while he is happily and loudly singing his version of "Twinkle, Twinkle, Little Star." Jeanette is flustered and rushing along the hallway as she talks nonstop to her son. Jeanette says, "Now, this is the library, so we can't yell or run. If you don't be good and listen to mommy, then we'll have to go home and you won't get to see Colleen." Colleen suppresses a wry smile as she hurries to help out. She thinks that she will once again need to review with Jeanette how to give clear commands. Paul is such an exuberant child, and Colleen wishes that Jeanette could enjoy his happy personality. She sees that Paul is in a stroller; he smiles a wide smile when he sees Colleen and says "up, up" while reaching his arms up to his mother to be taken from the stroller. Jeanette presses her lips together and hesitates.

"I don't think this will work out. He is just going to run around and he never listens to me when I try to stop him."

Colleen thinks carefully. She doesn't want to push Jeanette into something she is afraid to try and she definitely does not want to put Paul in a position of getting into trouble. However, she really thinks that Jeanette and Paul could get a lot out of a library visit. She also feels a little frustrated, as she knows that Paul can manage the library with just a little redirection and planning. "Why does Jeanette continue to give such long instructions when other methods work so much better?" she wonders. Colleen smiles and says, "It's so great that you guys made it all the way here. If you want to wait until a better day, we can. I am happy to help you try if you want, though." Jeanette looks dubious, but she starts to unbuckle Paul from the stroller, resuming her nonstop stream of instructions as she does.

Learning social skills such as how to cooperate and follow directions does not happen overnight. Parents and home visitors can be frustrated when young children do not comply or refuse to comply in ways that are perceived as "defiant" or "not respectful." Parents may worry that their child will have a hard time in school if he or she does not become more cooperative. In order for young children to cooperate and follow directions, many skills must be present. These include understanding instructions, being able to perform the behavior asked, and being able to inhibit behaviors the child would rather do. As in physical aggression, delays in development may play a role when young children do not follow directions. In addition, a certain degree of refusing to follow adult instruction is to be expected in younger children. As a result, it is important for home visitors to help parents know the difference between behaviors that signal a need for independence and those that suggest true problem behavior.

In Chapter 6, we discussed how a child's growing skills and temperament result in an initial increase in physical aggression around age 2 years. By age 3, physical aggression and behaviors such as tantrums are gradually shaped into more socially appropriate responses, both by improvement of developmental skills and by parent scaffolding and supports. In this chapter, we continue to look at how temperament, developmental skills, and parenting behaviors interact with and influence self-regulation related to the performance of positive or prosocial behaviors such as following directions, helping, and cooperating with others. Many factors underlie behavioral and emotion regulation—including brain changes, hormonal controls, cognitive and language development, temperament differences, and parenting environment (Thompson & Goodvin, 2007). As refraining from aggression is linked to better outcomes, so too are positive social behaviors. Children who show better early prosocial behaviors are likely to have enhanced longer-range outcomes, including getting along with others and even better school performance.

DEVELOPING PROSOCIAL BEHAVIORS

Young children may need guidance in developing the prosocial behaviors that help them succeed in life. In the following subsections, we discuss the development of the prosocial behaviors of compliance and self-regulation of feelings, as well as of other social and emotional skills.

Developing Compliance

The term *compliance* is used to describe a child doing what the parent or other caregiver wants, requests, or commands (Landy, 2009). This can include following directions to complete a specific task or instructions to stop doing or not do something. As any parent will attest, convincing a young child to do what the parent wants or getting them to stop doing what they want to do can be challenging. Both understanding what the parent wants and willingness to do it are involved in compliance.

Although most children are able to understand what a parent wants, in most situations, by age 3 years, they may not always perform to their potential ability. In younger children, normal deficits in self-control may contribute to lower compliance. This can confuse parents who may hear their 2-year-old correcting her dolls or telling others "no, no" and believe this behavior indicates full understanding of discipline. Being able to repeat a command is not the same as fully understanding it or being able to comply. In addition, of course, it is not unusual for the parent and the child to have different ideas about what the child should be doing. So, at times, a child may just not want to comply in given situations, even though they have the skill. An example might be the parent instructing a child to put away toys to get ready for bed. From the child's perspective, playing is fun or perhaps the tower is not finished. Although the child understands the command and is able to perform it, he or she does not want to because going to bed means missing out on more fun with toys.

Parents and other caregivers generally target the beginning of problems with compliance with commands to age 2 years. Thus, there are terms like "the terrible twos." However, compliance problems typically start much earlier. Very high levels of noncompliance are reported between 12 and 24 months (Landy, 2009). Once a child is able to walk, around the end of the first year, compliance becomes very important to parents. This is because as infants becomes toddlers, they are able to have more control over how close or far they are from parents, resulting in games of "catch me" and other safety concerns. Children in this age range can run, jump, climb, and explore; therefore, they can also find interesting and often possibly forbidden objects, resulting in the need for parents to monitor them closely. Parents who feel that they are in near continual conflict with their young children are probably right! From this rocky start between 12 and 24 months, most typically developing 3-year-olds will increasingly show skills such as knowing what behaviors adults expect, following rules, demonstrating self-control, and expressing feelings of pride and shame (Forman, 2007). These skills will continue to improve as the child approaches 4 years.

The combination of toddlers' greater ability to "get into things" and their higher interest in doing things their way results in increasing parent–child conflicts. As their infants become toddlers, parents find themselves greatly increasing the number of commands and prohibitions, (do and don't commands) they must make (Forman, 2007). Parents have to give commands repeatedly because young children frequently display behaviors that need correcting and often do not follow instructions. Specifically, children under the age of 2 years follow instructions less than half the time (Kochanska, Coy, & Murray, 2001). In addition, young children also do not follow prohibitions or "stop" commands very well; parents may have to tell a child in this age range to not do a specific behavior as many as 20 times in a single day (Landy, 2009).

Most of our discussion to this point has involved how young children comply when parents are present and giving the command. The top commands that parents give in this age range have to do with immediate needs, such as staying safe, instructions related to self-care, or taking care with objects or possessions. Common instructions include statements about here-and-now behaviors, such as "Don't run," "Let's get dressed," or "We don't take toys from friends" (Forman, 2007). However, parents and toddlers can experience conflictual interactions outside of discipline. For example, toddlers and parents can clash when the parent does not do something the toddler wants, such as allowing a piece of candy or letting them play with their cell phone. Toddlers and parents can also disagree over facts. A common example might be a parent announcing that the child needs a diaper change and the child insisting that he absolutely does not (Laible & Thompson, 2002). This behavior is most likely a form of avoidance and should be distinguished from actual lying.

Whatever the type, parent–toddler conflicts vary widely in frequency but have been reported to occur as much as 19 times an hour (Laible & Thompson, 2002). These many conflicts are opportunities for parents and children to learn how to come to resolution and for young children to begin the process of internalizing parental values and rules. Children who have internalized the parent's agenda begin to display committed compliance, described as willingness or even eagerness to cooperate (Kochanska, 2002). This type of compliance is distinguished from situational compliance, in which the child may only comply when the parent is present and enforcing the rule (Landy, 2009). See Table 7.1 for a picture of how developmental capacities affect compliance.

Language skills have been connected to emotion regulation and compliance. In order to follow a direction, young children have to understand what the parent is telling them. Children who have better verbal skills are better able to understand what they are to do and to actually do it (Vallotton & Ayoub, 2011). Language skill is also important in children's ability to internalize parental rules as part of their own self-regulation, in the present and in

Table 7.1. Links between development and compliance behaviors

Age	Emerging developmental skills		Parent response
	Physical	Cognitive and language	
<12 months	Child begins to move limbs but is still fairly stationary.	Cause-and-effect skills emerging; may understand more than can communicate	Able to leave child for a moment in a safe place; talk, sing, and play turn-taking games to build skills
12–24 months	Crawling, walking, running, jumping, and climbing skills develop.	Growing curiosity and interest in exploring surroundings; able to verbally refuse (e.g., "no!") and indicate possession (e.g., "mine")	Set new limits; monitor child activity more closely to ensure safety; expect to repeat commands
24–36 months	Movement becomes more coordinated; use of hands allows exploration of smaller objects and containers.	Can follow some rules and make requests to repeat enjoyable activities; more able to wait when requested, show some self-control, and express emotions	Use of routines; explain and predict activities to help with transitions and compliance

the future. As children gain in language comprehension, parents are able to talk about rules and expectations in more complex ways. An example might be, "When Nana gives you a present, be sure you say thank you." Early language capacity is also related to later self-regulation skills. For example, in one study, young children who had better overall language skills at 18 months later demonstrated less anger and better coping when in a frustrating situation at 4 years of age (Roben, Cole, & Armstrong, 2013). When young children have language delays, problems in compliance can stem from lack of understanding and may lead to long-term issues with compliance and emotion regulation.

Although noncompliance in early childhood is expected, not all forms of noncompliance are equal. Researchers distinguish between skilled and non-skilled forms of noncompliance. Skilled noncompliance, including negotiating with or attempting to redirect a parent, is more sophisticated than unskilled noncompliance, such as simple refusal. Noncompliance that includes defiance or aggression has been associated with later clinical behavior problems.

Young children spontaneously talk about emotions in themselves and others by 24 months but may have some sense of feelings earlier, as noted by some researchers (Brownell, Svetlova, Anderson, Nichols, & Drummond, 2013; Witmer, 2008). As with physical aggression and tantrums, parental responses are associated with children's abilities to build better skills, feelings, and emotion regulation. Parents' talk about their own feelings or feelings of others can promote sharing and other positive behavior at least by 2 years. Ideally, parents will provide an environment that helps young children identify and discuss emotions, gain coping skills to tolerate frustration, and manage other negative emotions such as fear. Parents will set up situations that reward children for compliance and other positive social skills. When parents provide this kind of support, children learn that upset feelings, although real, are not bad or dangerous and can be managed (Thompson & Goodvin, 2007).

Methods to Help Young Children Build Self-Regulation of Feelings

Methods to build self-regulation of strong feelings are varied and can include prevention strategies. Proactive or prevention methods include helping children to stay on a consistent routine that ensures predictability, reduces anxiety, and builds expectations. Parents can also avoid putting young children into situations in which they are likely to struggle, such as taking them to places that are not child friendly or scheduling activities when the child is likely to be tired and less cooperative (e.g., avoid taking a young child to a fancy restaurant, especially when dinner starts after bedtime).

It will not be possible for parents to completely avoid upsetting situations and, as discussed, a certain amount of difficult or challenging behavior is age appropriate and to be expected. Although it is not appropriate to expect toddlers to comply quickly or never have a tantrum, parents can use many strategies to help young children cope with their feelings and perform more competent social behaviors (Thompson & Goodvin, 2007). Parents may use distraction to attract attention away from something that might be scary or away from a tempting but forbidden object. Scaffolding and breaking down challenging tasks can help young children with frustration while gradually building skills that help them gain competence. Parents can coach children to use their highest skills, even when under pressure or stress. For example, parents can support the young child to use words to ask for help when frustrated or to give polite refusals, such as "no, thank you" instead of more defiant refusals. Providing additional information to reinterpret a child's view of a situation as threatening can also help (e.g., "It's just a shadow."). Methods to help young children build self-regulation are provided in Table 7.2.

The overall emotional climate in a family, including the parent's own responses to emotion-provoking situations, becomes important, as young children will typically use social referencing to determine how to feel about various people, events, and situations. A young child watches his or her parents to learn how to behave in specific situations (e.g., "Should I stay close, or is this a place to run and play?") and to gather information about how people handle emotion-provoking events generally. Home visitors can help parents recognize that their models of emotional language and emotional expression

Table 7.2. Methods to help young children build self-regulation

Method	Example
Prevention strategies	Providing routines
	Choosing environments where children will be successful
	Avoiding times when the child will be tired
Distraction	Redirecting the child to an activity that is less frightening
	Providing the child with something else to do instead of a forbidden activity or object
Scaffolding	Breaking down tasks into small components (e.g., "First put on your socks. Now let's put on your shoes.")
	Giving help to complete parts of tasks (e.g., "Mommy can pick up the blocks while you pick up your books.")
Coaching	Reminding the child what he or she can say and do when upset
	Giving words to the child's feelings (e.g., "You feel sad because you can't have a new toy.")
Providing information and modeling	"There is no monster. It is a shadow."
	"That lady is mommy's friend. It's okay to say hi to her."

are also important. In addition to providing a positive model, parents can coach and help young children practice emotional language to cope with situations. In a study by Brownell and colleagues (2013), parents were observed sharing picture books about emotions with their toddlers. The researchers found that when parents encouraged labeling and explanations about feelings, their toddlers were more likely to retrieve a needed item and share a toy or food with an adult when the opportunity presented later (Brownell et al., 2013). In the study, parent talk about emotions was less important than parental encouragement for the child to think, label, and explain emotions.

There are a variety of strategies that parents use to try to manage or change their child's behaviors. Methods that parents use include prohibitions (e.g., "Stop"), commands (i.e., "Do this"), physical control (e.g., pick up the child, prevent the child from touching something), modeling, redirection, corporal punishment, time-out, and loss of privileges (Livas-Dlott et al., 2010). Home visitors may help caregivers learn methods that are most effective. They can also support caregivers to fine-tune the methods that are used more often. For example, although young children have limited language, verbal commands are most used by parents of toddlers (Livas-Dlott et al., 2010). It therefore becomes important for home visitors to help parents learn to give commands that are effective. In most cases, a young child will be more likely to understand commands that are short, direct, and say what to do (McNeil & Hembree-Kigin, 2010; Webster-Stratton, 2001). For example, when a child begins to run in the store the parent can say, "Walk, please." When a child grabs a pet in a rough manner, the parent can say, "Easy hands." In addition, when children are just learning language, pairing of words with gestures may increase understanding and compliance (Rader & Zukow-Goldring, 2012). For example, a parent can touch or pat a chair while saying, "Sit down."

For younger children, and especially for children who have more challenging temperament or who are defiant, use of commands that tell what to do is recommended (Landy, 2009; Webster-Stratton, 2011). A command that is phrased in positive terms is easier for young children to understand than commands that include negative words such as *don't*. Parents should give the command up to two times and then support the child to complete the task if needed (McNeil & Hembree-Kigin, 2010). Long explanations, such as telling why a rule is needed, will be best understood by children over age 5. Talking about and explaining other people's feelings is probably not effective with young children during discipline situations, but is likely to be helpful at other times, as discussed earlier (Landy, 2009; McClelland & Tominey, 2014).

Once the child has followed the direction or instruction, the parent's job is not done. It is recommended to follow the child's compliance with a reinforcer. This does not mean that the parents have to follow their child around and hand out candy after every positive behavior. A more genuine and useful form of reinforcement is praise (Webster-Stratton, 2011). Many parents have heard that they should "catch the child being good." What they may not know is that global or vague praise is probably not very effective. Statements like "good job" or "way to go," although often appearing on motivational posters, are nice, but they probably will not increase the chances that the child displays the behavior again. A specific praise statement, called *labeled praise,* is more effective. Labeled praise tells the child what he or she did that you liked and would like to see again. Instead of saying, "good work," encourage parents to try "I like it when you pick up your cars" (Webster-Stratton, 2011). See Box 7.1 to learn about giving clear commands. Use these ideas to help parents practice reframing commands. Appendix 7A provides examples of commonly heard commands with suggestions about how to reframe them. Use this form to help parents and caregivers practice framing clear commands.

Jeanette takes Paul from the stroller and holds him on her hip. He looks excitedly at the children, books, and other interesting things in the library, jabbering and reaching out. Jeanette looks at Colleen doubtfully but puts Paul down on the floor. He immediately starts to run toward a shelf with puzzles. Jeanette runs after him and picks him up again while giving a long explanation about running and the library. Paul's face puckers up and he starts to cry. Jeanette raises her eyebrows as she looks at Colleen and says, "I knew this wouldn't work."

Colleen realizes that Jeanette is easily embarrassed by Paul's behavior, even when it is age appropriate. She says, "I think he was pretty excited to

---

BOX 7.1. Giving Good Commands to Increase Child Compliance

How to Act

- Stay calm.

- Speak in a low voice.

- Keep your facial expression relaxed (neutral).

What to Say

- Use few words (one to three is great).

- Say what to do.

- Follow up by saying what the child did that you liked (labeled praise).

What to Do

- Get at the child's level.

- Gain the child's attention with eye contact and gentle touch.

- When possible, show what to do.

---

see everything here. Maybe if you hold him while we walk over to the puzzles, we can help him play in a calmer way." Jeanette shrugs her shoulders but does it. Colleen coaches her to show Paul one toy at a time and to use one or two simple words to help direct his attention. Jeanette is surprised when Paul watches her, tries to say the words she models, and then is able to play with one toy for about 2 minutes while seated on the floor. "Wow, good boy!" Jeanette says. "Yes, you listened and stayed with mommy," Colleen adds.

During a later visit, Colleen and Jeanette talk about their trip. Colleen asks Jeanette to say what she liked and did not like. Jeanette explains that she actually had fun when Paul was able to stay near her and play with a toy for a time. Colleen asked Jeanette to think about what she did to help Paul play in a more organized way. "I guess I did a better job keeping it simple. I showed him what to do with a toy and used fewer words to talk to him," Jeanette said.

Supporting Other Social and Emotional Skills

So far, we have focused on how compliance develops and how it can be supported or encouraged in young children. However, there are other social and emotional skills that are demonstrated to at least some degree by almost all young children (Hay & Cook, 2007). Positive social behaviors are present in infancy and include participating in social games such as Peekaboo, sharing or giving something to another person, and early empathy shown by crying when another baby cries (Hay & Cook, 2007; Landy, 2009). More complex social behaviors occur as children get older.

Prosocial behaviors have been divided into three main types: doing something for others, working and playing with others, and feeling for others (i.e., empathy; Hay & Cook, 2007). Most babies and toddlers show interest in other people and will play simple games, share food or show objects, and follow simple directions. Between ages 2 and 3 years, young children are increasingly able to demonstrate other social behaviors that show they have some level of understanding of another person's perspective. Examples of these types of behaviors include sharing, cooperating in a game or tasks, trying to help with chores, and attempts to comfort another person (Hay & Cook, 2007). Thinking, language, self-regulation, and understanding about other people's inner experience (i.e., feelings, motivations, beliefs) combine to change very young babies' tendency toward social interest into a more deliberate social behavior (Hay & Cook, 2007). Older toddlers are pickier about whom they engage with socially and begin to understand social rules related to their own culture, for example.

It has been commonly understood that toddlers tend toward egocentricity, meaning that toddlers view everything from their own viewpoint and may have difficulty understanding or responding to needs of others (Gopnik, 2010). Cleverly designed research now helps us understand that young children's skills may have been significantly underestimated! Recent studies suggest that children younger than 3 years of age have better skills for understanding their own and other people's thinking than previously thought, according to the work of Alison Gopnik and colleagues (Gopnik, 2010; Gopnik, Slaughter, & Meltzoff, 1994). For example, in one study, children as young as 18 months old used an adult's facial expression to guide what kind of food they offered the adult (Repachouli & Gopnik, 1997). Through this kind of work that examines how babies solve problems, it has been shown that under the right circumstances, young children have a beginning understanding of the difference between real and pretend, people have wishes that are not always the same as their own, and things may be different than they appear. Young children's skills in peer relationships are also likely to be better developed than previously thought (Wittmer, 2008). Some of the examples of peer interactions that can be observed include infants and toddlers laughing together, teaching another person with explanations and modeling, and cooperating on a task.

All of these great skills can be developed through adult support and scaffolding (Landy, 2009; Wittmer, 2008). Home visitors can help parents build more positive or prosocial skills in early childhood simply by increasing awareness that young children have these capabilities (Wittmer, 2008). Taking a stance that a young child is likely to show a positive social behavior can help a parent see opportunities to reinforce good behavior when it occurs. Encouraging young children to use words and providing additional emotion words is also recommended (Wittmer, 2008). Adults can stay near young children to encourage and support their social interactions with others. Adult modeling of positive social interactions can help, including self-talk about emotions and helping children recognize other people's feelings and responses to their actions. Parents may be surprised by just how much their baby or toddler can do.

Jeanette was feeling a little more confident about taking Paul out to be around other children after the help she got from Colleen. She decided to try a local fast-food restaurant that had a play area. Jeanette and Paul arrived at the restaurant around 10:30 in the morning. Paul was excited and bounced in his stroller as they walked in the door. Jeanette was proud that she remembered to come in between breakfast and lunch so that it would not be too crowded and overwhelm Paul. Jeanette saw that there were a few other children in the play area, including a little girl who seemed close to Paul's age. Jeanette stayed near Paul and watched him closely. When Paul approached the little girl, Jeanette felt nervous and started to give him some directions and warnings. She remembered her talk with Colleen and instead tried out narrating what Paul might be thinking, saying, "Oh, here's a little friend to play with!" Paul and the little girl approached each other and smiled. The little girl was holding a small toy; Paul pointed at the toy and said "car." Jeanette felt an urge to remind Paul that the toy was not his, but instead she just said, "Yes, that is a little red car." Paul nodded and found a ball. He held the ball out to the little girl and said "ball." As Jeanette helped the children trade their toys, she thought about how nice it would be to tell Colleen about her success.

USING THE PAUSE FRAMEWORK

Using the vignettes in this chapter, imagine how Colleen might think through her experiences with Paul and his mother, Jeanette. See Figures 7.1 and 7.2 for examples of how this might look.

WHAT'S NEXT?

In Chapter 8, we apply the PAUSE problem-solving approach to fears and separation issues.

PAUSE WORKSHEET

pause

Child: Paul   Date: May 29, 2015

Parent: Jeanette   Provider: Colleen

PERCEIVE—Explore what is happening.

Parent/caregiver perspective:	Provider perspective:
Jeanette is struggling with how to handle Paul in public places like the library and how to deal with his loud voice and high energy levels.	Jeanette talks too much to Paul, giving him long instructions. He can't understand all of what she is saying.

ASK—Clarify what is happening.

Starting with the parent/caregiver's priorities and concerns, ask more detailed/specific questions to clarify what is happening.

What must Jeanette feel when Paul behaves this way? Is she worried about complaints from the neighbor if Paul is too loud? Is the neighborhood safe? Are there nearby, safe places for Paul to play?

How can we make the visit a success?

UNDERSTAND—Explore why it is happening.

With the parent/caregiver, explore explanations for what is happening. Consider possible explanations that include the environment, the child, and the parent. Listen and observe closely as you explore the situation in conversation with the family.

Parent/caregiver perspective:	Provider perspective:	Child's perspective:
Jeanette feels embarrassed about Paul's behaviors. She is overwhelmed and parenting with limited support.	Jeanette is missing out on a lot of fun with Paul. She is worried about how others will perceive her and Paul. She is not sure	Paul is ready to experience the world. He likes activity and has a lot of energy. He needs help regulating his energy and emotions.

(continued)

Figure 7.1. Colleen's PAUSE Worksheet for Jeanette and Paul.

Figure 7.1. *(continued)*

PAUSE WORKSHEET *(continued)*

UNDERSTAND *(continued)*

Parent/caregiver perspective:	Provider perspective:	Child's perspective:
	how to understand Paul and how to regulate his energy.	

STRATEGIZE and **EVALUATE**—Identify possible responses/solutions.

1. *Solution/action to try:*	
Direct Paul to one toy or book at a time, using the positive language and commands we have been practicing.	*How will we know if it works?* Paul will remain engaged and interested in one toy at a time.
	When will we evaluate if it works? At the next planned outing

2. *Solution/action to try:*	
Think about different places Jeanette can take Paul where they will be successful, such as a fast-food restaurant with a play area.	*How will we know if it works?* Jeanette will share about the experience and we will explore what worked and did not work.
	When will we evaluate if it works? At the session after she tries another outing

PROVIDER REFLECTION WORKSHEET

Child: Paul   Date: May 29, 2015

Parent: Jeanette

Provider: Colleen

1. How did I follow the parent's lead to learn what is most pressing or important to the family?	It was very hard for me to stop myself from instructing Colleen on how to be with Paul. She likes to give so many directions and explanations. When I slowed myself down, I was able to see that Colleen was very worried about not being successful when taking Paul out to different places and how people might look at her. She really wants to see Paul be successful.
2. How did I ask clarifying questions to help me understand the problem better?	I practiced the skills I have been working on to hold back and be with Colleen to better understand her perspective and how to see Paul in different ways. I feel I am doing well in asking questions that help Colleen see what is working and how to implement changes.
3. How did I provide information that may help the family better understand the child's behavior?	Colleen has noticed some successes after we tried some basic and simple things. We can build on these successes and help her better understand Paul's behaviors. I hope she can apply this learning to other situations.

(continued)

Figure 7.2.   Colleen's Provider Reflection Worksheet for Jeanette and Paul.

Figure 7.2. *(continued)*

PROVIDER REFLECTION WORKSHEET *(continued)*

4. *How did I engage the family to develop a response that may include a strategy to try, a resource to use, or more information to increase understanding?*	We were able to try a technique that worked for Colleen. When she helped Paul direct his excitement to a toy that he liked, he was able to play with it calmly for several minutes.
5. *How did I provide support and emotional containment if needed?*	I was aware that Colleen was becoming very upset and perhaps embarrassed that day at the library. It was helpful for me to stay calm and help direct her to find a way to help Paul navigate his experience that day. I think that when she found success, she felt good and learned something about how to better handle him in the future. It was so nice to see her having fun with her son.
6. *How do I plan to follow up on promised actions to maintain trust?*	Colleen was so excited to tell me about her successes when taking Paul to the play area at the restaurant. We talked about what worked well, including her plan to go in the middle of the morning, and how she helped him meet the little girl there. She was so excited that he shared a toy with her!
7. *What do I want to discuss in reflective supervision to improve my practice and outcomes with this child and family?*	I want to talk more about how to expand my reflective skills, as this relationship seems to be going very well and we are making a positive difference. How can I apply this to some other families on my caseload?

TIPS FOR PRACTICE

❱ Encourage parents to be good models of emotion regulation by staying calm, using appropriate emotion words, and being a supportive presence when children have strong feelings.

❱ Teach parents to support young children's positive behavior by avoiding situations that will be difficult for them (e.g., busy restaurants, stores with expensive items, activities scheduled at nap time).

❱ Teach parents to give clear commands and to follow up with specific praise to help children know what they are expected to do.

KEY POINTS TO REMEMBER

❱ Very young children have better skills in recognizing their own and other people's feelings than was understood in the past. Early prosocial behaviors are present in infants and toddlers and can be expected to increase and expand along with language, cognition, and self-regulation skills.

❱ Parents often focus on teaching their children compliance, or following the commands of others, but many other social skills are also important for smooth interactions with peers and adults. These include sharing, cooperating, and showing empathy.

❱ Caregivers can scaffold young children's social behavior in many ways. These include providing appropriate models, understanding typical development, applying suitable behavior methods (e.g., clear commands and labeled praise), and providing an environment that supports discussion of feelings and emotions.

SUGGESTED FURTHER READINGS

Gopnick, A. (2010). *The philosophical baby: What children's minds tell us about truth, love and the meaning of life.* New York, NY: Farrar, Straus & Giroux.

Wittmer, D. (2008). *Focusing on peers: The importance of relationships in the early years.* Washington, DC: ZERO TO THREE.

Practice Reframing Commands

Change these typical commands given by parents to commands that might be more easily understood by a toddler. In the blank spaces, add other examples of commands and practice reframing them.

Ineffective commands	Reframed commands	Your ideas to reframe
Johnny, stop running! You'll fall down and hurt yourself and we'll have to go to the hospital!	Johnny, walk!	
Don't throw your food! It makes a mess!	Give me your plate. Say "done."	
You can't take that toy from that boy. Give it back and say you are sorry.	You like that toy. That boy does too. Let's take turns.	
No yelling. You are giving me a headache. You are making me crazy.	Use your quiet (or inside) voice.	
Quit jumping on the couch! You'll break it and have to buy me a new one!	Sit on the couch. Jump on the floor.	

(continued)

Practice Reframing Commands

Ineffective commands	Reframed commands	Your ideas to reframe

When Parents Say...
Don't Be Such a Baby!

Fears and Separation Issues

Grace visits Amanda, a 27-month-old girl who is in the care of her grandmother Margaret, at her new child care setting. During a home visit the previous week, Margaret discussed her frustration with Amanda's clingy behavior and whining. She said, "This girl will not stay off of me for 1 minute. I can't get anything done around here. So I signed her up for day care starting next week." She hugged Amanda roughly and added, "Maybe being around the other kids will help her. I don't seem to be having any luck."

Grace is concerned about Amanda's ability to adapt to this new situation but does not share this worry with Margaret. Grace has noticed that Amanda is shy and quiet with her. She has seen that she stays close to her grandmother and that she is very hesitant to try toys that Grace brings to share. She wonders if Amanda has always been shy or if this behavior is part of a reaction to the loss of her mother, who was incarcerated several months earlier. Prior to the incarceration, Amanda lived with her mother in a different state. Margaret agreed to take Amanda in order to avoid foster care, even though Margaret had seen her granddaughter only one time before becoming her guardian. She admits being confused that Amanda has not warmed up to her and wonders aloud if she did the right thing in taking her.

In Chapters 5, 6, and 7, we discussed how problems in emotion and behavior self-regulation result in acting-out behaviors. Adults may think of children with acting-out behaviors, including aggression, low attention, oppositional behavior, and defiance, as lacking in self-control. Because it has been shown that challenging behaviors are often connected to a lack of parental control or support, it may seem that a solution is to simply crank up the level of emotional and behavior control, both on the part of the parent and the child. However, when thinking of emotion regulation, home visitors should help parents work toward a balanced approach, meaning that both the child and the parent should demonstrate balanced or a "just right" level of control and management. Otherwise, the child may demonstrate overcontrol, shown by fears, worry, physical symptoms, anxiety, depression, and withdrawn behaviors (Malik, 2012).

There are two main ways in which young children may act when they are overcontrolled in emotions: either too dependent or too independent. Clingy or dependent behavior is likely when parents do not allow autonomous behavior, perhaps due to their own fears and anxieties. Alternatively, the child may seem "independent" or as though he or she does not need or want adult help. The young child may have learned that adults will not provide help in frightening situations, so he or she has given up asking and simply handles things on his or her own. Other young children may lack skills needed to request help from adults. In either of these situations, the home visitor can help caregivers teach children how to make requests and support caregivers in recognizing and responding to those requests, as reviewed in Chapter 1. Finally, some young children may have had very difficult experiences that result in shutting down feelings that are too hard to tolerate and, ultimately, showing very little emotion. For these children, long-term emotional concerns are possible, including depression, poor social skills, and low self-esteem (Malik, 2012). We talk more about trauma later in this chapter and again in Chapter 9.

As we also discussed earlier, there are times when virtually any difficult behavior in a young child might be expected as part of typical developmental phases. This is as likely to be true of fearful behavior as it is of acting-out behaviors. In order to respond effectively, it is important to recognize when fearful behaviors are part of typical development and when they represent something more serious. Therefore, we now consider normal fears and anxieties in infants and young children.

NORMAL FEARS IN YOUNG CHILDREN

Fearful behavior is not unusual in young children and, as with any challenging behavior, the reasons are quite varied. Infants and toddlers' fearful behaviors may stem from any of the following:

- Typical developmental phases
- Cautious temperament style
- Genetic predisposition

- Exposure to trauma or loss

- Environmental issues, including parenting styles that are a poor fit for the child

Over time and with support, most young children learn skills to cope with people, objects, and situations they fear. Feelings of fear or anxiety occur when a person feels threatened or believes that something is dangerous and cannot be controlled or predicted. Although younger babies may react to many things with apparent fear, serious anxieties or trauma responses are unlikely prior to 9 months of age (Scheeringa, 2004). Fears and anxieties increase over the early childhood period, peaking at about age 3 years (Landy, 2009). This pattern shows that both developmental capacities and experience in the world are needed for fear and anxiety to occur. A baby who does not realize that he or she could be hurt or injured is unlikely to fear harmful things or events.

The timing of specific fears makes sense when you consider what is important and what young children are learning to do at different times. For example, fears typical of very young babies reflect their need for almost total physical and emotional support from adults; fears of heights, loss of physical support, separation from caregivers, and strangers are common in babies (Lieberman &Van Horn, 2013). Toddlers, who are able to move around more autonomously, also fear new people and places, as well as water, baths and drains, the toilet, and falling. In addition, toddler fears of being hurt can show up as struggles with haircuts or cutting fingernails (Lieberman & Van Horn, 2013). As children get closer to age 3 and even more mobile, they begin to fear things that may have represented danger to our ancestors, including snakes, animals, and bugs, along with people they see infrequently but who may be associated with discomfort, such as doctors and dentists (Landy, 2009). Three-year olds, with their better language and cognitive skills, also fear imaginary creatures such as ghosts or monsters. Table 8.1 provides a summary of typical fears and anxieties in very young children, along with some ideas for caregivers to help children cope.

Starting at about 6 months and gradually increasing through the end of the first year, most babies show an apparent fearful response to new people that is called *stranger anxiety* (Brooker et al., 2013). Stranger anxiety is a good example of a behavior that is reliant on attainment of new cognitive skill. In this case, the infant has developed a skill called *object permanence,* or the ability to recognize that people and things continue to exist even when out of sight. Once this happens, babies begin to demonstrate selective preferences for specific caregivers and to recognize that some people are not known, or strangers. Being wary of strangers is a protective behavior for infants, who have likely become mobile at this age and could be at risk. However, young children who have higher levels of stranger fear or a sharply escalating level of stranger fear are at increased risk for anxiety (Brooker et al., 2013). Let's

Table 8.1. Common fears and helpful responses

Age	Common fears	How to help
Infants over 9 months	Heights	Stay close.
	Loss of physical support	Provide physical comfort.
	Separation from caregivers	Play coming-and-going games (e.g., Peekaboo).
	Strangers	
Young toddlers	New people and places	Stay close in new settings until the child is comfortable; follow the child's lead.
	Water, baths, and drains; the toilet	Let the child watch another person do the new thing first.
	Falling	
	Being hurt (haircuts or cutting fingernails)	Read books or tell stories about new or feared things, people, and events.
Older toddler to early preschool	Insects, snakes, animals	Provide chances to see and learn about feared objects and settings.
	Doctor or dentist	Take short practice visits to the doctor and dentist.
	Imaginary beings (ghosts, zombies)	Provide play materials related to fears, such as a doctor kit.
		When the child is calm, explain about real and pretend.

Sources: Landy (2009); Lieberman and Van Horn (2013).

check in with Grace to see how she uses observation to begin to understand Amanda's fearful behaviors.

Grace asks Margaret how she thinks Amanda is responding to the new child care program. Margaret reports that Amanda had a hard time separating from her. She tells Grace, "I usually just have to sneak off or she screams. I just can't take that." Margaret adds that the child care provider has told her that Amanda is quiet and that there are no problems. She expressed relief that the program has worked out so well. "Now if she would just stop following me around at home!"

Curious, Grace visits the child care center, where she is concerned to see that Amanda sits alone and is sucking her thumb. The child care provider reports enthusiastically that Amanda is "sweet and easy to take care of" compared with her other 2-year-olds, who display a good deal of activity and frequently fight over toys. Grace sits near Amanda and shows her some toys. She has chosen ones that Amanda has seen before and likes. Amanda looks at Grace with a somber facial expression and cautiously touches the toys but does not play right away. Other children, seeing the new toys, approach curiously. Amanda hurriedly drops her hand and looks away. Grace wonders again if she should have challenged Margaret's plan to enroll Amanda in child care.

TEMPERAMENT

In Chapter 5, we briefly mentioned temperament, or inborn styles of responding to people, events, and situations. Along with developmental level and previous history, temperament style contributes to the response that infants and young children have to events, people, and experiences. Current discussions of temperament focus on two main issues, reactivity and regulation, that work together to create behavioral styles (Rothbart & Posner, 2006). It is helpful to think about each of these responses as falling on a continuum from high to low. When children's responses are very high or very low, clinical diagnosis might be considered; high reactivity or low inhibition may result in impulsivity and other acting-out behaviors, whereas low reactivity or high inhibition may connect to anxiety and other internalizing problems. Table 8.2 illustrates how reactivity and regulation interact.

Inhibited Temperament and Anxiety

Kagan, Reznick, and Gibbons (1989) estimated that between 10% and 20% of typical children are classified as behaviorally inhibited (i.e., shy and withdrawing in new social situations, less likely to approach new things, and more anxious with new things). These babies and toddlers have been described in many ways, including slow to warm, fearful, cautious, and shy. Babies who have this temperament pattern may show more intense or persistent stranger fear. As they become toddlers, shy or inhibited children tend to hang back and are less likely to try new things or to interact socially with peers (Grady & Karraker, 2014). As a result, they may have fewer opportunities to learn social interaction skills, such as conversation and cooperation, which are useful later. Home visitors can reassure parents that although temperamentally cautious young children may need attention and adult support, most do not develop anxiety disorder (Buss, 2011). In fact, research indicates that most slow-to-warm infants typically do not continue to show this tendency by first grade. An interesting finding was that infants with a difficult temperament style actually had more shyness long term than their slow-to-warm peers (Grady, Stoltzfus, Karraker, & Metzger, 2012).

Table 8.2. Temperament features and child behaviors

	Regulation	
Reactivity	High	Low
High approach:	Social	Impulsive, low attention
uninhibited; likely to approach, touch, and try new things	Extroverted	Aggressive
Low approach:	May appear worried but can cope	Withdrawn
inhibited; likely to hang back, hesitant to try new things, appears cautious	Can self-calm	Has trouble interacting

Adults often think about shyness as a challenge, and much of the available research has been focused on the problems associated with this temperament style. However, recently researchers have begun to think about shy behaviors in more positive ways. Home visitors can help caregivers to view cautious behavior as a coping strategy that can help lower the risk for anxiety disorders. When the home visitor observes a young child showing shy behaviors such as looking away while smiling or nervously touching his or her hair, clothes, or body, the home visitor can explain to parents that these actions help the child calm down. These types of behaviors allow the child to stay available to interaction and may also signal to caregivers that some kind of support or help is needed (Colonnesi, Napoleone, & Bogels, 2014). Home visitors can also reassure caregivers that these behaviors are fairly common; in one study, slightly more than half of 2 year olds and more than 80% of 3 year olds showed this kind of shyness in situations, including seeing themselves in a mirror and when a stranger smiles or compliments them (Geppert, 1986).

Finally, it is also important to recognize that shy behavior may have a different meaning in various cultures (Colonnesi et al., 2014). In some Eastern cultures, for example, including Chinese and Indian, what we may think of as a "shy" appearance may be seen as modesty, a valued trait. When working with families from backgrounds that are different from their own, home visitors should remember to ask about the meaning of any behavior. Overall, being able to recognize forms and levels of inhibited behavior may help home visitors understand and respond to young children who demonstrate different kinds of shyness.

Communication and Cognitive Milestones and Anxiety

In Chapters 6 and 7, we recognized that children's emerging language and cognitive development gradually improve their ability to manage challenging behaviors such as aggression and not following commands. Similarly, these developmental milestones also help children get better with managing anxious feelings. The home visitor should recognize the ages when children begin identifying their own and other people's feelings. Children improve their ability to recognize emotions between 2 and 5 years, beginning with happiness and sadness (Denham & Couchoud, 1990). By age 5, typically developing children recognize these basic feelings, along with others such as anger and fear. Lack of recognition of basic emotions in preschool children has been associated with the presence of serious behavior problems; furthermore, such children may have some biases toward negative emotions, particularly sadness (Martin, Boekamp, McConville, & Wheeler, 2010). This means that the child may be more likely to incorrectly interpret another person's facial expression and emotion as a negative emotion. As a result, the child's responses do not match with the actual events. Home visitors can encourage parents to recog-

---

BOX 8.1.   Helping Support Emotional Development

Examples of caregiver statements that help children learn emotion labels

Model emotional statements.

- "I am happy to see you!"
- "I am upset because my car is broken."

Point out emotional states in other people.

- "That girl got a present and she is excited."
- "That boy's mommy had to go in the other room and he was worried about where she was."

Name emotional states in the child.

- "You are frustrated. That puzzle is hard."
- "You are so excited to go to the park! Tell your feet to be calm so they can go into their shoes so we can leave."

Engage in activities to practice learning emotions.

- Read books that label emotions.
- Make "emotion" faces with the child. Say "show me your happy face" or "show me your surprised face."
- Play with dolls or action figures and include emotions in the narrative. Say, "Superman feels sad when the building falls down" or "Sally feels happy when the family works together to dig the garden."

---

nize and respond to child feelings and teach children to name feelings as part of developing emotion regulation. Box 8.1 provides examples of ways caregivers can help children learn to recognize emotions.

PARENTING STYLE AND RESPONSES

Clinging to the parent or caregiver when in new situations or when frightened is very typical of an infant or toddler (Malik, 2012). A caregiver response style that provides support as the fearful child warms up or comfort when the child is too dysregulated by fear is needed for these children to feel comfortable enough to interact with other people, approach new toys, or explore new situations. Caregivers who try to push the child to interact too soon, insist on interactions with new people, or leave the child too quickly in new situations will find that these methods do not work or may even make things worse. However, parents who are overprotective and never challenge the fearful young child are missing an opportunity to help the child learn the skills needed to regulate their anxieties.

Most research examining the effects of parenting behaviors on young children's anxiety have focused on parental and especially maternal anxious behaviors. Maternal anxiety is connected to increased infant anxiety, from both behavioral and genetic perspectives (Aktar, Majdandzic, de Vente, & Bogels, 2014; Brooker et al., 2013). Caregivers can transmit tendencies to be anxious by showing fearful behaviors, giving many warnings, and keeping children from trying things. For example, caregivers may pass on caution through social referencing as babies watch their parents to learn how to feel about new people, places, things, and situations (Aktar et al., 2014). Social referencing is especially important around age 12 months, as this is the time when the baby is becoming mobile. Anxious parents may send a signal with their facial expressions, postures, and tone of voice that people, situations, and places are unsafe. Other fearful parent behavior such as frequent expressions of anxiety (e.g., "be careful," "don't get hurt"), use of avoidant coping (i.e., choosing to stay away from certain places or people), and little ability to encourage the child to approach something new are other ways that anxiety can be developed in children. These are forms of caregiver overprotection that can result in the child developing overcontrol of emotions and behaviors, leading to child anxiety (Aktar et al., 2014).

A particular form of parental anxiety disorder, called *social anxiety disorder,* may be most involved in toddler anxious behaviors. Social anxiety disorder in both mothers and fathers has been associated with parents and their children both demonstrating more anxiety in a new situation. This may look like avoidance (i.e., hiding or hanging back) or showing fear relating to social and nonsocial events, such as saying hello to a stranger or trying out a new toy that seems scary or unpredictable (Aktar et al., 2014).

Many—if not most—times, anxious behavior has a developmental or temperament basis, may decrease in time, and may actually be adaptive. In all of these situations, home visitor strategies discussed earlier that support parents to demonstrate sensitive caregiving and avoid anxious models are helpful and may be sufficient. However, some young children may demonstrate anxious behaviors that go beyond these descriptions and that may reach a level that suggests a behavioral health disorder. Next, we consider how to recognize when a fear extends beyond what can be explained by development or temperament.

As with other challenging types of behaviors, anxieties or fears that are more intense and frequent compared with those of peers, occur across situations, or persist after adult intervention may signal a problem. High levels of fearful behavior that occur consistently from infancy until early school age are most likely to reflect risk for anxiety in later years, including adulthood (Brooker et al., 2013; Buss, 2011).

Another red flag is showing fear responses to things or events that most young children would not view as dangerous (Buss, 2011). In one study, over-cautious young children reacted similarly to a friendly stranger and to a scary spider or robot and failed to use self-coping strategies or seek out a caregiver for comfort. Children who show the same response to different threat levels may have trouble accurately interpreting threats, or they may lack flexibility in responding. Toddlers who showed undifferentiated fear at 2 years of age were more likely to be rated with anxious behaviors by parents and teachers when the children were followed up in preschool and kindergarten (Buss, 2011). Finally, irritable behavior (i.e., being easily frustrated or angered) has been associated with mental health diagnoses, including depression and anxiety, in older children; recent studies are beginning to demonstrate similar findings in early childhood (Dougherty et al., 2013).

Severe anxiety and avoidant behavior can also interfere with daily activities of the child or of the family as a whole. Examples include anxiety that prevents a child from having an experience that leads to learning or something that the child would actually like to do. At times, the young child's fearful behavior is so debilitating that the entire family schedule is arranged around accommodating the child, interfering with family functioning or even simply the ability to go out to dinner (ZERO TO THREE, 2005). At this point, the diagnosis of an anxiety disorder may be considered. Box 8.2 provides some

---

BOX 8.2. Red Flags for Possible Anxiety Disorder

- There is a family history of anxiety disorder.

- Anxiety starts in infancy and continues in early childhood or school age.

- Compared to peers, the child's fears are more intense and frequent and occur across settings.

- The child's fears are undifferentiated (i.e., occur with dangerous and nondangerous things).

- The child's anxiety or avoidant behavior interferes with family functioning (e.g., the family cannot go out due to extreme child reactions to new places and people).

- The child is so fearful, he or she is unable to do something he or she likes or wants to do.

- The child displays excessive clinginess with caregivers, refusing to be alone or left with others.

- The child experiences sleep disturbance due to anxiety about sleeping, dreams, or being alone at night.

examples of red flags to watch for regarding anxiety in very young children. Referral to a child's physician or a mental health specialist may be indicated when red-flag behaviors are observed.

Let's see how the home visitor, Grace, continues to explore Amanda's slow-to-warm behavior and to share her ideas with Margaret.

Grace visits Amanda at the child care center a few more times and is glad to see that she is slowly starting to seem more comfortable. Grace even sees Amanda protest when another child takes a toy. Grace realizes that she has assumed that all of Amanda's behaviors are connected to her recent experiences, but now she wonders if some of the behavior is connected to temperament. She asks Margaret if she knows much about Amanda's behavior before she came to live with her, but Margaret has little information to share. She remembers that Amanda's mother, Jody, was an active and outgoing little girl, just like most people in their family. "Amanda is kind of different from the rest of us, I guess," Margaret says. "I only met her dad once and he was pretty shy," she adds. "It must be really different for you to have a child that is so quiet," Grace suggests. "I don't mind the quiet, but I can't stand how she just hangs on me," Margaret says. Grace wonders out loud, "You said she might be shy, like her dad. Maybe Amanda needs help to get used to all this new stuff she has to manage." Margaret thinks and then says, "Well, she did have a lot of changes and we really don't know how long it will go on. I mean, I'd like to know how long she'll be here, too." Grace thinks a bit too and adds, "It has been a lot for both of you."

WHAT ABOUT TRAUMA?

New fears that do not seem typical of the child or that do not correspond with a typical developmental phase deserve a closer look, as they may have a trauma component (Malik, 2012). Growing evidence has led to a consensus among researchers and clinicians that acute and chronic trauma exposure in early childhood is common and has the potential to have lifelong effects on development, behavior, and physical health (Briggs-Gowan, Carter, & Ford, 2012; Lieberman, Chu, Van Horn, & Harris, 2011). Experiences that may be traumatic are varied, but include directly or indirectly experiencing events or circumstances that pose psychological or physical threat. Some examples include the following:

- Abuse

- Severe neglect

- Witnessing domestic and community violence

- Car or other accidents

- Medical procedures

- Natural and manmade disasters

- Exposure to media violence such as commercial television, cable, and adult-level video games (Osofsky, 2011)

Adverse childhood experiences (referred to as ACEs) are known to relate to many later problems in adulthood, including mental and physical health challenges (Felitti et al., 1998). The unfortunate results of early ACEs begin to appear much sooner than adulthood, however. For example, abuse prior to age 5 years has been connected to both internalizing and externalizing behavior problems (Keiley, Howe, Dodge, Bates, & Pettit, 2001). In another study by Clarkson Freeman (2014), children with child welfare contact were followed 5 or more years after the initial investigation. Those who had three or four ACEs were more than four times as likely to have problems such as anxiety and depression as those with no ACEs (Clarkson Freeman, 2014). Very young children, children who live in poverty or who have other risk factors, and children representing ethnic minorities may be most affected (Lieberman et al., 2011).

Healthy young children can be expected to learn to manage and recover from typical stressful events, including physical, emotional, and relational stressors, when they live in a supportive family and in safe and predictable environments (Lieberman & Van Horn, 2013). For some children, the environment is not safe and their parents do not have the emotional resources to provide the needed support. Difficult child behaviors are common and could include any of the behaviors that we have discussed so far, including sleep and feeding problems, aggression, tantrums, lack of compliance, and anxiety characteristics. Many parents may struggle to respond appropriately, often due to their own histories of trauma exposure, either in the past or concurrent with their children. Therefore, in addition to being aware of the potential effects of trauma on children, home visitors need to consider the possibility that parents are also affected. In Chapter 9, we talk more about how parenting can be affected by trauma and how home visitors can help families affected by these issues.

PARENTAL LOSS AS A FORM OF TRAUMA

A special form of trauma for infants and young children is loss of a parent or other primary caregiver. Because babies and toddlers are entirely dependent upon their caregivers, losing a caregiver, even temporarily, can be very distressing. Young children expect and need a parent to be available, both physically and psychologically, in order to feel safe. Parents may be separated from young children for various reasons that are expected to be temporary, such as military deployment, foster care placement, parental incarceration, and parent serious illness. Permanent reasons for parent loss include death, abandonment, and permanent removal through court actions. Although from an adult perspective the meaning of these separations may be very different, to infants and toddlers, the core issue may be the same: the primary caregiver is suddenly not available. These types of separations affect hundreds of thousands of American children (Child Trends Data Bank, 2014; Glaze & Maruschak, 2008; Lieberman & Van Horn, 2013; Williams & Fraga, 2011).

Children may experience repeated separations and reunions in many of these situations. For example, many families have experienced repeated deployments, leading to a series of separations and reunions (Lieberman & Van Horn, 2013). For children in foster care, visits can be experienced as a reminder of loss for both child and parent. For those children who have a parent in prison, high rates of recidivism may mean that the parent returns only to leave again. In one survey, 45% of parents in prison reported being under supervision such as probation or parole at the time of the present arrest and 75% had prior arrest histories (Glaze & Maruschak, 2008). These results suggest that parents and children may be likely to endure repeated experiences of little, no, or inconsistent contact as a result of incarceration.

For families in which one parent is absent for any reason, the remaining parent's emotional health is critical to the child's resilience and may be connected to the child's ability to cope with stress related to the separation. Relationships between the absent parent and the current caregivers and reintegration of the absent parent back into the family can be difficult (Harris, Harris, Graham, & Carpenter, 2010; Lieberman & Van Horn, 2013). Home visits can be an important part of the support that is given to the caregiver who remains, either directly through a positive relationship or through encouragement to connect to other supports and to use self-care.

Responses to separation may vary based on the child's developmental level, temperament, previous experiences, and other individual factors. Some children may adapt to frequent separation, but others may struggle and even eventually show more generalized anxiety symptoms (Lieberman & Van Horn, 2013). Developmental level can also affect how a child understands a separation. Due to their tendency toward egocentricity, young children may believe that they are responsible for a parent leaving or for the reactions of the remaining caregiver. Home visitors can help caregivers and parents consider the experiences of young children when a parent is away temporarily or will not return.

Margaret tells Grace that she has heard from Amanda's mother, who would like Amanda to visit her in prison. The prison is several hours away and Margaret is not sure a visit is a good idea. Grace asks, "Do you think that Amanda misses her mom?" Margaret says no, and then tells Grace that she has not really said anything to Amanda about her mother because she thought it would be upsetting and did not think Amanda could understand anyway. Grace talks about how young children become connected to their parents, and she explains that they could miss them even if they don't understand everything. Margaret is surprised. She says, "Then wouldn't the visit just make it worse? How would I explain why Jody didn't come back home with us?"

WHAT HELPS ANXIOUS INFANTS AND CHILDREN?

Children who are anxious for reasons such as shyness, temperament characteristics, anxiety, or history of trauma can be helped by supportive parents and other caregivers (Rice & Groves, 2005). Home visitors can suggest that families provide increased structure, which is likely to ease anxiety in any child. This is because structure, including a routine, lets children feel that the world is predictable. Recognizing and naming feelings can also help anxious young children, who may not have a vocabulary to express the feelings that they have (Malik, 2012). Parents should avoid rushing or pressuring the child who hangs back or shows fear to do something before he or she is ready, whether that is speaking to a new adult or trying out an unfamiliar activity. Home visitors can use similar actions to support parents to be more regulated and calm so that they can be better able to provide calming behavior toward the child.

Home visitors can provide parents with information that helps prevent anxious responses and that normalizes shy behavior. Babies are likely to react to loud noises, so coach parents to avoid noisy places if needed. When the infant is upset by a loud noise, encourage the parent to provide comfort and move away from the noise. If possible, show the baby where the sound came from. For infants who struggle with separation, traditional children's games that involve "coming and going," such as Peekaboo, help infants have fun with mini-separations (Landy, 2009). When parents are dropping off for child care or leaving children to go out, encourage them to avoid dragging out the moment of separation. Rather, the parent should settle the child with the caregiver and/or activity and then follow three steps: say you are going, say that it is okay to stay with this person, and say that you will be back. Parents should be advised not to sneak out and to try to avoid looking afraid or worried, as children will take their lead from their parents as to how to feel about the separation.

Talk to parents about the importance of taking a balanced approach with toddlers: encourage, but do not push too hard. Cautious toddlers will do better with new things when given plenty of time and preparation. Use books, DVDs when appropriate, or other indirect ways to get a child used to a feared object, person, or situation. We can use the example of a visit to the doctor, which may be anxiety provoking because it involves close contact and touch with a person who is not seen frequently and who may have caused discomfort with a shot in the past. To help a toddler prepare to visit the doctor, read books and watch children's programs about doctors to gain familiarity. Take the child to the doctor's office for a visit that does not involve a check-up. It might also help to see an older sibling successfully complete a doctor's visit. Provide a doctor's kit and encourage the child to pretend to give the caregiver, doll, or stuffed animal a checkup. See Box 8.3 for tips to share with caregivers.

As always, preventing anxiety through positive parenting practices and safe environments is best. This may not always be possible, as many anxiety provoking situations that are part of the everyday environment are out of the family's control. Of course, providers would like for families to have safe housing and live in nonthreatening environments, although this is recognized as often outside of the home visitor's ability to influence. Despite these real issues that parents face, there are many aspects of the environment and parent reactions that can be improved. Home visitors can encourage parents to have balanced reactions to people, events, and situations so that children learn to accurately perceive relative danger or risk. They can work with families to teach parents to refrain from making fun of their young children's fears and to sensitively support exploration when appropriate. Also, parents can be sup-

---

Box 8.3. Tips for Caregivers to Reduce Young Children's Anxiety

- Prevent anxiety by creating a safe and healthy environment.
- Play games that involve coming and going, such as Peekaboo.
- Provide increased structure and routine.
- Recognize and name feelings.
- For the child who hangs back or shows fear, avoid rushing or pressuring to do something before he or she is ready.
- Avoid noisy places; offer comfort, distraction, or a way to escape if you must be in a noisy place.
- Recognize children's activities and accomplishments.
- Encourage children's curiosity and play, and choose age-appropriate activities.
- Remember that anxiety may run in families; explore one's own issues when warranted.
- Work toward the "right balance" when encouraging children to engage socially and when providing discipline (i.e., supportive yet firm).

ported to choose age-appropriate activities, such as shielding young children from scary movies and video games used by adults or older children in the home.

As we have discussed, child and parent anxieties may interact. Remember that anxiety runs in families (Buss, 2011). When you observe anxiety in the young child, consider if the parent is also showing symptoms. It is likely that some of the families that participate in home visiting include parents with clinical diagnoses of anxiety or depression, or who have symptoms that are not well managed. Encouraging parents to participate in evaluations and treatment when warranted is recommended.

Research has shown that moderate but not too intense levels of parental encouragement can help behaviorally inhibited or shy children engage socially. Home visitors can help parents find the right balance. In particular, encouraging statements have been found to be more helpful for shy children than just warm statements. Examples of encouraging statements include providing a specific suggestion about what to do (e.g., "You can sit and play in the sand box with that little girl.") instead of simply making warm or praise statements (e.g., "You're doing great!"; Grady & Karraker, 2014). Because some types of shy behaviors are perceived more positively (Colonessi et al., 2014), parents can coach their inhibited toddlers to perform low-contact but appropriate methods of interacting. For example, parents can teach toddlers to smile and wave to strange adults when making eye contact or speaking is too hard. With family members, a child who does not want to give a kiss or hug could give a high five or fist bump instead.

Children who have experienced trauma may or may not have strong reactions. Although many children experience trauma, not all develop a traumatic stress response or disorder. About 30% have reactions severe enough to lead to a diagnosis and need for treatment (Cohen & Scheeringa, 2009). For these children, reactions to people, experiences, or situations connected to the trauma in some way may lead to anxious responses. It is always advisable to ask about any recent situations or activities the child has experienced that could represent a trauma. When fearful behaviors are present, home visitors can gently ask about possible difficult experiences that occurred directly to a child or that the child observed happening to another person. Any actions that the home visitor can take to understand a child's reactions as trauma related and help a family to be in a safe environment and return to a typical routine can be helpful.

Remember that temporary separations or permanent loss of the parent are significant stressors for very young children. Children who must repeatedly separate and reunite with parents for parenting time due to shared custody or visitation within a context of foster care, or even as a result of military deployment, can develop anxious behavior (Lieberman & Van Horn, 2013). In many of these situations, the parent may also have strong feelings about the other parent, a foster parent, or the visiting situation. Even when parents have angry, sad, or other negative feelings related to these experiences, the child's needs for support must be addressed. Developing a standard way of talking about the situation can be helpful, even when a child is very little. Lieberman and Van Horn (2008) suggest that parents explain to their children that a judge or court has decided that it has to be this way, for example. Parents can be encouraged to explain that they feel sad about leaving and will miss them. Keeping the visit schedule consistent will be helpful in the long run, as the child can learn that the parent will come back.

Lieberman and Van Horn (2013) offer suggestions about how to help families when parents must be away for military deployment. This information can also help families who are separated for other reasons. First, if the family is aware of the pending separation, some preparation may be helpful. Home visitors can encourage the parents to recognize that children attend to and pick up on adult behaviors and conversations and to watch for child reactions. Encourage parents to spend time together in order to build up a cache of positive memories by taking photos or making recordings for younger children who may need more concrete materials to support their memory. Parents should be encouraged to provide a verbal explanation of what is happening and describe what each person will be doing while apart. Some free and easily accessible examples of how to speak with children about difficult issues, including separation, have been developed by the Public Broadcasting Service (http://www.pbs.org/parents/parenting/). In addition, Sesame Workshop has developed a number of materials for helping children affected by parental incarcerations (http://www.sesamestreet.org/parents/topicsandactivities/toolkits/incarceration#).

At the beginning of the separation, young children may show increased emotionality, behavior issues, and sleep problems (Barker & Berry, 2009). These are most likely to occur in the first month but may improve somewhat thereafter. As the time apart continues, children will benefit from routine, structure, and visual depictions of time passing, such as a calendar. To keep the absent parent in mind, build in time to talk about that person in daily routines, such as during bedtime prayer if that is part of the family traditions (Lieberman & Van Horn, 2013). Contacts with the parent through mail or Skype/FaceTime can be helpful. When parents are in prison, visitation is often not very child friendly, so this needs to be carefully planned. Foster care visits can be stressful too, especially when supervised, as parents may feel awkward and confuse their children by behaving differently than expected.

Parents should be helped to understand a range of reactions that a child might show during visits. The home visitor should coach the parent to be patient, as the child may appear not to recognize the parent or may look afraid and confused. If a returning military parent is injured and looks different, the young child's age-typical fears of injury are likely to be activated (Lieberman & Van Horn, 2013). Again, young children's egocentric thinking may lead them to believe that they are responsible for the injury in some way. When a parent's injuries are severe, about a third of the time the other parent needs to travel to see them or provide caregiving, causing another separation (Cozza et al., 2010). Providing explanations appropriate to the child's developmental level and helping the temporary caregiver to keep the routines the same will help.

When the parent returns, reintegration into home routines can also be challenging for everyone. The family has had to adapt while one parent was absent. When that parent returns, it may take time before the person can reclaim specific roles and responsibilities. The returning parent may need time to catch up to the changes at home, including the child's changed development and new abilities (Lieberman & Van Horn, 2013).

For some families, the ultimate separation may happen when a parent dies. Although it may be very difficult for adults to discuss the death of a loved one, truthfulness is recommended (Lieberman, Compton, Van Horn, & Ghosh Ippen, 2003). Family members will need support to explain the loss of the parent in clear terms. They will also need to be prepared for the likelihood that children will repeatedly ask questions about what happened and when they will see the parent again. These questions can reappear periodically for a long time. Parents often feel confused about how the child is feeling, because young children cannot sustain long periods of continual sadness. Parents should be helped to know that a young child can appear sad, then seem to play normally, and then suddenly ask if the parent will be home to tuck them in, for example (Lieberman & Van Horn, 2013). The home visitor should take advantage of reflective supervision when supporting families through these kinds of situations in order to maintain clear perspectives and boundaries while identifying and dealing with any potential issues of their own.

USING THE PAUSE FRAMEWORK

Using the scenario presented in the vignettes, examine how Grace thinks through her experiences with Amanda's grandmother, Margaret. See Figures 8.1 and 8.2 for examples of how this might look.

WHAT'S NEXT?

In Chapter 9, we apply the PAUSE problem-solving approach to family challenges and issues that affect the work of home visitors.

TIPS FOR PRACTICE

▶ Help parents recognize when anxious behavior is part of typical development or a child's temperament style. Coach parents to provide sensitive supports and to avoid teasing or belittling a child who is anxious.

PAUSE WORKSHEET   pause

Child: Amanda   Date: July 14, 2015

Parent: Margaret (grandmother)   Provider: Grace

PERCEIVE—Explore what is happening.

Parent/caregiver perspective:	Provider perspective:
Amanda's grandmother (temporary guardian) wants her to be less clingy and more outgoing.	Amanda has had a traumatic experience, having lost her mother to incarceration and been moved to a different state to live with a relative she does not know.

ASK—Clarify what is happening.

Starting with the parent/caregiver's priorities and concerns, ask more detailed/specific questions to clarify what is happening.

What information is available about Amanda prior to the move, such as her personality, activities, relationship with her mother, and so forth?

What is Amanda's temperament style? And her mother's? And father's? Other family members'?

Have other family members experienced traumatic events? How did they respond?

UNDERSTAND—Explore why it is happening.

With the parent/caregiver, explore explanations for what is happening. Consider possible explanations that include the environment, the child, and the parent. Listen and observe closely as you explore the situation in conversation with the family.

Parent/caregiver perspective:	Provider perspective:	Child's perspective:
Amanda is being needy, which can be annoying and interrupts the family schedule.	Amanda has experienced a trauma and needs some structure/routine and reassurance that all is going to be okay.	Amanda misses her mommy and doesn't understand the loss.

(continued)

Figure 8.1. Grace's PAUSE Worksheet for Margaret and Amanda.

Figure 8.1. *(continued)*

PAUSE WORKSHEET *(continued)*

UNDERSTAND *(continued)*

Parent/caregiver perspective:	Provider perspective:	Child's perspective:

STRATEGIZE and **EVALUATE**—Identify possible responses/solutions.

1. *Solution/action to try:*	*How will we know if it works?*
Introduce some information about loss so Margaret and the child care provider can see Amanda's behavior in a different way.	Margaret and the child care provider use alternative strategies to support Amanda.
	When will we evaluate if it works?
	In 1 month

2. *Solution/action to try:*	*How will we know if it works?*
Work with Margaret to set a routine to introduce some structure for Amanda.	Amanda's clinginess decreases at home; separation for child care is less stressful.
	When will we evaluate if it works?
	In about 6 to 8 weeks, after implementing a plan

PROVIDER REFLECTION WORKSHEET

Child: Amanda   Date: July 14, 2015

Parent: Margaret (grandmother)

Provider: Grace

1.	How did I follow the parent's lead to learn what is most pressing or important to the family?	Although it was difficult for me to be patient because of Amanda's needs, I was very mindful to try to fully understand Margaret's concerns.
2.	How did I ask clarifying questions to help me understand the problem better?	I think I have done well to stay in a place of exploration with this family and child care provider by asking a lot of questions. This seems to help them better understand Amanda's individual experience and situation.
3.	How did I provide information that may help the family better understand the child's behavior?	I have been able to introduce some information about trauma and loss and temperament style that may help the family better respond to Amanda's needs.

(continued)

Figure 8.2. Grace's Provider Reflection Worksheet for Margaret and Amanda.

Figure 8.2. *(continued)*

PROVIDER REFLECTION WORKSHEET *(continued)*

4. *How did I engage the family to develop a response that may include a strategy to try, a resource to use, or more information to increase understanding?*	The family has been open to various ideas and is willing to set up a more defined routine and schedule. The grandmother and child care provider seem willing to partner so that the schedules complement each other between home and child care.
5. *How did I provide support and emotional containment if needed?*	I have been able to support Margaret in better understanding her own strong emotions regarding having Amanda come to her home, her daughter's incarceration, and Amanda's clinginess.
6. *How do I plan to follow up on promised actions to maintain trust?*	By going to the child care setting several times, I feel I demonstrated a commitment to supporting this family in fully understanding their concerns and issues.
7. *What do I want to discuss in reflective supervision to improve my practice and outcomes with this child and family?*	I want to learn more about trauma-informed work and how I can be supportive to families when young children struggle with loss. I am also curious about children's temperament and how this influences parent–child interactions.

▶ Encourage parents to use structure and routine to help children who are anxious for any reason, including a developmental phase, temperament, or a stressor.

▶ Assist caregivers to recognize that children will notice and may mirror adult anxieties. For those caregivers whose anxiety is significant, encourage personal treatment.

KEY POINTS TO REMEMBER

▶ Some level of anxiety is typical for infants and young children, especially in certain developmental stages.

▶ Many factors may increase the chances that a child develops anxious behaviors, including temperament and trauma exposure.

▶ Home visitors can help parents learn strategies that allow young children to feel safe and to gain skills needed to manage anxious feelings.

SUGGESTED FURTHER READINGS

Pincus, D. (2012). *Growing up brave: Expert strategies for helping your child overcome fear, stress, and anxiety.* New York, NY: Little, Brown.

Rice, K.F., & Groves, B.M. (2005). *Hope and healing: A caregiver's guide to helping young children affected by trauma.* Washington, DC: ZERO TO THREE.

What Else Might This Be?

Family Challenges

Jackie, a physical therapist in an early intervention system, arrives for her scheduled visit with Chloe, a 10-month-old girl with motor delays and torticollis. The door is opened by Chloe's 10-year-old sister, Olivia, who is holding her and helping her with a bottle. Jackie is surprised to see Olivia, as it is a school day. Looking in, Jackie notices that the floor is covered with piles of clothing, stacks of toys, and many partially filled boxes and trash bags. Olivia tells her, "We are moving to grandma's apartment. They have a pool!"

Chloe's mother, Desiree, appears, carrying a box of dishes. She seems surprised to see Jackie, and says, "Is it Wednesday already?" Jackie feels irritated and wonders why Desiree did not tell her about this move last week! She also wonders where Chloe's father is, as he is typically present for sessions. He does not often participate, but Jackie has noticed that he does usually listen in. "So, Olivia says you are moving. It seems pretty busy here with all this activity. Would another time be better?" Desiree takes the baby and tells Olivia to take the box into a different room. In a low voice, she explains to Jackie that they were evicted and will be going to her mother's apartment for a few days. After that, she is unsure where they will be. Olivia thinks they are packing up, but actually Desiree is sorting their things because she has no place to keep most of it. "If you want to work with Chloe today, that would be okay. I'm just not sure when we'll be able to see you again," Desiree says.

Jackie feels overwhelmed by the young family's situation and unsure if she could or should try to help. Thoughts and ideas come quickly. She wonders where Chloe's father is in all this, if she should offer to contact the service coordinator or maybe a social worker, or whether someone at her church could help. Feeling even more uncomfortable, Jackie tells Desiree that she is sorry for her troubles and agrees to go ahead with the session. As she sits down with Chloe, Jackie is relieved to be focused on something familiar.

In the last few chapters, we focused on how to explore difficult child behavior with families using the PAUSE problem-solving approach, incorporating reflection and relationship-based methods. Throughout, we recognized the possibility that parenting behaviors may contribute to difficulties in children's behaviors. In this chapter, we delve into some of the more common stressors that families face, discuss how these stressors affect parenting behavior and child outcomes, and present some suggestions for home visitors working with families in these situations.

Home visitors must bear in mind that families that experience risk factors may be reluctant to disclose struggles with mental illness (MI) or substance abuse, due to concerns about being labeled or judged. Those with identified issues of MI or addiction may fear asking for help with parenting due to potential for reporting to authorities and fear of having children removed (Boursnell, 2014). When home visitors are able to work with families over the long term, the potential for building a positive relationship is increased. Over time, the professional can get to know the parents in a deeper way that includes recognition of family strengths and their successful ways of coping. Families are more likely to experience the relationship with the home visitor as supportive, which may increase their willingness to take advantage of offered help. However, program requirements that force home visitors to press families for sensitive information too soon can backfire, leading families to give inaccurate information or to leave the program before getting truly started (Barak, Spielberger, & Gitlow, 2014).

Before we cover specific stressors, it is important to acknowledge that many families that use early childhood services may experience more than one stressor across time or concurrently. For example, trauma experience is associated with borderline personality disorder (BPD) and substance abuse. In addition, military and returning veteran populations have much higher rates of depression, anxiety, and suicide than the general public (Lieberman & Van Horn, 2013). Combinations of risk factors may reduce the effectiveness of home visiting programs. In one study, children of mothers who had either depression or who lacked trust in the home visiting providers showed improvement in cognition and behavior. However, children whose mothers had both concerns did not improve, even though both groups received the same number of visits (Cluxton-Keller et al., 2014).

In some home visiting programs, screening for certain types of risk factors is part of the standard activities. Knowing which stressors and risk factors are related may help the home visitor be more alert to other potential issues after screening identifies a concern. For example, prenatal and postnatal maternal screening for depression is helpful, but we may miss other important information if the screening ends there. In this instance, mothers with depression may also benefit from screening to check for coexisting stressors, trauma, or anxiety as well as the availability of social supports (Price & Masho, 2014).

Although it is important to find safe ways for families to share the issues that concern them, it is also fair to say that the presence of multiple risk factors that complicate families' lives will also complicate the home visitor's work with them. It may be difficult to determine where to start when the problems are so interconnected (Monahan, Beeber, & Jones Harden, 2012). Providers may have long-term goals related to program requirements, often tied to grant funding, that differ from priorities families might identify as preferred. Families are often distracted from long-term goals by acute issues (Boursnell, 2014). Programs may frame work with "at risk" families from deficit models that can challenge a home visitor's desire to think about families from a strengths perspective (Mills et al., 2012). In one study, individuals with mental illness reported that they would like help that is not too intrusive and recognition that their needs are different at different times (Perera, Short, & Fernbacher, 2014).

In the following sections, we apply recommendations from recovery approaches to MI and substance abuse strategies that fit well with relationship-based practice principles: emotion support, sharing knowledge of crisis resources, and helping family members develop problem-solving skills (Substance Abuse and Mental Health Services Administration [SAMHSA], 2009). First let's see how Jackie is progressing with Chloe's family as we begin to discuss what it is like for home visitors to interact with families whose needs are many.

On the way to her next visit, Jackie calls Chloe's service coordinator to alert her to the family's impending homelessness. The service coordinator has several ideas about how to help and agrees to call the family. Jackie feels relieved but wonders if she should have been able to take more directive action. She is also concerned that Chloe's family might be hard to contact in the future. She wonders if she will ever the see the family again.

SORTING THROUGH A MYRIAD OF POSSIBLE FAMILY RISK FACTORS

Jackie, the home visitor in the chapter vignette, is faced with helping this family gain some much-needed supports for issues outside her direct work with Chloe but that may influence Chloe's development. Home visitors see many different caregivers and families and are likely to encounter a variety of challenging situations like Jackie's experience with Chloe's family. The following subsections identify some of the potential issues families face and describe some ways the home visitor can support the child and family.

Parents with Mental Illness and Disability

MIs of any kind are common. According to surveys conducted by SAMHSA (2014a), about 4% of the U.S. population has a serious mental illness that influences functioning, and the overall prevalence of MI is close to 18%. Because many of these individuals are of child-bearing age, it is likely that many children grow up with a parent with MI. A recent Canadian study estimated that about 12% of children have a parent with MI (Bassani, Padoin, Philipp, & Veldhuizen, 2009). The majority of interest and research on parental MI has focused on mothers, and specifically on maternal depression. There is also a sizable body of research on the effects of BPD and trauma, which are related to each other and to depression. In recent years, researchers and clinicians have begun to consider the needs of parents with schizophrenia and substance abuse. As mentioned in Krumm, Becker, and Wiegand-Grefe (2013), two recent reviews completed in 2006 and 2009 reported growing interest in the effects of paternal MI. These reviews and other studies are helping to establish that paternal MI also is associated with negative child outcomes. They also add to our understanding of the risks for child neglect and abuse that are present when fathers have MI. Although knowledge of the effects of parental MI is growing and expanding, for the purposes of this discussion we briefly consider depression and BPD, as these are among the most common MIs and most likely to be encountered by home visitors. As we review these potential risks, keep in mind that parents who have MI and other risks are able to take care of their children, but they may need additional supports to do so effectively (Krumm et al., 2013).

Depression and Parenting

Depression is common in the general population and more likely in people who have other life stressors. For example, 40%–60% of low-income mothers report depression, which is twice the rate in general samples (Knitzer, Theberge, & Johnson; 2008). Unfortunately, most of these women do not seek treatment (Knitzer et al., 2008). Women are especially vulnerable to depression during pregnancy and the postpartum period. Early childhood programs have often attended to depression and especially maternal depression, due to their high association with negative child outcomes. Depressive and the often co-occurring anxious symptoms may interfere with a mother's performance of many daily activities, including appropriate parenting behaviors. With infants, the main concern is the mother's low reciprocity and sensitivity, which can impair attachment. For toddlers, concerns center on discipline and behavior management styles that can lead to ongoing challenging behaviors. The research is extensive and complex, with efforts to consider both direct effects and interplay among many factors, including child characteristics such as temperament and delays in development, parental histories, and stressful family context and overall environment (Alvarez, Meltzer-Brody, Mandel, & Beeber, 2015). To address these types of concerns, the home visitor should focus on the following:

- Keep goals simple to avoid overwhelming the parent with depression.

- When working with families with infants, support parents to read and respond to babies' cues to maximize positive attachments.

- When working with families with toddlers, provide support related to appropriate behavior management.

Borderline Personality Disorder

All people have personality styles or traits that might include tendencies toward eccentric, dramatic, or fearful thinking and behavior (American Psychiatric Association [APA], 2013). When a person's typical ways of thinking and feeling about him- or herself and others significantly interfere with daily life, a personality disorder (PD) may be present (APA, 2013). Many people display more than one PD, and it is common for PD to be present with other psychiatric disorders (Zimmerman, Rothschild, & Chelminski, 2005), such as depression and anxiety. Often the PD is not diagnosed, leading to less effective treatments.

One of the best known and most researched forms of personality challenges is BPD. Important for home visitors who use a relationship-based model, BPD includes feelings and behaviors that interfere with all close relationships. Understanding BPD is particularly critical for workers in early childhood fields, as it is related to problems with parenting behaviors that affect parent–child relationship and discipline methods that result in adverse child outcomes (Tomlin, 2002). Finally, BPD frequently co-occurs with depression, trauma, and substance abuse, meaning that home visitors should consider it when working with families with these other risk factors.

The core features of BPD include intense and conflictual relationships, poor control of impulses and emotions, and problems with thinking and sense of self (APA, 2013). Because BPD includes problems with affect regulation and unusual beliefs, the person may show impulsive behaviors and a low level of consistency. Due to the extreme level of inconsistency that parents with BPD may demonstrate, their children are at high risk for insecure attachment patterns and subsequent challenging behaviors. Parents with BPD, unable to manage their own emotions, lack skills to scaffold child emotional experiences. They are likely to need help to learn how to accurately recognize, tolerate, and respond to child emotions. When faced with negative child emotions such as fear or sadness, parents with BPD frequently push away the feelings with criticism and mocking. At the extreme, disorganized attachment may occur (Hobson, Patrick, Crandell, García-Pérez, & Lee, 2005; Stepp, Whalen, Pilkonis, Hipwell, & Levine, 2012). Mothers with BPD are likely to need assistance to recognize typical child development and to have appropriate expectations. In addition, due to extreme swings between harsh discipline and laxness, they may need help to maintain a stable and nurturing environment, including guidance on how to establish and sustain a routine and to be consistent in setting limits (Stepp et al., 2012).

Interpersonal characteristics that interfere with the parent–child relationship can also significantly challenge the provider's ability to form and maintain an effective working relationship with affected parents (Tomlin, 2002). Inappropriate perceptions about other people can lead parents to react strongly to a home visitor's attempts to set limits or boundaries, typically interpreting these behaviors as abandonment. As a result of these misperceptions, parents may demonstrate maladaptive behaviors that can include ones that seem to push the home visitor away. These may include not answering or returning calls, failing to follow through with recommendations, or refusing to continue services. At other times, the parent may behave in ways that seem intended to force the home visitor to give more attention, commonly with threats of self-harm or attempted suicide. In these types of instances, the home visitor should take the following steps:

- Set limits and keep strong boundaries (e.g., let the parent know when you can accept phone calls and resist adding extra appointments when parents are highly stressed).

- Help the parent to build routines and consistently set limits with his or her child.

- Monitor his or her own feelings and behaviors, as people with BPD may provoke feelings of frustration and anger.

Parents with Disability

More than 4 million parents in the United States have a disability (Kaye, 2011). Increasingly, there is recognition that having a disability does not mean that parenthood is impossible, and research on the effects of disability on parenting, although limited, is growing (Kleinmann & Songer, 2009). Disability alone does not present risk for successful parenting; instead, those with disabilities who have problems parenting most likely also struggle with additional issues, including poverty, trauma histories, and other risk factors (Kirshbaum & Olkin, 2002). Home visiting services, when properly individualized and adapted, can be one of the supports that helps parents with all types of disabilities retain custody of their children and parent safely and successfully (Kleinmann & Songer, 2009).

People with disabilities including motor or sensory impairment, or intellectual disability, can become parents and may need specialized supports. Individuals who have sensory impairment, including vision or hearing loss, may successfully parent with few accommodations and community supports. Home visitors can help caregivers identify supports including:

- Technology, such as visual alarms for people who are deaf, to allow independent parenting.

- Other providers such as occupational therapists and physical therapists who can provide adaptive equipment to increase mobility and accessibility.

- Community programs to access accessible housing, transportation, and other resources.

Parents with intellectual disability may concern home visitors the most, as they are more likely to have involvement in the child welfare system. However, evidence suggests that most parents with intellectual disability, given sufficient support, can successfully parent their children (Lightfoot, Hill, & LaLiberte, 2010). Home visitors can support parents with intellectual disability by:

- Breaking down tasks into steps and planning for frequent repetition and practice.

- Providing information in alternative formats that match literacy levels, including picture supports and video recordings.

- Supporting parents in developing routines and accomplishing necessary parenting tasks and activities (e.g., daily hygiene, getting ready for daily activities, administering medications, keeping appointments).

Substance Use, Abuse, and Addiction

A reported 9% of the U.S. population use illegal drugs (SAMHSA, 2014b). This includes drugs such as cocaine, heroin, marijuana, and prescription drugs used for nonmedical reasons. Excessive use and abuse of substances, whether legal or illegal, is likely to impair a person's daily functioning across all areas of life, including parenting. When substances are used during pregnancy, there are also a variety of possible effects on the unborn child, many of which result in lifelong developmental, behavioral, and physical challenges.

Researchers who study substance use differentiate among use, abuse, and addiction. It is possible for a person to both use and abuse drugs without being addicted. The term *addiction* typically means that the person is no longer in control of their use (Baldwin, Songer, & Ensher, 2009). Both genetic and family risk factors contribute to risk for developing an addiction versus use or abuse without addiction. Likelihood of use of more than one substance is high (Baldwin et al., 2009).

Home visitors should recognize the potential effects of both legal (e.g., prescription drugs, cigarettes, alcohol) and illegal (e.g., heroin, cocaine, methamphetamine) drugs on the child directly and through impaired parenting behavior. Alcohol, though legal, is the most commonly used addictive substance. Use of alcohol during pregnancy is known to lead to serious birth defects that include problems in growth and the nervous system, leading to a cascade of developmental and behavioral problems. Perhaps surprisingly, close to 20% of women smoke during pregnancy. Smoking during pregnancy can lead to many problems for the fetus, including prematurity, miscarriage, and small size, which are risk factors for medical and learning issues (Hackshaw, Rodeck, & Boniface, 2011). Similar concerns have been reported for second-hand exposure to smoke (Hayashi, Matsuda, Kawamichi, Shiozaki, & Saito, 2011).

Babies born to using mothers may be physically dependent on the drug, leading to withdrawal symptoms. Depending on the drug used, the baby might have physical symptoms, such as breathing problems, vomiting, diarrhea, trembling, excessive sleeping, or behaviors such as crying and irritability (Baldwin et al., 2009). Early on, babies born with substances in their systems may have feeding and sleep problems that make them hard to care for. Continuing irritability and problems with soothing can interfere with bonding, especially when parents' confidence is undermined by a lack of success (Baldwin et al., 2009). As children grow older, both behavioral and learning issues may become apparent.

Parents who continue to use substances may engage in risky behaviors that lead to concerns for child safety. Examples include driving while under the influence or allowing children to be exposed to dangerous chemicals through second-hand smoke or ingestion. Some parents who are impaired by the effects of drugs or alcohol may fail to provide needed supervision or use funds for drugs instead of providing sufficient food or other needed resources. Parents using substances may also have difficulty providing a basic routine or a stable home environment.

When substance abuse concerns are present or suspected, the home visitor can offer some ideas and resources and should consider the following guidelines and strategies:

- Set clear limits and boundaries regarding contact and appointments and stay clear about the goals of the home visiting program.

- Carefully ask if any family members use alcohol or other drugs as part of regular assessment activities. If the family answers yes, be prepared to offer resources and referral for information, assessment, diagnosis, treatment, family counseling, self-help groups, and other community-based supports.

- Support parents with substance use issues in their parenting needs as you would other parents seeking to enhance their skills.

- If abuse and/or neglect are observed, contact authorities, as defined by federal and state statutes.

- Avoid becoming overinvolved or codependent, and discuss reactions to families experiencing substance abuse issues in reflective supervision.

Domestic Violence or Trauma

We discussed how young children respond to trauma exposure in Chapter 8. In this subsection, we acknowledge that parents can be affected by trauma in several ways. Caregivers may be directly affected by traumatic events that occurred during their own childhood or events that are currently occurring. Common examples of such trauma include community or interpersonal violence, loss, accidents, or natural disasters. Parents can also be indirectly affected, showing symptoms after their children experience a traumatic event (Appleyard & Osofksy, 2003). For some families, trauma is pervasive and chronic, including chaotic and unsafe environments and poverty (Appleyard & Osofsky, 2003).

Because trauma has the potential to affect all aspects of functioning, skills related to parenting may not be spared. According to the National Child Traumatic Stress Network, trauma may reduce a person's ability to engage in relationships, dampen cognitive skills, and reduce emotion regulation, all of which may be important to sensitive and effective caregiving (http://www.nctsn.org/). Parents may struggle with decision making and planning, for example. When the parent and the child are both traumatized, parents may respond in several maladaptive ways: becoming withdrawn and unavailable, becoming overprotective, and repeatedly talking about or even actually reenacting the events (Scheeringa & Zeanah, 2001). These reactions affect not only parenting behavior and the parent–child relationship; they may also make it hard for families to engage in services offered by home visitors.

Providing stability and routine is frequently recommended as a strategy to help young children begin to heal when trauma occurs. Unfortunately, for some children this is not possible, when poverty and domestic violence combine to result in homelessness. Women who are homeless are highly likely to have experienced violence or trauma. About 90% reported at least one trauma event, with up to 50% of homelessness in women due to interpersonal trauma. More than 2.5 million American children experienced homelessness in 2014, with about half of these reported to be less than 6 years old (Bassuk, DeCandia, Beach, & Berman, 2014; Samuels, Shinn, & Buckner, 2010). These figures include families that do not have their own homes but "doubled up" with friends or extended families, with frequent moves from place to place, as well as families that live in cars, shelters, or the open. As might be expected, parents who are homeless may have other stressors or risk factors, including depression, trauma disorders, and substance abuse. These issues are known to have the potential to affect parenting behavior, and homelessness on its own can also have an impact on a parent's ability to support his or her children.

When families have experienced trauma, home visitors can help the parent prioritize immediate and longer term needs, such as the following:

- Physical safety, including a safe place to live and protection from injury or threat

- Return to routines and schedule

- Access to therapies needed to heal from the trauma experience

Stress During Pregnancy

The stressors that we have discussed so far are likely to be present prior to the child's birth, meaning that many women experience stress during their pregnancies. For example, it is estimated that about 10%–15% of women have anxiety or depression in the prenatal period. Researchers have been interested in understanding if and how maternal stress during pregnancy affects the fetus and if effects are long lasting.

Fetal exposure to maternal stress has been related to higher infant reactivity or vulnerability to stress (Davis & Thompson, 2014). This increased reactivity occurs through fetal programming, a process in which the prenatal environment permanently affects the baby's development, putting him or her at risk for physical and health issues that can be long lasting (Barker, 1998). The babies exposed to maternal stress in utero appear more fearful, react more strongly to novelty, and are at higher risk for depression and anxiety later as preteens or teens. For mothers whose anxiety or depression is in the top 15% in terms of severity, the risk for the fetus to have behavior problems in childhood or adolescence is doubled from 5% to 10% (O'Donnell, Glover, Barker, & O'Connor, 2014). Some gender differences have been reported. For example, boy babies exposed to prenatal stress are less likely to survive and are more likely to have developmental problems; girl babies were more prone to anxiety and affective disorders (Davis & Thompson, 2014).

Pregnant women may have many types of worries and concerns; some are related specifically to the pregnancy and others are more general. When discussing worries during pregnancy, home visitors may notice that some mothers worry about the pregnancy itself, such as whether it was planned or desired, about the health of the baby, and about the experience of delivery. Mothers tend to worry about miscarriage early in pregnancy, switching to concern about the fetus in the middle and then, near the end, about the delivery.

Anxiety that is related to the pregnancy has been linked with premature birth and child outcomes such as problems in cognition, emotion, temperament, anxiety, and executive functions (Guardino & Schetter, 2014). Mothers who are younger, have less education, and have lower incomes are more likely to have pregnancy-related anxiety, as are mothers who are in relationships that end more quickly. African American and Latina mothers may be more vulnerable to this kind of anxiety. In addition, mothers' personal characteristics, including lower self-esteem, lower mastery and optimism, and less social support (especially from a partner), are also risk factors for pregnancy-related anxiety (Guardino & Schetter, 2014).

When they support pregnant mothers, home visitors help prevent physical changes to infants that cause problem behaviors in early childhood. These supports should include the following:

- Providing education and resources to help mothers stay healthy, such as nutrition and prenatal care

- Contributing to a supportive social environment through building a positive relationship

- Screening for maternal depression, anxiety, and pregnancy-specific anxiety

Supports that help prevent anxiety and depressive symptoms related to pregnancy include the following:

- Providing childbirth education to alleviate worries

- Giving support related to diagnostic tests

- Encouraging healthy practices balanced with assurances that most babies are born healthy

Environmental Risk Factors

Many families face economic uncertainties that can dramatically affect their ability to be in the present moment to meet the needs of their children. When a family is struggling to make ends meet (e.g., pay rent, utilities, car notes, insurance; purchase food and diapers), it can be challenging for parents to notice the developmental nuances that occur in very young children. Following the 2007 economic recession and slow recovery, many families continued to struggle with economic conditions that led to unemployment, underemployment, and a shift with families moving from the "middle class" to poverty. As a result of the fiscal crisis, a staggering number of children lived in poverty and were food insecure. According to the National Center for Children in Poverty, in 2010 more than 20% of American children lived in families with incomes below the poverty level and another 25% lived in families with significantly low incomes (Wight, Chau, & Aratani, 2010). Home visitors are likely to be very aware of the struggles of such families, feeling the tension of how to balance attention to program goals with fulfilling basic needs for housing, food, and medical care.

Family financial instability is also often related to several other common stressors, including parental mental health and addiction concerns, and family situations including incarceration, divorce, and domestic violence.

EXTENDING YOUR SKILL SET TO SUPPORT PARENTS AND CAREGIVERS

In addition to knowledge of specific risk factors and how they interact, home visitors can provide supports for families who struggle with chronic stressors. In the following subsections, we detail a set of strategies that are targeted for helping individuals in recovery and that complement home visitors' efforts to provide relationship-based and reflective approaches (SAMHSA, 2009).

Provide Emotional Support

Home visitors must be aware that, for many families, additional time and effort will be needed in order for the family to develop enough trust in the relationship to accept emotional and other supports. Research indicates that people with various forms of MI or other risk factors often struggle with initiating and maintaining relationships (SAMHSA, 2009; Stepp, et al., 2012). These studies, although often focused on family relationships, provide information that may also help inform relationships between caregivers and home visitors. Expectations about what relationships with home visitors might be like are formed through prior experiences with all kinds of relationships, whether personal (e.g., parents, friends, partners) or professional (e.g., teachers, doctors, case managers). Individuals with MI and disability often reported believing that others do not understand their problems and that they lack trust in their ability to be helped. Reports of being criticized about parenting or other skills in ways that damage confidence were also noted (Kleinmann & Songer, 2009; Perera et al., 2014). As a result, such individuals may need more time and support in order to feel comfortable with the home visitors. Home visitors can use the relationship-building strategies outlined in Chapter 1, understanding that forming the relationship may take longer.

Biases about common risk factors may interfere with the home visitor's ability to demonstrate emotional supports needed to build relationships. Some home visitors may have negative attitudes or beliefs about mental illness (e.g., believing that people with MI should not be parents) that are likely to interfere with building positive partnerships (Perera et al., 2014). Attitudes about addiction, such as viewing it as a weakness rather than an illness, might also lead to misunderstandings about parents' intentions or abilities to meet their children's needs. Stigma related to mental illness and disabilities may lead home visitors to have lowered expectations for affected individuals. Thoughts about "foster care kids" might interfere with supporting positive reunification efforts with the child's primary caregivers. Also, hearing about parents who are in prison may bring up biased ideas about these individual's abilities to care for their children and to watch out for their best interests. Home visitors who are aware of the potential for bias can monitor their own reactions to family characteristics and behaviors. Research about specific populations can be used as a starting place in learning about individual families, but in the end, to avoid stereotyping, every family must be understood as unique.

Within a positive relationship, home visitors can provide emotional supports to vulnerable families. In Chapter 1, we discussed the importance of developing relationships and how home visitors can act in ways that build relationships through consistent and reliable responses. For families that have multiple risk factors and have had few positive relationships with professionals, behaviors that signal respect and recognition of family strength are needed. Home visitors can demonstrate respect by behaviors such as the following:

- Arriving on time

- Respecting family boundaries

- Asking permission to be in the family's home

- Asking what name to use when referring to the child and family members

- Talking openly and honestly with the family

- Asking permission to share and gather information

Jackie texts and calls Desiree several times over the next couple of weeks but does not hear back. She checks in with the service coordinator, who fortunately has the grandmother's contact information. When Jackie reaches Desiree, Desiree expresses surprise to hear from her. Desiree lets Jackie know that she is not in a position to meet, but she tells Jackie how much she appreciates hearing from her. "I thought you would just forget about us," she says. Jackie assures her that she has not forgotten Chloe or her and that she would like to restart visits when possible.

Gain Skills with Difficult Topics

In order to help families who live with many stressors or risk factors, home visitors must be able to recognize and talk about the issues. For example, many parenting programs attend to maternal depression through screening and referral. When staff have additional training about these topics, they and parents are more satisfied and communicate more about mental illness and its effect on parenting (Knitzer et al., 2008). This necessitates gaining a level of comfort with difficult topics through training, experience, and practice. Training needs to include content knowledge and, more important, ideas for assessing parent readiness to discuss an issue, practice so that information can be shared smoothly, and supervision and self-reflection so that home visitors can assess their own level of comfort (Monahan et al., 2012). When talking about these topics, try to find a balance of words that are professional yet understandable to families. Use of the same words that the family uses can be productive. Introducing new words, just like introducing new ideas, can be successful when done with care and support. Figure 9.1 provides examples of how to discuss challenging topics and an opportunity to capture your own ideas.

Have Reasonable Expectations

Families with severe or multiple challenges may make progress at slower rates than others, may experience repeat problems, and may require more of the home visitor's time overall. For example, parents with depression may have a hard time following through to implement strategies shared by the home visitor (Alvarez et al., 2015). In parallel, the home visitor may need additional training and support to be effective (Monahan et al., 2012). Home visitors would be wise to strive to tolerate patterns that involve ups and downs, or one step forward, one back, as this is the nature of work with families with complex lives and multiple stressors. Being able to recognize and celebrate small changes can help home visitors tolerate the slower pace that these families have. These small changes are often quite meaningful for a specific family. For example, the home visitor can help the family celebrate trying out a bedtime routine, even if they do not yet implement it every night. A caregiver might demonstrate a great time-out during one visit and then go back to yelling at his child during the next. In this situation, the home visitor can remind the caregiver of his or her previous success and encourage him or her to try again next time. These acts of acknowledging and highlighting small changes can contribute to a positive relationship with the parent. In turn, the parent is

PRACTICE DISCUSSING DIFFICULT TOPICS

Use this form to think about words and questions to discuss and learn more about difficult topics parents and caregivers face. Review the sample wording and add your own ideas in the space provided. It might be helpful to discuss your ideas with a colleague or in reflective supervision or consultation sessions.

Topic	Sample wording	Your turn
Depression	How have you been feeling lately? Are there times when you feel down or not able to enjoy your baby?	
Incarcerated family member	I understand that Sally's father is incarcerated at this time. How has that been for you and your son? How might you talk with Sally about this?	
Family struggling economically	How are you getting your everyday needs met? What kinds of help could your family use (e.g., food, shelter, transportation, health care)?	
Domestic violence	Do you feel safe? Is your child safe? Is anyone hurting you? Are there weapons in your home? Do you have a place to go if you feel unsafe? Do you have someone to call to help you?	

(continued)

Figure 9.1. Practice worksheet for discussing difficult topics.

Figure 9.1. *(continued)*

Topic	Sample wording	Your turn
Substance use/abuse	Does anyone in the home use alcohol or other substances? Does anyone have a problem with using?	
Parent deployment	Is anyone serving in the military? Is there a plan for deployment? *If yes:* What has been shared with the rest of the family about the deployment? How might you talk with the children about this?	
Parent relationship problem	How do you both get along? How do you solve problems? How much do you agree about parenting and other important family decisions?	
Other topics		

better able to hear and take action on recommendations that are made after the home visitor has joined him or her in seeing and appreciating this small improvement (Landy & Menna, 2006).

Often, the home visitor may think that his or her own effectiveness is lacking when families make slow progress. Learning to see your role as part of the bigger web of support that is needed can be beneficial (Yoches, Summers, Beeber, Jones Harden, & Malik, 2012). For example, your role may be to get the family to the point that they could choose to use another service. A component of a person's MI, disability, addiction, or trauma response can include lashing out at providers, blaming them for problems, or accusing them of not helping enough. It is important to learn not to take these emotional responses personally and avoid letting them get in the way of the work to be done (Landy & Menna, 2006). Talking over these experiences with a supervisor can help. We review more about these and other benefits of supervision in Chapter 10.

Share Information

Families with multiple challenges have many needs, and these can be experienced by the family as well as the home visitor as emergencies. Having referral information and resources for a variety of potential issues can help build your relationship with the family, as it allows the family to see you as a responsive and reliable source of support. It can also help you, as the provider, to feel calmer and better prepared.

Although the need to provide concrete supports and help in a crisis is very real, it is not the only form of information that can be shared. Information about child development and behavior are also important components of most home visiting programs. Many home visitors and early intervention providers have very detailed knowledge about child development and may not be aware of how little some parents know about expected skills for babies and toddlers. Lack of knowledge about typical development can lead parents to have inappropriate expectations. One important role is to gently challenge incorrect perceptions or assumptions about children in general or about the specific child (Landy & Menna, 2006). Some parents believe their children can do activities that they actually are not developmentally ready to perform. For example, a parent might say, "She is 18 months old already and should be ready to potty train." The home visitor might respond in one of the following ways:

"What does her doctor recommend?"

"Tell me more about how you plan to teach her."

"How has she shown you she is ready to learn this new skill?"

Questions or statements like these lead the parent to think about the issue from different perspectives and provide the home visitor with the opportunity

Table 9.1.　Home visitor responses to assumptions about children

Caregiver expectation of child's development	Home visitor response
A mother tells the home visitor that she believes her 2-month-old baby is ready to eat solid foods such as cereal, saying, "She should be sleeping through the night by now and I'm exhausted!"	"A lot of moms I talk with are tired and wonder about how to help their baby sleep better. Usually, I hear doctors talk about adding cereal when babies are a little older, but you could check with your doctor to see what is recommended. I wonder if you would like to talk about some ideas to help you get some more rest."
A caregiver shouts angrily at a 30-month-old child who is running off in a park, "You are doing this on purpose to embarrass me!"	"It's hard when little kids have so much energy! Even though running off is pretty normal, sometimes parents worry that other people think they are not doing their job."
A mother cries when her toddler hits her during discipline. She says, "He is bad and will never be good."	"I know it is frustrating for you when he hits. I wonder if he is frustrated, too. Maybe he is really trying to tell us what he wants, but he doesn't have the words yet."

to share more accurate information that matches the child's developmental skills. In this example, perhaps the parent's motivation to potty train at this age is to save money on diapers. By knowing this information, the home visitor can identify a resource that addresses this concern while working on an appropriate potty training plan. Table 9.1 provides some additional examples of how a home visitor might respond to assumptions about the child.

Build Problem-Solving Skills

At times, rushing to solve problems and providing resources is not the answer. When a home visitor too quickly provides a resource or solution, there is a risk that he or she is not on the same page as the family. The solution the home visitor identifies may not be one the family would have chosen. Even less helpful, the home visitor might not even know what the family thinks is the main problem, meaning that his or her suggestions are not aligned with family goals and are likely to be ignored. Furthermore, when the home visitor is always the problem solver, families lose a chance to build problem-solving skills and to have a sense of efficacy that comes from taking charge of issues themselves.

Parents with the risk factors we have discussed may have difficulty with planning and problem-solving; as a result, their normal life may involve moving from crisis to crisis. Slowing down and providing opportunities to help a family work through a problem step by step can help families gain skills in these areas. Depending on the family, a home visitor may need to be patient and allow mistakes to happen. This is hard, as it is common to feel frustrated when a family fails to take actions that would avoid a problem, even when the home visitor offers to help. So the family may miss appointments, lose important forms, or forget to apply a strategy that the home visitor suggested. For these families, the provider may need to step back even further. Helping a family think about what might be getting in the way of planning or implementing an action step, such as being too stressed, sad, or angry, may be a big first step forward (Landy & Menna, 2006).

As she drives to a visit with Maureen and her family, Kathryn thinks about the plan they made the previous week to talk to the family doctor about the baby's hearing. Kathryn reviews in her mind the steps she laid out for Maureen to follow and feels relieved that this will finally be resolved. Kathryn has been worried about the baby's hearing for months.

When Maureen answers the door, Kathryn immediately asks about the doctor's appointment. Maureen looks a little embarrassed. She tells Maureen, "I never called the doctor. We had some other things come up. Our heat got shut off, and then my mom's car broke down. It's been crazy." Kathryn feels disappointed and concerned. She doesn't understand how Maureen can be so disorganized. At the same time, she recognizes that Maureen's family has encountered some unavoidable stressors. She wonders if Maureen is aware of the importance of getting the baby's hearing checked.

Kathryn says, "Well, it sounds like you have had a wild week. I can understand how things got away from you." "Yes, they did," Maureen answers. She seems to relax. "I thought you would be mad since I didn't get the call made to the doctor. I know you think it's important. This is like the second or third time we made a plan about it."

Kathryn realizes that Maureen may have reasons other than the ones that she stated for not making the call. She decides to work toward getting a conversation started about things that get in the way instead of just making another plan. She says, "Yes, I do think it is important and I think you do, too. We could just make a new plan, but I wonder if we should try to think about this in another way. An awful lot of things seem to get in the way of making that call."

At this point, Kathryn may learn a number of different reasons for Maureen's failure to make the call. Maureen really might have been distracted by the stressful events that happened. She may be uncomfortable talking on the phone or she may be afraid to find out whether the baby has a hearing problem. Maureen also may not be worried about the baby's hearing at all, leaving her little motivation to go for a checkup. By starting a conversation instead of continuing to repeat the plan, Kathryn may learn more about how Maureen sees things.

Accept the Unexpected: What Is Needed Now?

Once home visitors step across the threshold into a family's home, anything can happen. As much as a home visitor would like to have a good plan for a session, circumstances may interfere so that the plan may no longer be appropriate. Many home visitors report that flexibility is an important key to working with high-risk families. Being willing to give up the planned session in favor of what the family needs right now or is capable of doing may be the right and most effective strategy. This requires a willingness to step outside of one's role, at times. It is recognized that this reality may cause tension when one is working in a program that involves evaluation or research requiring fidelity to a program model. Home visitors may feel caught between an action that supports relationship and adherence to the program model (Barak, Spielberger, & Gitlow, 2014). When this happens, home visitors should discuss the situation with a supervisor, as their agency may have general policies or guidance for this issue. If there is no policy, the home visitor and supervisor can discuss options that would be acceptable.

Providers and agencies should consider whether it is a good use of resources to continue providing parent training or curriculum as planned when a parent will not be able to do his or her part due to depression or other mental illness (Alvarez et al., 2015). Instead, stopping to ask questions and creating a space for exploring the current concern or family priority is needed. If family priorities are left unaddressed, the family is unlikely to be willing or able to attend to issues they believe are less important. The case example in the previous subsection reviewed a few examples of the caregiver and the home visitor having different agendas; the home visitor could shift his or her work to better attend to the parent's agenda. The home visitor might find that identifying resources would be effective (e.g., helping the family to get the heat turned back on or locate a source for help with transportation). In other situations, the home visitor could discover that the family is working with another agency. Coordinating plans between agencies would be useful in this situation; we will talk more about coordination in Chapter 10.

Know Your Limits

Although home visitors may not think they have the specialized skills needed to help parents with significant stressors, one of the main wishes of mothers who struggle with MI is long-term in-home supports by someone who could provide practical help and be available to talk about problems (Krumm et al., 2013). This combination of a long-term relationship, good listening skills, and practical knowledge is certainly in the repertoire of a home visitor or early intervention professional and will be enough to meet the needs of many families. However, even with training and supervision, early childhood professionals are not a substitute for other specialized providers, and coordination with other professionals is essential (Yoches et al., 2012).

One difficulty is that participants in home visiting and early intervention programs often do not view the parent–professional relationship in the same way. This may lead to differences in expectations about what will and can occur. About three quarters of participants in home visiting programs report viewing the visitors as a friend. This differs from the perspective of the home visitor, who is more likely to describe their role as a resource for information, a person who cares or helps, or a friend with boundaries (Mills et al., 2012; Riley, Brady, Goldberg, Jacobs, & Easterbrooks, 2008). Agency policies are likely to address boundary issues; if they do not, this should be part of supervision. Overall, it can be helpful to know that even though parents and professionals see the roles differently, there tends to be a high level of family satisfaction with home visits. We return to this issue in more detail in Chapter 10.

HOW WE ENGAGE WITH FAMILIES

Despite the home visitor's best efforts and skill, there are some families who will continue to resist offers of relationship, support, and concrete help. When families seem hard to engage, disengaged, distant, or overwhelmed, home visitors may become frustrated and discouraged by their perceived lack of effectiveness. To cope, the provider may push too hard or let go too soon. Unfortunately, these responses may be all too familiar to the family, which has many times experienced personal and professional relationships that do not meet its needs. It is not surprising, then, if the family implements a coping strategy from its own past, such as choosing to terminate the relationship. This result may reinforce the home visitor's view that the family did not want help after all. For these families, the emphasis should be on building relationship in a very basic way, by being reliable, consistent, and containing. Frequently, this will start with attention to the parent's emotional experience.

Many of the parents that home visitors work with may have trouble with emotion regulation. They may lack an ability to tolerate negative emotions along with difficulties recognizing positive ones. These parents will benefit from provider actions aimed at their own emotional experience. This suggestion may send up a red flag, with home visitors running off shouting, "I'm not a therapist!" It is true that early intervention workers are unlikely to have backgrounds or licenses that prepare them to deliver psychotherapy, and that careful attention to professional boundaries and appropriate scope of practice is important. However, a home visitor can function in a way that provides some emotional containment, not as a friend or as a therapist, but in a way that lets the parent share their emotions that are directly related to their child and about what it is like for them to be a parent (Weatherston, 2000).

A home visitor sits listening to a mother and father discuss their concerns about the behavior of their 14-month-old son, who had been biting peers at child care. The mother states, "He is so mean; kind of like a bully." The home visitor, who has been listening to the parents' complaints about this boy for 45 minutes, notices that her own response to this statement was a flash of annoyance or even anger. She realizes that she believes the parents' expectations are unreasonable and that she is irritated because this topic has been discussed many times before. Although her initial impulse is to remind the parents of her previous teaching about typical development, instead she decides to respond to their emotional states. The worker asks, "What is it like for you to see your son act like a bully?" This question leads to a discussion of the mother's fears that her son would hurt someone and what would happen if he was kicked out of child care.

Parents who have multiple challenges may not respond as well to structured teaching activities as others. Some parents, especially young mothers, for example, are more open to information when it is presented "in the moment." Parents who have cognitive challenges due to trauma or intellectual disability may need tasks broken down and repeated. Home visitors who can be flexible, who use active strategies such as demonstration or modeling directly with the child, and who choose topics based on what is currently happening with the family may be more effective in engaging harder to reach parents (Mills et al., 2012). Allowing the family to be "the driver" may increase attention and future application of learning, as the family more clearly recognizes the relevance of the instruction to its daily life.

We have often discussed the importance for parents with young children to implement a parenting strategy that blends routine and limit-setting with warmth. Similarly, home visitor behaviors such as expressive, animated, and warm interactions with parents are favored. In addition, these warm interactions between parent and home visitor are likely to increase parent responsiveness to babies, which is related to enhanced child developmental outcomes (Trivette, Dunst, & Hamby, 2010).

In a related vein, we advise parents to provide labeled praise for their children, meaning to talk specifically about behaviors they are happy to see. An example of labeled praise to encourage sharing in a young child might be, "I like it when you let Karen have a turn with the ball." In parallel, home visitors can specifically point out or emphasize parent strengths, with statements such as "It's so great how you are using that bedtime routine we talked about" or "That was a really terrific redirection you just gave to Tina." Home visitors who express confidence in a mother's competence help her recognize what she is doing well; this in turn builds confidence in parenting skills (Landy & Menna, 2006; Mills et al., 2012).

USING THE PAUSE FRAMEWORK

Using the vignettes presented in this chapter, consider how Jackie processes her experiences with Chloe and her family. See Figures 9.2 and 9.3 for examples of how this might look.

WHAT'S NEXT?

In Chapter 10, we reflect on taking care of ourselves, establishing good boundaries in our work, and participating in reflective supervision or consultation.

TIPS FOR PRACTICE

▶ Be aware that a family with one risk factor is likely to also be experiencing others that may require different kinds of attention.

▶ Home visitors who can step back, evaluate situations, and consider multiple perspectives, using methods such as PAUSE, will be most effective with families that have multiple risk factors and stressors.

▶ When the home visitor experiences strong feelings, he or she should take time to wonder how the situation is being experienced by the caregiver and the child.

KEY POINTS TO REMEMBER

▶ A large number of American families are living with significant stressors that may make it difficult to meet basic needs. These families may need to obtain concrete supports before they are able to fully attend to the emotional needs of their young children.

▶ Parental issues such as mental health concerns, disabilities, and addiction may interfere with caregiving behaviors. Nevertheless, individuals with these challenges most likely can successfully parent with supports, including home visiting.

PAUSE WORKSHEET   pa**᳁**se

Child: _Chloe_   Date: _August 21, 2015_

Parent: _Desiree_   Provider: _Jackie_

PERCEIVE—Explore what is happening.

Parent/caregiver perspective:	Provider perspective:
The family is overwhelmed with being evicted and having to move quickly.	I am unclear what my role should be in this situation. Do I focus on my role as a physical therapist or should I offer to help in a concrete way to address the emergency situation?

ASK—Clarify what is happening.

Starting with the parent/caregiver's priorities and concerns, ask more detailed/specific questions to clarify what is happening.

The family has been evicted. What are their immediate needs? How can I help?

They are moving in with Desiree's mother. Will visits continue there? How long will they live in that location?

Where is Chloe's father? What is the plan for all of their belongings?

Who else could help the family at this time?

How can the team minimize the impact of the move on the children and their development?

UNDERSTAND—Explore why it is happening.

With the parent/caregiver, explore explanations for what is happening. Consider possible explanations that include the environment, the child, and the parent. Listen and observe closely as you explore the situation in conversation with the family.

Parent/caregiver perspective:	Provider perspective:	Child's perspective:
The family is in crisis now and does not have time to address Chloe's specific needs. Desiree has to look out for the entire family.	There is a short window to help Chloe reach her developmental milestones. Is there a way to continue to	It might be confusing for Chloe to be moving so quickly. Is there any way I can help her with the transition while still

(continued)

Figure 9.2. Jackie's PAUSE Worksheet for Desiree and Chloe.

Figure 9.2. *(continued)*

PAUSE WORKSHEET *(continued)*

━━━━━━━━━━━━━━━━━━━━━━━━━━━━━━━━━━━━━━

UNDERSTAND *(continued)*

Parent/caregiver perspective:	*Provider perspective:*	*Child's perspective:*
	offer physical therapy services? Do I have any other roles to play?	including therapeutic goals?

STRATEGIZE and **EVALUATE**—Identify possible responses/solutions.

1. *Solution/action to try:*	
Refer this family to a local resource for supports and services.	*How will we know if it works?* The family will have their needs met. *When will we evaluate if it works?* By phone when scheduling the next visit

2. *Solution/action to try:*	
Ask the family how the home visitor could have been more helpful.	*How will we know if it works?* Team members will learn ways to help in similar situations. *When will we evaluate if it works?* When a similar situation occurs

PROVIDER REFLECTION WORKSHEET

Child: Chloe   Date: August 21, 2015

Parent: Desiree

Provider: Jackie

1. How did I follow the parent's lead to learn what is most pressing or important to the family?	It was very difficult for me to know how to respond to this family's crisis. I felt uncomfortable and uncertain. I did ask if I should leave or continue with the session.
2. How did I ask clarifying questions to help me understand the problem better?	When I asked if there might be a better time to meet, as they seem very busy, I found out more about what would happen. I think the family felt heard.
3. How did I provide information that may help the family better understand the child's behavior?	I was surprised and unsure how to respond. I did not think to ask about Chloe's experience in this situation.

(continued)

Figure 9.3. Jackie's Provider Reflection Worksheet for Desiree and Chloe.

Figure 9.3. *(continued)*

PROVIDER REFLECTION WORKSHEET *(continued)*

4. *How did I engage the family to develop a response that may include a strategy to try, a resource to use, or more information to increase understanding?*	I don't feel I did a good job managing my own feelings, so I did not problem-solve with the family. I actually felt relieved when Desiree suggested I just have my session with Chloe, as that was familiar and I felt competent. How can I learn from this experience in case something like this happens again?
5. *How did I provide support and emotional containment if needed?*	I had trouble with my own feelings, so I did not support the family. I was surprised at my strong reaction of irritation. I am worried that the family sensed my discomfort with not knowing how to help.
6. *How do I plan to follow up on promised actions to maintain trust?*	I did offer to explore some resources and called the family when I got back to the office, after speaking with some other staff members.
7. *What do I want to discuss in reflective supervision to improve my practice and outcomes with this child and family?*	I want to explore my reaction to this situation, learn about possible resources for families, and discuss how to better react in these kinds of situations.

▶ Relationship-based practices and reflective skills can help home visitors find ways to engage families who struggle with stressors that challenge parenting.

SUGGESTED FURTHER READING

Ensher, G.L., Clark, D.A., & Songer, N.S. (Eds.). (2009). *Families, infants, and young children at risk: Pathways to best practice.* Baltimore, MD: Paul H. Brookes Publishing Co.

You Can't Do this Alone

Boundaries, Self-Care, and Supervision

Anna drives away from a home visit with a mix of feelings. She notices how tight her shoulders are feeling and tries to relax her jaw, as she is gritting her teeth. "This family is going to make me crazy," she thinks. Every time Anna thinks she has a handle on things with this family, something else comes up. Anna started working with Anthony's mother, Tessa, during her pregnancy. Reflecting back, Anna realizes that she has worked with the family for 8 months so far in her role as a home visitor for a prevention program. Over this time period, Anna has found herself frustrated and even angry many times.

Anna cannot understand how Tessa can be so compliant and cooperative one day and then appear completely unmotivated and disinterested the next time she sees her. Sometimes, Tessa tells Anna she does not remember things that have been discussed repeatedly. At other times, she calls Anna multiple times in a day with questions and demands. Often, this is followed by missed appointments and calls for several weeks. Luckily, Anthony is an adorable and responsive baby that Anna very much enjoys seeing and playing with. Whenever Anna thinks about asking to have the family reassigned, she remembers Anthony and his needs. "Someone needs to put this baby first," she often says to herself.

This week, Tessa was completely disconnected during the appointment. The apartment was cluttered and dirty. Anthony was in a car seat and needed a change. Anna feels a little surge of anger when she recalls seeing Anthony sleeping in the car seat. She knows she had told Tessa repeatedly that this is not safe. Anna did not even try to address the issue with Tessa this time; she took the baby from the car seat, gave him a bath, and put him in clean clothes. As she bustled around doing these tasks, Anna did not notice that Tessa sat quietly and just watched her.

As she pulls into her own garage, Anna remembers noticing that Anthony had grown and that many of his clothes were too small. "I'll have to remember to bring those outfits I got for Anthony next week," Anna thinks. She suddenly realizes she cannot recall whether she confirmed the next appointment with Tessa. Anna thinks back to when she left. She remembers that Tessa had followed her to the door and recalls saying to Tessa, "Did you want something?" in a voice that she now thinks might have been a little rough. Anna has a picture of Tessa pulling back slightly and shaking her head no. "I wonder what her problem was today, anyway," Anna thinks briefly as she begins her own evening routine.

In this chapter, we return to the topics of relationship and reflective practice, including challenges to maintaining these practices, such as secondary trauma, setting limits and boundaries, finding personal and professional balance, and avoiding burnout. These are important issues for all kinds of providers; you can't do your best work if you don't take care of yourself. As part of this discussion, this chapter details how reflective supervision can provide support to home visitors as well as serve as a form of professional development (Jones Harden, 2010; Watson et al., 2014). Finally, we explore ideas to manage miscommunication and conflicts between team members as well as between provider and family, with suggested steps for repair when things go wrong.

Increased emphasis on serving children in early childhood has resulted in an expansion of home visiting in general. Across the country, more programs are available, serving a variety of families. For most participating families, a risk factor led to their eligibility for services. Risk factors vary widely and can include having a child with a disability or delay (Part C of the Individuals with Disabilities Education Improvement Act of 2004, PL 108-446), being a young or vulnerable parent, or experience with or risk for child welfare involvement (Maternal, Infant, and Early Childhood Home Visiting program of the Patient Protection and Affordable Care Act of 2010, PL 111-148). In addition to the challenges that the work with families brings, the characteristics of the work itself may be difficult for home visitors for several reasons.

Many home visitors are trained in models that involve working with individual clients and may have trouble shifting to working with a parent–child dyad. In fact, many home visitors and early education providers may have had only child-focused training and subsequently struggle when required to perform in a coaching format with parents (Tomlin, 2002). These providers may have a hard time understanding how to help parents work with the child in a facilitation model rather than giving direct instructions. Parents may also expect the provider to "do work" with their child. As a result, service delivery may involve the home visitor interacting with the child while the parent watches but does not have a chance to practice the methods being demonstrated (Jones Harden, Denmark, & Saul, 2010).

Often, home visitors speak about the frustration of figuring out facilitating the parent–child relationship when other things seem more important, such as getting basic needs met (Jones Harden et al., 2010). Early intervention workers have much information and many resources to share with families and may get impatient for parents to start taking advantage of those resources. The previous chapters highlight the importance of developing a relationship with families that will serve as a vehicle for sharing knowledge, skills, and resources. This link between the parent–provider relationship and the delivery of the services is at the core of successful intervention (Lee et al., 2013). It is helpful to consider three interrelated sets of strategies or actions borrowed from infant mental health practice that build relationship and skills in parents across time (Tomlin & Viehweg, 2003; Weatherston, 2000, 2005). These sets of strategies include 1) provide support, 2) build skills, and 3) promote positive interactions.

First, the home visitor should plan and intentionally act in ways that provide support. Needed supports include those that are concrete and practical, such as helping a family obtain resources (e.g., diapers) or an advocate (e.g., access a waiver program, find a child care program). Home visitors can also provide psychological or emotional supports simply by being consistent and reliable. When parents experience the home visitor as a supportive presence, they are better able to participate in activities needed for the next type of interaction, teaching, and skill building to improve outcomes in child behavior and development. Activities to improve outcomes may include noticing a baby's cues, gently challenging inaccurate beliefs, speaking for the baby, highlighting strengths of the parent-child relationship, and explaining and modeling appropriate discipline strategies. Ultimately, once the parent feels safe in concrete and psychological ways and has a basic skill base, then the parent is ready to apply the skills and build his or her own relationship and positive interactions with the child (Tomlin & Viehweg, 2003; Weatherston, 2000; Woods, Wilcox, Friedman, & Murch, 2011). This sequence should not be thought of as a linear one. Providers should not anticipate getting to an "end," but instead should view working through these three strategies as a process. It is important to remember that with very complex family situations or with young children who have significant needs, it is very unlikely that any one parent–provider relationship will be all that is needed to achieve every family goal. Home visitors would do well to understand their role in helping a family as only a piece of the work to be done.

BOUNDARIES IN EARLY CHILDHOOD WORK

Home visitors are sometimes unprepared for the level of difficulty that some families live with (Tandon, Mercer, Saylor, & Duggan, 2008; Zeanah, Larrieu, & Boris, 2006). As reviewed in earlier chapters, families may struggle with shocking problems on a daily basis (e.g., parental incarceration, domestic violence, unsafe housing, extreme poverty, debilitating substance abuse/use or mental illness). Home visitors who grew up in more secure circumstances may have no frame of reference for understanding these types of experiences. Other home visitors who were exposed to difficult events and situations similar to those of some families they serve may have personal biases that are not helpful or that may interfere with the work (Zeanah et al., 2006). For example, a home visitor who overcame difficult life circumstances may have the attitude that anyone could do the same, leading to frustration with clients who are not making progress the provider believes is appropriate (Jones Harden et al., 2010). Other times, home visitors may unexpectedly become reactive to challenging family circumstances that remind them of their own difficult times. It can be hard for the home visitor to separate out what is happening to the family from his or her own experiences (Seligman, 2014).

There is a level of intimacy that is part of working with families with very young children (Tomlin & Viehweg, 2003; Watson & Gatti, 2012). For many providers and families, the fact that the work occurs in the family's home adds another layer of closeness to the work and the relationship. Family members may view the home visitor, who has worked diligently from a relationship-based perspective, as a friend, rather than as a professional (Mills et al., 2012; Riley et al., 2008). Home visitors need to clearly define the relationship, providing boundaries that protect the family and themselves. This could include having written explanations of the home visitor's role and expectations about family participation in sessions. It can be helpful to specify how and when communication will occur, such as when the caregiver can expect that the home visitor will answer calls. The home visitor may also need to discuss program policies regarding the use of texting, Facebook, Twitter, or other forms of social media to clarify up front what communication methods will be used. Home visitors may be invited to family gatherings such as a child's birthday party or offered a meal or snack. Families may ask for favors such as a ride to the store or to watch the children while the parent takes a shower or runs an errand. Understanding agency policies and guidelines can help you know how to respond to situations and requests like these. Home visitors must make the best decisions possible for each situation based on their understanding of their role, their program's policies, and the specific family.

Early childhood providers' consideration of boundaries varies. In one study with Early Head Start home visiting staff, some reported that they think about boundaries and are aware of the need to avoid crossing them. These providers also reported attending to their own emotional involvement with families. However, others in the sample reported directly helping families in concrete ways, such as providing a ride to the store or even cash in an emergency. Others reported making an effort to solve a family problem that was clearly outside of their scope of practice. For example, one provider barred an abusive partner from participating in the home visit (Jones Harden et al., 2010). Behaviors such as these may be considered ethical violations in many professional disciplines. In these examples, the home visitor has moved from a professional to a more personal relationship which can set up inappropriate expectations, interfere with achieving the planned outcomes, and cause missed opportunities for parents to build problem-solving skills. Maintaining awareness about one's scope of practice and skill set and clarity about the role and responsibilities of a home visitor can help avoid ethical errors.

Home visitors also need to be clear about roles and responsibilities when families are working with multiple providers and agencies. For example, families with parents with MI or developmental disorders may be involved with multiple professionals from early intervention, mental health, and child welfare, among other programs. Beeber and Canuso (2012) state that home visitors should request clarification of the "margins of authority" (p. 164) from supervisors or program managers in order to fully understand where their own authority starts and ends. In some cases, agencies have articulated agreements that explain how their staff communicate and work together. It is helpful to have clear communication about when and by whom various decisions are made. Understanding the roles and activities of other providers can also help the home visitor maintain awareness of when and how he or she may appropriately make changes to his or her specific work to accommodate the needs of a parent in crisis or with chronic issues before the problems undermine effectiveness. Clear communication and coordination within and across agencies and professionals is crucial. However, it is important to emphasize that information sharing for coordination efforts needs to be done sensitively and with the parent's permission. Home visitors who struggle with information that parents may share should avoid the temptation to process this information with other workers, respecting the family's privacy across all aspects of this work, especially when discussing trauma and other difficult subjects (Yoches et al., 2012). However, it is certainly appropriate to discuss challenging situations in reflective supervision sessions, where confidentiality can be assured.

Another aspect of the intensity and closeness of this work occurs when the home visitor and parent have similar characteristics or backgrounds. Some home visiting programs have emphasized similarities between workers and the populations they serve, such as ethnicity and, especially, languages spoken. The shared experience of being a parent can establish helpful common ground between the home visitor and family and may help facilitate trust

(Mills et al., 2012). Regardless of the type of similarity a home visitor and parent share, there are times when the use of a personal story is thought to have some benefit, such as increasing provider credibility and showing an understanding of parent feelings in a way that may help a parent accept a suggestion. Sharing a personal story may not always be useful, however. Some parents may feel less competent if the home visitor seems to know everything. When self-disclosing, it is probably best to focus on the child's issues and share only your experiences that are directly related to the work. It might be appropriate to share the activities you did at the zoo with your own child to promote learning about animals, but inappropriate to discuss the shopping trip you had with your best friend. When using this method, monitor how comfortable the parent seems to feel and make sure that the sharing is not a distraction (Woods et al., 2011). Refer to Box 10.1 for some suggestions on how to develop and maintain appropriate boundaries.

Lack of clear boundaries may increase the stress and likelihood of experiencing burnout in those who work with young families (Tandon et al., 2008; Zeanah et al., 2006). However, it is also true that the higher the level of risk and more problems that the family has, the greater the likelihood the home visitor will have strong feelings about the family (Seligman, 2014; Watson & Gatti, 2012). As a result, the home visitor may feel pressed to do more and stretch a boundary. Nurses in a Nurse Family Partnership program reported that families in which parents have mental health issues need more time and it was harder to stay on the planned schedule (Zeanah et al., 2006). When dif-

---

BOX 10.1. Suggestions for Developing and Maintaining Appropriate Boundaries

- Know and follow ethical guidelines of the profession.

- Know personal preferences regarding boundaries in relationships with families.

- Understand how a family's sense of boundaries might affect the home visitor.

- Consider the preferences of families and what will help them feel safe and engaged.

- Discuss issues of boundaries with families as necessary in certain situations.

From Weldum, J.R., Songer, N.S., & Ensher, G.S. (2009). The family as foreground. In G.L. Ensher, D.A. Clark, & N.S. Songer (Eds.), *Families, infants and young children at risk* (pp. 39–58). Baltimore, MD: Paul H. Brookes Publishing Co.; reprinted by permission.

ficult topics must be addressed, home visitors may struggle with concern that they do not have the background or training to address these areas adequately (Tandon et al., 2008; Yoches et al., 2012). It can be helpful to focus on what the home visitor provides that is helpful, such as child guidance and general supports, while maintaining the perspective that one is not responsible for every challenge a family faces. Reflective supervision can help the home visitor manage these concerns.

MANAGING MISSTEPS

No matter how carefully home visitors approach their work, mistakes will happen. These can include something as simple as a misunderstanding or communication problem about a scheduled appointment or something more serious that threatens the relationship. Parents could become frustrated with a home visitor who set a limit due to an agency rule, disappointed and disengaged when the service does not meet their expectations, or angry when a home visitor brings up a safety concern. For their part, home visitors may have similar feelings of disappointment when a family does not attain set goals, frustration when a family misses appointments, and anger when a family does something the home visitor perceives as potentially dangerous for the child. When working in collaboration with other professionals, similar breaches are possible. For example, workers can experience frustration when a task is incomplete due to lack of clarity about role responsibility. At other times, workers from different backgrounds may view a family differently, causing disagreement about what approach is likely to be most effective.

When partners have strong feelings or do not take care in communicating, relationships can suffer. It is important to note that occasional "ruptures," such as disagreements, miscommunications, or one partner having hurt feelings, are a completely normal part of any close relationship. Acknowledging and addressing a rupture is needed in order to move toward repair of the breakdown in the relationship (Friedlander, 2014). For many families in the care of home visitors, the notion that such a repair is possible is foreign. Naming and taking steps to mend a misstep or misunderstanding can provide an example of being responsive and correcting an error that the parent can use with their child or within other relationships. To round out the parallel process, this type of rupture and repair can occur in other relationships, including with colleagues and supervisors (Heffron & Murch, 2010).

Addressing breaks in a relationship requires more than technical skills. It also necessitates an openness and willingness to discuss what happened and one's own role in it (Friedlander, 2014). It is possible to notice a change in another person without recognizing what started it. Being willing to address that change and consider one's own possible role are good steps toward repair. Friedlander (2014), a psychologist who often writes about therapeutic and supervision processes, offers an approach to managing relationship ruptures that can be helpful for home visitors: Once you have noticed and pointed out that something seems to be happening, make a statement about what you think could be occurring. Next, ask if the other person is willing to discuss the situation. Last, take responsibility for your part in the situation. The next part of the vignette gives an example of how this might look in an early childhood context.

In supervision later that week, Anna vents her frustration about Tessa's lack of engagement during the visit. She shares that she had only focused on the baby and his needs. Instead of just reminding Anna that her role was to help both parent and child, Anna's supervisor listens carefully and sympathizes with how frustrated she must have felt. "It is difficult to feel that you are working so hard and no one is listening," the supervisor says. After a bit, the supervisor asks Anna to describe more about what was happening during the visit. She adds that she does not have a good feel for what Tessa was doing or how she was reacting while Anna helped Anthony. Anna recalls again that Tessa was quiet and describes Tessa following her to the door at the end of the visit. "This seems a little different from what you usually describe about Tessa. What was that like for you when you noticed her difference?" the supervisor asks.

"Well, actually, I did not notice that at the time. I thought about it later when I got home," Anna admits. "Right now, I kind of think she wanted to say something." After talking with her supervisor, Anna recognizes she missed some cues Tessa was giving during the last visit. When she arrives for the next visit, Tessa is still cool and distant. Anna tries out the plan she developed with her supervisor.

Observe/notice:

Anna: "I feel like you seem a little upset today."

Tessa: "I am okay."

State what you think or feel might have happened (if you think you know):

Anna: "I am concerned that I was not very responsive to you the last time we met."

Tessa: "You were kind of rude."

Ask if the person is willing to discuss what happened or is happening:

Anna: "Would it be okay if we talked about what is happening between us?"

Tessa: "I guess."

Self-correct when needed:

> Anna: "In thinking back to last week, I feel like I missed that you wanted to tell me something. I am sorry about that. Is there something that you would like to say?"

> Tessa: "I was feeling down and then you just went straight to Anthony. I know I should not have him in the seat. I could tell you were mad and that made me more down."

> Anna: "You are right that I was frustrated about the car seat. But I should have asked about it so I could understand what was going on with you. Are you still feeling down today? If it's okay, I'd like to hear what is going on with you."

SECONDARY TRAUMA AND BURNOUT

Many types of professionals who function in challenging environments can develop a prolonged response to chronic stressors inherent in their work. This response is called *burnout*. Burnout is typically defined as having three components: emotional exhaustion, cynicism or depersonalization, and inefficacy (Maslach, Schaufeli, & Leiter, 2001). Worker burnout is very common in high-stress human service fields such as nursing and child welfare. Burnout characteristics such as feelings of being emotionally overwhelmed and ineffective may contribute to worker turnover. When experiencing burnout, workers report a number of physical and psychological symptoms, including headaches, stomach pain, panic symptoms (e.g., heart racing, dry mouth), problems sleeping, and changes in appetite (Denmark & Jones Harden, 2012). Trauma responses are also possible for professionals. This could happen when the professional directly experiences a traumatic event, such as a personal or on-the-job experience of being threatened, or when the provider sees someone else being hurt or threatened. In addition, workers who spend time with traumatized individuals and hear the stories and see the results of traumatic events may eventually develop trauma symptoms (Denmark & Jones Harden, 2012).

Although there is a good deal of work on secondary trauma and burnout in other fields, there is limited exploration of these phenomena among home visitors or other early intervention professionals (Lee et al., 2013). This is unfortunate, as the intensity and the quality of this work, especially with higher risk populations, means that home visitors who serve young families may be vulnerable to these experiences. In one study, home visiting nurses discussed the impact of their work (Zeanah et al., 2006). Despite acknowledging feelings of satisfaction that come with seeing things work out for families and knowing that they helped, the home visiting nurses reported many negative emotions, such as disappointment, sadness when a family could not reach its own potential, struggling with one's own feelings when a family's goals and worker's goals are not aligned, and the overall problem of laying down the work at the end of the day. In another study, Early Head Start reported concerns including the burden of large caseloads and limited ability to make decisions and take actions (Jones Harden et al., 2010).

There are several ways to address the stress of this work in order to reduce the potential for and address symptoms of burnout and secondary trauma when needed. Basic self-care should be a priority for all who work with families with very young children and especially those whose caseloads are high or include multirisk families. Most people are able to name the main areas of self-care, including taking care of oneself physically and emotionally. These main areas typically include getting enough sleep, eating a reasonably healthy diet, and making room for some relaxation, exercise, and fun. Others frame this as creating a healthy work–life balance so that both work and personal activities are pleasurable and enjoyable. Home visitors can be supported by program-focused methods that help as well. These include the program having safety protocols in place, offering stress management classes, providing emotional supports such as retreats and mental health days, acknowledging accomplishments, and providing formal mental health supports as needed (Denmark & Jones Harden, 2012). It is helpful to spend some time reflecting on your own work–personal-life balance. Figure 10.1 is one way you can examine your current work and life activities and consider whether you are in balance.

In one study, home visitors specified a desire for more supervision that included emotional support provided by someone able to understand the work (Jones Harden et al., 2010). Workers who serve families with multiple issues may benefit from reflective supervision over time to manage their own feelings. When emotions are high and distressing, single or inconsistent sessions are often not enough to manage the worker's response. Supervision needs to be ongoing and include both social and organizational supports to be most effective. Without these types of supports, home visitors can feel "isolated and overwhelmed" (Yoches et al., 2012, p. 95) and, as a result, the work does not move forward. In the next section, we discuss reflective supervision as a way to gain support for these kinds of situations as well as a useful method of professional development.

REFLECTIVE SUPERVISION

There is general consensus that reflective supervision involves three characteristics: collaboration, regularity, and reflection (Fenichel, 1992; Tomlin et al., 2014). A supervisory relationship that is collaborative is egalitarian. The supervisor, although typically more experienced, does not provide a prescriptive or directive approach. Instead, the supervision is characterized by the pair working together with an emphasis on the supervisee's exploration and discovery with support. Regularity in supervision has several meanings. From a practical

REFLECTION ON WORK–LIFE BALANCE

Exercise: Review your calendar for at least 2–4 weeks, placing each event into one of the three columns. Total the number in each column and compare; consider the balance between what you do for others and what you do that supports your own well-being. Discuss your results with a trusted colleague or in reflective supervision.

Things I do for work	Things I do for others outside work	Things I do for me
Ex: Meetings with colleagues	Ex: Drive children to sports event	Ex: Doctor appointment
Ex: Sessions with clients	Ex: Volunteer at church	Ex: Go to a movie with spouse or friend
Ex: Paperwork	Ex: Serve on local board for not-for-profit organization	Ex: Plan a family vacation
Ex: Research resources and useful information for families	Ex: Lawn care for aging parents	Ex: Massage, exercise, pedicure/manicure

(continued)

Figure 10.1.   Reflection worksheet on work–life balance.

Figure 10.1. (continued)

Things I do for work	Things I do for others outside work	Things I do for me
TOTAL: _____	TOTAL: _____	TOTAL: _____

standpoint, the supervision should be regularly scheduled. The time should be set aside and interruptions or cancellations avoided. The supervisee should come to experience the supervisor as consistent and reliable. Finally, the supervision must include a reflective component that allows the supervisee to have time and support to consider his or her own responses to the work, to link those responses back to previous experiences, to consider how those responses may guide future action, to wonder about what is happening for the parents and the baby, and to consider a variety of possible links between all of these factors (Heffron & Murch, 2010; Shahmoon-Shanok, 2010; Weatherston & Barron, 2010).

This consideration of links and influences between various facets of the work, especially among relationships, is related to the concept of parallel process. *Parallel process* describes how relationships are interconnected (Heffron & Murch, 2010). It has been described for more than 100 years in the psychotherapy literature, and an understanding of it is now a conventional component of reflective practice and supervision or consultation. Recent empirical work with psychotherapists has demonstrated the theory that interaction patterns that occur in supervision are taken back to work with clients (Tracey, Bludworth, & Glidden-Tracey, 2012). In infant and toddler fields, including home visiting, there is a small but growing effort to explore how reflective supervision supports the workers and improves the work (Watson & Gatti, 2012; Watson et al., 2014; Weatherston, Weigand, & Weigand, 2010).

Most home visitors would agree that we are changed by our experiences, both personal and professional. When we are able to use reflection, we make connections between experiences and learn what works and what doesn't, changing what we do based on experience (Heatherington, Friedlander, & Diamond, 2014). A good reflective coach, supervisor, consultant, or facilitator is typically a more experienced practitioner who will help the supervisee improve his or her ability to step back and reflect. This involves gaining skills in the ability to think broadly and deeply in order to combine internal knowledge (including one's own experience of thoughts, feelings, and reactions) with external knowledge (e.g., scientific knowledge, best practice guidelines) in a way that improves or advances practice (Brandt, 2014). Being able to integrate information at this level takes time and experience and is often achieved through a supervisory relationship that takes a reflective approach. In reflective supervision, the supervisor will assist the supervisee to move between considering different relationships using many methods. A coach or supervisor may accomplish this feat through a variety of means, ranging from more direct activities (e.g., direct instruction, modeling, asking questions, providing feedback, facilitating problem solving) and less obvious (e.g., remaining silent in order to provide space for the supervisee's own thoughts to emerge; Brandt, 2014; Heffron & Murch, 2010; Knoche, Kuhn, & Eum, 2013; Shahmoon-Shanok, 2010; Weatherston & Barron, 2010).

BENEFITS OF REFLECTIVE SUPERVISION

As mentioned, the empirical research basis for reflective coaching, supervision, and facilitation, although an active area of growth, remains small (Watson et al., 2014). However, there is some evidence not only of how it works, but also of how it may improve recipient skills and benefit organizations. Reflective supervision and coaching have been associated with more effective implementation of programming (McAllister & Thomas, 2007), transformed practice for providers, and more positive outcomes for young children (Knoche et al., 2013). In home visiting and early education and care, the importance of reflective supervision generally, and especially with more vulnerable families, has been highlighted (Jones Harden, 2010; Watson & Gatti, 2012).

Everyone has an individual point of view that comes from a blend of many things: personal characteristics and experiences, training, personality, values, and beliefs (Weldum et al., 2009). Although it is not possible or even desirable for home visitors to keep their own responses and views out of the work, sometimes those views or responses can get in the way. Reflective supervision or consultation provides a way to address thoughts and feelings of the home visitor in order to better address family and young child needs (Watson & Gatti, 2012). Examples of some of the benefits of reflective supervision have been summarized as "clarifying the family situation, increasing self-awareness regarding one's work with families, debriefing and regrouping after a crisis, and gaining new perspectives for use in refining interventions" (McAllister & Thomas, 2007, p. 205).

Reflective supervision is likely to be particularly important for areas in which home visitors or other early childhood professionals may not be formally prepared, such as parental mental illness (Jones Harden et al., 2010). Even when a home visitor suspects the problem, without opportunities for reflective consultation, he or she may not know what to do or may fail to appreciate the need to take actions such as making community referrals (Jones Harden et al., 2010; Tandon et al., 2008). Similarly, younger and less experienced home visitors, who are more likely to report burnout symptoms (Lee et al., 2013), are seen as likely to significantly benefit from supervision. The quality of the supervision is also important. When workers are satisfied with supervision and feel more empowered in work, less burnout is reported (Lee et al., 2013).

Beyond benefits to individual workers, supervision is also useful for employers and agencies. Supervision has been associated with enhanced worker-reported job satisfaction and lower burnout (Mena & Bailey, 2007), and with better worker retention (McGuigan, Katzev, & Pratt, 2003). Less frequent turnover of workers benefits families, due to the consistency of the service provided. Agencies also benefit through the cost savings with avoiding expenses associated with recruitment and retraining.

Reflective supervision, consultation, and coaching methods, although valuable and increasingly recognized as effective, are not universally implemented for a variety of reasons. Barriers include practical concerns, such as making time for the sessions, and worries or fears about self-examination and the potential for being judged (Heffron & Murch, 2010; Norman-Murch & Ward, 1999). Home visitors should take time to make sure they understand what reflective supervision involves and clearly understand how it is different from personal therapy. Implemented skillfully, reflective supervisory relationships will increase ability to slow down, back up, take a careful look at the whole picture, explore emotions as part of the work, and learn new skills (Neilsen Gatti, Watson, & Siegel, 2011; Shahmoon-Shanok, 2010; Weatherston & Barron, 2010).

USING THE PAUSE FRAMEWORK

Using the vignettes in this chapter, think about how Anna processes her experiences with Anthony and his mother, Tessa. See Figures 10.2 and 10.3 for examples of how this might look.

WHAT'S NEXT?

After working through these chapters, the "what's next" question is now directed to you. What will you do with this information and how will you incorporate the PAUSE framework into your work with families and children?

TIPS FOR PRACTICE

▶ Mistakes happen in any relationship. Home visitors can learn to repair breaks in relationships that occur with families they serve.

▶ In order to effectively serve families and prevent burnout, home visitors must attend to their own emotional responses and practice self-care.

▶ Reflective supervision is a way for home visitors to receive support to grow professionally and better serve challenging families.

KEY POINTS TO REMEMBER

▶ Due to the intense nature of home visiting with vulnerable families, home visitors are at risk for experiencing strong emotional responses such as burnout or secondary trauma.

PAUSE WORKSHEET

pause

Child: Anthony

Date: October 30, 2015

Parent: Tessa

Provider: Anna

PERCEIVE—Explore what is happening.

Parent/caregiver perspective:	Provider perspective:
Tessa has a lot on her plate. She seems to love Anthony and want the best for him. She has periods where she seems very engaged and other times when she is preoccupied.	I am worried about Anthony getting everything he needs. Tessa seems to miss some of the important cues he gives her about his needs. I feel frustrated when she misses appointments or doesn't call to cancel, and also when she calls multiple times in a row asking for something.

ASK—Clarify what is happening.

Starting with the parent/caregiver's priorities and concerns, ask more detailed/specific questions to clarify what is happening.

I could ask more about how things are going for Tessa now, such as "How are you handling all of the things you have to do with Anthony?"

I might start a conversation about how much he is growing and changing. I could reflect that I remember when my own children outgrew their clothes so quickly.

UNDERSTAND—Explore why it is happening.

With the parent/caregiver, explore explanations for what is happening. Consider possible explanations that include the environment, the child, and the parent. Listen and observe closely as you explore the situation in conversation with the family.

Parent/caregiver perspective:	Provider perspective:	Child's perspective:
Tessa may have worries about finances or other family issues. She may not have enough information about Anthony's development.	Tessa may be struggling with family or other issues I am not aware of.	Anthony may be confused by his mother's varied and inconsistent responses to his needs.

(continued)

Figure 10.2. Anna's PAUSE Worksheet for Tessa and Anthony.

Figure 10.2. *(continued)*

PAUSE WORKSHEET *(continued)*

UNDERSTAND *(continued)*

Parent/caregiver perspective:	Provider perspective:	Child's perspective:
She may not know how to support him to reach his next developmental milestones.		

STRATEGIZE and **EVALUATE**—Identify possible responses/solutions.

1. Solution/action to try:	
Explore how Tessa sees Anthony and his current development to find out more about what she would like to see happen so we can update his plan.	*How will we know if it works?* Tessa's perspective about Anthony is shared. New needs are identified. *When will we evaluate if it works?* By the next regular plan review date

2. Solution/action to try:	
Discuss adding a social worker to our team to gather more information and identify resources.	*How will we know if it works?* Social work is added. *When will we evaluate if it works?* When we review the assessment report from the social worker together

PROVIDER REFLECTION WORKSHEET

Child: Anthony   Date: October 30, 2015

Parent: Tessa

Provider: Anna

1.	How did I follow the parent's lead to learn what is most pressing or important to the family?	I missed her lead this time. I realize I am struggling to understand what is most important for Tessa. She seems inconsistent and sometimes not attentive enough to Anthony's needs.
2.	How did I ask clarifying questions to help me understand the problem better?	I did not ask questions. Instead, I jumped to solve the immediate issues and didn't even realize Tessa was watching me. I wonder what she was thinking. I don't think I even confirmed our next appointment.
3.	How did I provide information that may help the family better understand the child's behavior?	I did not share any information other than simply doing what needed to be done. I have no idea whether Tessa will learn from my simply bathing and changing Anthony when he needed that.

(continued)

Figure 10.3. Anna's Provider Reflection Worksheet for Tessa and Anthony.

Figure 10.3. *(continued)*

PROVIDER REFLECTION WORKSHEET *(continued)*

4. *How did I engage the family to develop a response that may include a strategy to try, a resource to use, or more information to increase understanding?*	I did not engage with Tessa. I think we might need to invite another service to the team. Maybe a social worker could help us better understand what is happening with this family and whether other resources are necessary.
5. *How did I provide support and emotional containment if needed?*	I did not do very well with containing emotions, as I realize I was too upset myself when Tessa did not take proper care of Anthony. How can I be more present in the moment and then more helpful to Tessa?
6. *How do I plan to follow up on promised actions to maintain trust?*	I made a plan to provide clothing, but I did not discuss it with Tessa. I will discuss the clothing plan with my supervisor to make sure that is allowed. I need to contact the family to confirm the next appointment. I wonder how I can check in with Tessa on how she is feeling about our working relationship.
7. *What do I want to discuss in reflective supervision to improve my practice and outcomes with this child and family?*	I want to better understand Tessa's ups and downs and why this is so challenging for me. I know I am motivated to stay involved because I like Anthony, although I secretly wish the family would fire me or just exit the program. Why am I so frustrated?

▶ Self-care is necessary to be most effective in this work.

▶ Attention to boundaries is difficult due to the intensity and intimacy of the work of home visitors. Boundary issues may be present with families, co-workers, and supervisors as well as across agencies. Clear communication of roles and responsibilities can avoid boundary violations.

▶ Mistakes and missteps are normal in all relationships, and the relationships between home visitors and families are no exceptions. These types of missteps can be addressed and repaired.

▶ Home visitors are working in a complex environment and may experience strong emotions and other responses related to the work. Reflective supervision can help home visitors manage their feelings, allow for integration of emotion and thinking, and build skills that improve practice.

SUGGESTED FURTHER READINGS

Heffron, M.C., & Murch, T. (2010). *Reflective supervision and leadership in infant and early childhood programs.* Washington, DC: ZERO TO THREE.

Heller, S.S., & Gilkerson, L. (Eds.). (2010). *A practical guide to reflective supervision.* Washington, DC: ZERO TO THREE.

Summers, S.J., & Chazan-Cohen, R. (2012). *Understanding early childhood mental health: A practical guide for professionals.* Baltimore, MD: Paul H. Brookes Publishing Co.

Last Reflection

As a home visitor, you know that this work is extremely important in helping families provide the best they can for their children despite living with difficult and complex circumstances. We hope that you have found the PAUSE framework—as well as the other ideas, resources, and concepts provided— helpful as you seek to improve your practice and partnerships with parents and caregivers.

Throughout this book, we encouraged you to slow down, think more deeply, consider multiple perspectives, and use reflective supervision or consultation. We hope that reading this book has caused you to think and wonder about your own practice as a home visitor. Maybe you have found validation for some of your current practices, new ideas for improving practice, and even permission to ask for help when something is outside of your scope of responsibilities. Please accept one final opportunity to pause and think about what you will take from your reading and what steps you might take next in your journey as a practitioner. Here are some questions to help you organize your thoughts:

What else do you want to know about?

Which suggested books and resources will you read and refer to?

What strategies will you incorporate into your home visiting practice?

What might you do differently now?

Which ideas will you share with your colleagues and supervisor?

How did you see yourself in the examples provided? What does this tell you?

Which practices were affirmed for you or help you know you are on the right track?

Finally, we encourage you to find ways to continue to expand your skills and knowledge by participating in reflective supervision or consultation. Through the support of such a learning relationship, you will achieve better understanding of your own and other people's perceptions of situations and events, and you will increase your ability to support parents and caregivers to address the needs of their children. Thank you for your work as a home visitor!

References

Ainsworth, M.D.S. (1979). Infant–mother attachment. *American Psychologist, 34*(10), 932–937.

Aktar, E., Majdandzic, M., de Vente, W., & Bogels, S.M. (2014). Parental social anxiety disorder prospectively predicts toddlers' fear/avoidance in a social referencing paradigm. *Journal of Child Psychology and Psychiatry, 55*(1), 77–87.

Alink, L.R., Mesman, J., van Zeijl, J., Stolk, M.N., Juffer, F., Koot, H.M.,...van Ijzendoorn, M.H. (2006). The early childhood aggression curve: Development of physical aggression in 20- to 50-month-old children. *Child Development, 77*(4), 954–966.

Alvarez, S.L., Meltzer-Brody, S., Mandel, M., & Beeber, L. (2015). Maternal depression and early intervention: A call for an integration of services. *Infants and Young Children, 28*(1), 72–87.

American Academy of Pediatrics Task Force on Sudden Infant Death Syndrome. (2011). SIDS and other sleep-related infant deaths. Expansion of recommendations for a safe infant sleep environment. *Pediatrics, 128*(5), 1030–1039.

American Academy of Sleep Medicine. (Ed.). (2006). *International classification of sleep disorders, revised: Diagnostic and coding manual* (2nd ed.). Darien, IL: Author.

American Psychiatric Association. (2013). *Diagnostic and statistical manual of mental disorders* (5th ed.) Washington, DC: Author.

Appleyard, K., & Osofsky, J. (2003). Parenting after trauma: Supporting parents and caregivers in the treatment of children impacted by violence. *Infant Mental Health Journal, 24*(2), 111–125.

Baldwin, H.A., Songer, N.S., & Ensher, G.L. (2009). The cycle of substance abuse. In G.L. Ensher, D.A. Clark, & N.S. Songer (Eds.), *Families, infants, and young children at risk: Pathways to best practice* (pp. 249–272). Baltimore, MD: Paul H. Brookes Publishing Co.

Bandura, A. (1977). *Social learning theory.* New York, NY: General Learning Press.

Barak, A., Spielberger, J., & Gitlow, E. (2014). The challenge of relationships and fidelity: Home visitors' perspectives. *Children and Youth Services Review, 42,* 50–58,

Barker, D. (1998). In utero programming of chronic disease. *Clinical Science, 95,* 115–128.

Barker, L.H., & Berry, K. (2009). Developmental issues impacting military families with young children during single and multiple deployments. *Military Medicine, 174,* 1033–1040.

Bassani, D.G., Padoin, C.V., Philipp, D., & Veldhuizen, S. (2009). Estimating the number of children exposed to parental psychiatric disorders through a national health survey, *Child and Adolescent Psychiatry and Mental Health, 3*(6), doi:10.1186/1753-2000-3-6.

Bassuk, E., DeCandia, C., Beach, C., & Berman, F. (2014). *America's youngest outcasts: A report card on child homelessness.* Waltham, MA: The National Center on Family Homelessness at American Institutes for Research. Retrieved from http://www.homelesschildrenamerica.org/mediadocs/280.pdf

Beeber, L.S., & Canuso, R. (2012). Intervening with parents. In S.J. Summers & R. Chazan-Cohen (Eds.), *Understanding early childhood mental health: A practical guide for professionals* (pp. 159–177). Baltimore, MD: Paul H. Brookes Publishing Co.

Belden, A., Thompson, N.R., & Luby, J.L. (2008). Temper tantrums in healthy versus depressed and disruptive preschoolers: Defining tantrum behaviors associated with clinical problems. *Journal of Pediatrics, 152*(1), 117–122.

Bernstein, V.J., & Edwards, R.C. (2012). Supporting early childhood practitioners through relationship-based, reflective supervision. *National Head Start Association Dialog, 15*(3), 286–301.

Bonuck, K.A., Hyden, C., Ury, G., Barnett, J., Ashkinaze, H., & Briggs, R.D. (2011). Screening for sleep problems in early intervention and early childhood special education: A systematic review of screening and assessment instruments. *Infants and Young Children 24*(4), 295–308.

Bordin, E.S. (1979). The generalizability of the psychoanalytic concept of the Working Alliance. *Psychotherapy: Research, Theory, and Practice, 16*(3), 252–260.

Boursnell, M. (2014). Assessing the capacity of parents with mental illness: Parents with mental illness and risk. *International Social Work, 57*(2), 92–108.

Brandt, K. (2014). Transforming clinical practice through reflection work. In K. Brandt, B.D. Perry, S. Seligman, & E. Tronick (Eds.), *Infant and early childhood mental health: Core concepts and clinical practice* (pp. 293–307). Washington, DC: American Psychiatric Publishing.

Bridgett, D.J., Oddi, K.B., Laake, L.M., Murdock, K.W., & Bachman, M.N. (2013). Integrating and differentiating aspects of self-regulation: Effortful control, executive functioning, and links to negative affectivity. *Emotion, 13*(1), 47–63.

Briggs-Gowan, M.J., Carter, A.S., & Ford, J.D. (2012). Parsing the effects violence exposure in early childhood: Modeling developmental pathways. *Journal of Pediatric Psychology, 37,* 11–22.

Brooker, R.J., Buss, K.A., Lemery-Chalfant, K., Aksan, N., Davidson, R.J., & Goldsmith, H.H. (2013). The development of stranger fear in infancy and toddlerhood: Normative development, individual differences, antecedents, and outcomes. *Developmental Science, 16*(6), 864–878.

Brown, L.F., Pridham, K.A., & Brown, R. (2014). Sequential observation of infant regulated and dysregulated behavior following soothing and stimulating maternal behavior during feeding. *Pediatric Nursing, 19,* 139–148.

Brownell, C.A., Svetlova, M., Anderson, R., Nichols, S.R., & Drummond, J. (2013). Socialization of early prosocial behavior: Parents' talk about emotions is associated with sharing and helping in toddlers. *Infancy, 18*(1), 91–119.

Bruer, J.T., & Greenough, W.T. (2001). The subtle science of how experience affects the brain. In D.B. Bailey, J.T. Bruer, F.J. Symons, & J.W. Lichtman (Eds.), *Critical thinking about critical periods* (pp. 209–232). Baltimore, MD: Paul H. Brookes Publishing Co.

Bruns, D.A., & Thompson, S.D. (2010). Feeding challenges in young children. *Infants and Young Children, 23*(2), 93–102.

Bull, M.J. (2014). Car safety seats and the First Steps provider. *UTS Training Times, 10*(2), 8–9. Retrieved from http://www.in.gov/fssa/files/TT_2014_2_May.pdf

Buss, K. (2011). Which fearful toddlers should we worry about? Context, fear, regulation, and anxiety risk. *Developmental Psychopathology, 47*(3), 804–819.

Chess, S., & Thomas, A. (1996). *Temperament: Theory and practice.* New York, NY: Brunner/Mazel, Inc.

Child Trends Data Bank. (2014). *Foster care: Indicators on children and youth.* Retrieved from http://www.childtrends.org/wp-content/uploads/2014/07/12_Foster _Care.pdf

Clarkson Freeman, P.A. (2014). Prevalence and relationship between adverse childhood experiences and child behavior among young children. *Infant Mental Health Journal, 35*(6), 544–554.

Cluxton-Keller, F., Burrell, L., Crowne, S.S., McFarlane, E., Tandon, S.D., Leaf, P.J., & Duggan, A.K. (2014). Maternal relationship insecurity and depressive symptoms as moderators of home visiting impacts on child outcomes. *Journal of Child and Family Studies, 23,* 1430–1443.

Cohen, J., & Scheeringa, M. (2009). Post-traumatic stress disorder diagnosis in children: Challenges and promises. *Dialogues in Clinical Neuroscience, 11*(1), 91–99.

Colonnesi, C., Napoleone, E., & Bogels, S.M. (2014). Positive and negative expressions of shyness in toddlers: Are they related to anxiety in the same way? *Journal of Personality and Social Psychology, 106*(4), 624–637.

Cozza, S.J., Guimond, J.M., McKibben, J.B.A., Chun, R.S., Arata-Maiers, T.L., Schneider, B.,... Ursano, R. J. (2010). Combat-injured service members and their families: The relationship of child distress and spouse-perceived family distress and disruption. *Journal of Traumatic Stress, 23,* 112–115.

Daro, D.A., & Harding, K.A. (1999). Healthy Families America: Using research to enhance practice. *The Future of Children, 9,* 152–176.

Davis, E.P., & Thompson, R. (2014). Prenatal foundations: Fetal programming of health and development. *Zero to Three, 34*(4), 2–22.

DeKlyen, M., Biernbaum, M., Speltz, L., & Greenberg, M. (1998). Fathers and preschool behavior problems, *Developmental Psychology, 34,* 264–275.

Denham, S.A., & Couchoud, E.A. (1990). Young preschoolers' understanding of emotions. *Child Study Journal, 20,* 171–192.

Denmark, N., & Jones Harden, B. (2012). Meeting the mental health needs of staff. In S.J. Summers & R. Chazan-Cohen (Eds.), *Understanding early childhood mental health: A practical guide for professionals* (pp. 217–226). Baltimore, MD: Paul H. Brookes Publishing Co.

Denno, D.M., Carr, V., & Bell, S.H. (2010). *Addressing challenging behavior in early childhood settings: A teacher's guide.* Baltimore, MD: Paul H. Brookes Publishing Co.

DiStefano, G., Gino, F., Pisano, G.P., & Staats, B.R. (2014). *Learning by thinking: Overcoming the bias for action through reflection.* Harvard Business School NOM Unit Working Paper No. 14-093; Harvard Business School Technology and Operations Management Unit Working Paper No. 14-093. Retrieved from http://dx.doi.org/10.2139/ssrn.2414478

Dougherty, L.R., Smith, V.C., Bufferd, S.J., Stringaris, A., Leibenluft, E., Carlson, G.A., & Klein, D.N. (2013). Preschool irritability: Longitudinal associations with psychiatric disorders at age 6 and parental psychopathology. *Journal of the American Academy of Child and Adolescent Psychiatry, 52*(12), 1304–1313.

Dunlap, G., Ostryn, C., & Fox, L. (2011). *Preventing the use of restraint and seclusion with young children: The role of effective, positive practices.* Retrieved from http://challengingbehavior.fmhi.usf.edu/do/resources/documents/brief_prevent ing.pdf

Durrant, J., & Ensom, R. (2012). Physical punishment of children: Lessons from 20 years of research. *Canadian Medical Association Journal, 1849*(12), 1373–1377.

Edelman, L. (2004). *A relationship-based approach to early intervention.* Retrieved from http://cacenter-ecmh.org/wp/wp-content/uploads/2012/03/relationship_based _approach.pdf

Egger, H., & Angold, A. (2006). Common emotional and behavioral disorders in pre-school children: Presentation, nosology, and epidemiology. *Journal of Child Psychology and Psychiatry, 47,* 313–337.

Evanoo, G. (2007). Infant crying: A clinical conundrum. *Journal of Pediatric Health Care, 21,* 333–338.

Felitti, V.J., Anda, R.F., Nordenberg, D., Williamson, D.F., Spitz, A.M., Edwards, V.,… Marks, J.S. (1998). Relationship of childhood abuse and household dysfunction to many of the leading causes of death in adults. The Adverse Childhood Experiences (ACE) Study. *American Journal of Preventive Medicine, 14*(4), 245–258.

Fenichel, E. (Ed.). (1992). *Learning through supervision and mentorship to support the development of infants, toddlers, and their families: A source book.* Washington, DC: ZERO TO THREE.

Fleming, P.J., & Blair, P.S. (2015). Making informed choices on co-sleeping with your baby. *BMJ, 350*:h563. doi: http://dx.doi.org/10.1136/bmj.h563

Fonagy, P., Gergely, G., Jurist, E., & Target, M. (2002). *Affect regulation, mentalization, and the development of the self.* New York, NY: Other Books.

Fonagy, P., Steele, H., Steele, M., Leigh, T., Kennedy, R., Mattoon, G., & Target, M. (1995). Attachment, the reflective self, and borderline states: The predictive specificity of the Adult Attachment Interview and pathological emotional development. In S. Goldberg, R. Muir, & J. Kerr (Eds.), *Attachment theory: Social, developmental, and clinical perspectives* (pp. 233–278). New York, NY: Analytic Press.

Fonagy, P., & Target, M. (1998). Mentalization and the changing aims of child psychoanalysis. *Psychoanalytic Dialogues, 8,* 8–114.

Forman, D. (2007). Autonomy, compliance, and internalization. In C.A. Brownell & C.B. Kopp (Eds.), *Socioemotional development in the toddler years: Transitions and transformations* (pp. 285–319). New York, NY: Guilford.

Friedlander, M.L. (2014). Use of relational strategies to repair alliance ruptures: How responsive supervisors train responsive psychotherapists. *Psychotherapy, 52*(2), 174–179. Retrieved from http://dx.doi.org/10.1037/a0037044

Garon, N., Bryson, S.E., & Smith, I.M. (2008). Executive function in preschoolers: A review using an integrative framework. *Psychological Bulletin 134*(1), 31–60.

Geppert, U. (1986). *A coding system for analyzing behavioral expression of self-evaluative emotions.* Munich, Germany: Max Planck Institute for Psychological Research.

Gilkerson, L., & Gray, L. (2014). Fussy babies: Early challenges in regulation, impact on the dyad and family, and longer-term implications. In K. Brandt, B.D. Perry, S. Seligman, & E. Tronick (Eds.), *Infant and early childhood mental health: Core concepts and clinical practice* (pp. 195–208). Washington, DC: American Psychiatric Publishing.

Gilkerson, L., Hofherr, J., Steir, A., Cook, A., Arbel, A., Heffron, M.C.,…Paul, J.J. (2012). Implementing the Fussy Baby Network approach. *Zero to Three, 32*(2), 59–65.

Glaze, L.E., & Maruschak, L.M. (2008). *Parents in prison and their minor children.* Bureau of Justice Statistics Special Report. Retrieved from http://www.bjs.gov/content/pub/pdf/pptmc.pdf

Gomby, D.S., Larson, C.S., Lewit, E.M., & Behrman, R.E. (1993). Home visiting: Analysis and recommendations. *The Future of Children, 3*(3), 6–22.

Goodlin-Jones, B.L., Sitnick, S.L., Tang, K., Liu, J., & Anders, T.F. (2008). The Children's Sleep Habits Questionnaire in toddlers and preschool children. *Journal of Developmental and Behavioral Pediatrics, 29*(2), 82–88.

Gopnick, A. (2010). How babies think. *Scientific American, 303,* 76–81.

Gopnick, A., Slaughter, V., & Meltzoff, A. (1994). Changing your views: How understanding visual perception can lead to a new theory of the mind. In C. Lewis & P. Mitchell (Eds.), *Children's early understanding of the mind: Early developments* (pp. 157–181). Hillsdale, NJ: Lawrence Erlbaum.

Gottman, J.M. (1991). Chaos and regulated change in families: A metaphor for the study of transitions. In P.A. Cowan & M. Hetherington (Eds.), *Family transitions* (pp. 247–272). Hillsdale, NJ: Lawrence Erlbaum.

Grady, J.S., & Karraker, K. (2014). Do maternal warm and encouraging statements reduce shy toddler's social reticence? *Infant and Child Development, 23,* 295–303.

Grady, J.S., Stoltzfus, J., Karraker, K., & Metzger, A. (2012). Shyness trajectories in slow-to-warm infants: Relationship with child sex and maternal parenting. *Journal of Applied Developmental Psychology, 33*(2), 91–101.

Green, M., & Palfrey, J. (2000). *Bright futures: Guidelines for health supervision of infants, children, and adolescents.* Washington, DC: Georgetown University.

Guardino, C.M., & Schetter, C.D. (2014). Coping during pregnancy: A systematic review and recommendations. *Health Psychology Review, 8*(1), 70–94.

Guralnick, M.J. (2001). Connections between developmental science and intervention science. *Zero to Three, 21*(5), 24–29.

Hackshaw, A., Rodeck, C., & Boniface, S. (2011). Maternal smoking in pregnancy and birth defects: A systematic review based on 173,687 malformed cases and 11.7 million controls. *Human Reproduction Update, 17,* 589–604.

Harris, Y.R., Harris, V., Graham, J.A., & Carpenter, G.J.O. (2010). The challenges of family reunification. In Y.R. Harris, J.A. Graham, & G.J. Oliver Carpenter (Eds.), *Children of incarcerated parents: Theoretical, developmental and clinical issues* (pp. 255–275). New York, NY: Springer.

Hay, D.F., & Cook, K.V. (2007). The transformation of prosocial behavior from infancy to childhood. In C.A. Brownell & C.B. Kopp (Eds.), *Socioemotional development in the toddler years: Transitions and transformations* (pp. 100–132). New York, NY: Guilford.

Hayashi, K., Matsuda, Y., Kawamichi, Y., Shiozaki, A., & Saito, S. (2011). Smoking during pregnancy increases risks of various obstetric complications: A case cohort study of the Japan Perinatal Registry Network database. *Journal of Epidemiology, 21,* 61–66.

Heatherington, L., Friedlander, M.L., & Diamond, G. (2014). Lessons offered, lessons learned: Reflections on how doing family therapy can affect therapists. *Journal of Clinical Psychology, 70*(8), 760–767.

Heffron, M.C., Ivins, B., & Weston, D.R. (2005). Finding an authentic voice—Use of self: Essential learning processes for relationship-based work. *Infants and Young Children, 18*(4), 323–336.

Heffron, M.C., & Murch, T. (2010). *Reflective supervision and leadership in infant and early childhood programs.* Washington, DC: ZERO TO THREE.

Henderson, J.M., France, K.G., Owens, J.L., & Blampied, N.M. (2010). Sleeping through the night: Consolidation of self-regulated sleep across the first year of life. *Pediatrics, 126*(5), e1081–1087, doi:10.1542/peds.2010-6875d.

Hirshkowitz, M., Whiton, K., Albert, S.M., Alessi, C., Bruni, O., DonCarlos, L… Adams Hillard, P.J. (2015). National Sleep Foundation's sleep time duration recommendations: Methodology and results summary. *Sleep Health, 1*(1), 40–43.

Hobson, P.R., Patrick, M., Crandell, L., García-Pérez, R., & Lee, A. (2005). Personal relatedness and attachment in infants of mothers with borderline personality disorder. *Development and Psychopathology, 17,* 329–347.

Individuals with Disabilities Education Improvement Act (IDEA) of 2004, PL 108-446, 20 U.S.C. §§ 1400 *et seq.*

Jones Harden, B. (2010). Home visitation with psychologically vulnerable families: Developments in the profession and in the professional. *Zero to Three, 30*(6), 44–51.

Jones Harden, B., Denmark, N., Holmes, A., & Duchene, M. (2014). Detached parenting and toddler problem behavior in Early Head Start families. *Infant Mental Health Journal, 35*(6), 529–543.

Jones Harden, B., Denmark, N., & Saul, D. (2010). Understanding the needs of staff in Head Start programs: The characteristics, perceptions, and experiences of home visitors. *Children and Youth Services Review, 32,* 371–379.

Jones Harden, B., & Lythcott, M. (2005). Kitchen therapy and beyond: Mental health services for young children in alternative settings. In K.M. Finello (Ed.), *The handbook of training and practice in infant and preschool mental health* (pp. 256–286). New York, NY: Jossey-Bass.

Kagan, J., Reznick, J.S., & Gibbons, J. (1989). Inhibited and uninhibited types of children. *Child Development, 60,* 838–845.

Kaley, F., Reid, V., & Flynn, E. (2011). The psychology of infant colic: A review of current research. *Infant Mental Health Journal, 32*(5), 526–541.

Karp, S.M., & Lutenbacher, M. (2011). Infant feeding practices of young mothers. *Maternal Child Nursing, 36*(2), 98–103.

Kaye, S.H. (2011). *Population estimates and demographics of parents with disabilities in the United States.* Berkeley, CA: Through the Looking Glass.

Keiley, M.K., Howe, T., Dodge, K., Bates, J., & Pettit, G. (2001). Timing of abuse: Group differences and developmental trajectories. *Development and Psychopathology, 13,* 891–912.

Kelly, R.J., Marks, B.T., & El-Sheikh, M. (2014). Longitudinal relations between parent–child conflict and children's adjustment: The role of children's sleep. *Journal of Abnormal Child Psychology, 42,* 1175–1185.

Kirshbaum, M., & Olkin, R. (2002). Parents with physical, systemic, or visual disabilities. *Sexuality and Disabilities, 20*(1), 65–80.

Kleinmann, A.E., & Songer, N.S. (2009). Parents with developmental disabilities caring for infants and young children. In G.L. Ensher, D.A. Clark, & N.S. Songer (Eds.), *Families, infants, and young children at risk: Pathways to best practice* (pp. 287–315). Baltimore, MD: Paul H. Brookes Publishing Co.

Knitzer, J., Theberge, S., & Johnson, K. (2008). *Reducing maternal depression and its impact on young children: Toward a responsive early childhood policy framework.* Retrieved from National Center for Children in Poverty website: http://www.nccp.org/publications/pdf/text_791.pdf

Knoche, L.I., Kuhn, M., Eum, J. (2013). "More time. More showing. More helping. That's how it sticks": The perspectives of early childhood coaches. *Infants and Young Children, 26*(4), 349–365.

Kochanska, G. (2002). Committed compliance, moral self, and internalization: A mediational model. *Developmental Psychology, 38*(3), 339–351.

Kochanska, G., Coy, K.C., & Murray, K.T. (2001). The development of self-regulation in the first 4 years. *Child Development, 72,* 1091–1111.

Krumm, S., Becker, T., & Wiegand-Grefe, S. (2013). Mental health services for parents affected by mental illness. *Current Opinion in Psychiatry, 26*(4), 362–368.

Laible, D.J., & Thompson, R. (2002). Mother–child conflict in the toddler years: Lessons in emotion, morality and relationship. *Child Development, 73*(4), 1187–1203.

Landy, S. (2009). *Pathways to competence: Encouraging healthy social and emotional development in young children* (2nd ed.). Baltimore, MD: Paul H. Brookes Publishing Co.

Landy, S., & Menna, R. (2006). *Early intervention with multi-risk families: An integrative approach.* Baltimore, MD: Paul H. Brookes Publishing Co.

Lee, E., Esaki, N., Jeehoon, K., Greene, R., Kirkland, K., & Mitchell-Herzfeld, S. (2013). Organizational climate and burnout among home visitors: Testing mediating effects of empowerment. *Children and Youth Services Review, 35,* 594–602.

Lieberman, A.F., Chu, A., Van Horn, P., & Harris, W.W. (2011). Trauma in early childhood: Empirical evidence and clinical implications. *Development and Psychopathology, 23*(2), 397–410.

Lieberman, A.F., Compton, N.C., Van Horn, P., & Ghosh Ippen, C. (2003). *Losing a parent to death in the early years: Guidelines for the treatment of traumatic bereavement in infancy and early childhood.* Washington, DC: ZERO TO THREE.

Lieberman, A., & Van Horn, P. (2008). *Psychotherapy with infants and young children: Repairing the effects of stress and trauma on early attachment.* New York, NY: Guilford.

Lieberman, A., & Van Horn, P. (2013). Infants and young children in military families: A conceptual model for intervention. *Clinical Child and Family Psychology Review, 16,* 282–293.

Lightfoot, E., Hill, K., & LaLiberte, T. (2010). The inclusion of disability as a condition for termination of parental rights. *Child Abuse and Neglect, 34,* 927–934.

Livas-Dlott, A., Fuller, B., Stein, G.L., Bridges, M., Mangual Figueroa, A., & Mireles, L. (2010). Commands, competence, and cariño: Maternal socialization practices in Mexican American families. *Developmental Psychology, 46*(3), 566–578.

Magee, C.A., Gordon, R., & Caputi, P. (2014). Distinct developmental trends in sleep duration during early childhood. *Pediatrics, 133,* e1561–1566, doi: 10.1542/peds.2013-3806.

Main, M. (1996). Introduction to the Special Section of attachment and psychopathology: Part 2, An overview of the field of attachment. *Journal of Consulting and Clinical Psychology, 64*(2), 237–243.

Malik, N. (2012). The challenging child: Emotional dysregulation and aggression. In S.J. Summers & R. Chazan-Cohen (Eds.), *Understanding early childhood mental health: A practical guide for professionals* (pp. 25–39). Baltimore, MD: Paul H. Brookes Publishing Co.

Mann, K., Gordon, J., & MacLeod, A. (2009). Reflection and reflective practice in health professions education. *Advances in Health Science Education, 14,* 595–621.

Martin, S.E., Boekamp, J.R., McConville, D.W., & Wheeler, E.E. (2010). Anger and sadness perception in clinically referred preschoolers: Emotion processes and externalizing behavior symptoms. *Child Psychiatry and Human Development, 41,* 30–46.

Maslach, C., Schaufeli, W.B., & Leiter, M.P. (2001). Job burnout. *Annual Review of Psychology, 52*(1), 397.

Maxted, A.E., Dickstein, S., Miller-Loncar, C., High, P., Spritz, B., & Liu, J. (2005). Infant colic and maternal depression. *Infant Mental Health Journal, 26*(1), 56–68.

McAllister, C.L., & Thomas, T. (2007). Infant mental health and family support: Contributions of Early Head Start to an integrated model for community-based early childhood programs. *Infant Mental Health Journal, 28*(2), 192–215.

McClelland, M.M., & Tominey, S.L. (2014). The development of self-regulation and executive function in young children. *Zero to Three, 35*(2), 2–8.

McGuigan, W.M., Katzev, A.R., & Pratt, C.C. (2003). Multi-level determinants of mothers' engagement in home visiting services. *Family Relations, 52*(3), 271–278.

McKenna, J., & McDade, T. (2005). Why babies should never sleep alone: A review of the co-sleeping controversy in relation to SIDS, bed sharing, and breast feeding. *Paediatric Respiratory Reviews, 6,* 134–152.

McNeil, C.B., & Hembree-Kigin, T.L. (2010). *Parent–child interaction therapy* (2nd ed.). New York, NY: Springer.

Meltzer, L.J., Mindell, J.A. (2014). Systematic review and meta-analysis of behavioral interventions for pediatric insomnia. *Journal of Pediatric Psychology, 39,* 932–948.

Mena, K.C., & Bailey, J.D. (2007). The effects of the supervisory working alliance on worker outcomes. *Journal of Social Service Research, 34*(1), 55–65.

Mence, M., Hawes, D.J., Wedgewood, L., Morgan, S., Barnett, B., Kohlhoff, J., & Hunt, C. (2014). Emotional flooding and hostile discipline in the families of toddlers with disruptive behavior problems. *Journal of Family Psychology, 28*(1), 12–21.

Mills, A., Schmied, V., Taylor, C., Dahlen, H., Schuiringa, W., & Hudson, M.E. (2012). Connecting, learning, leaving: Supporting young parents in the community. *Health and Social Care in the Community, 20*(6), 663–672.

Monahan, C.I., Beeber, L.S., & Jones Harden, B. (2012). Finding family strengths in the midst of adversity: Using risk and resilience models to promote mental health. In S.J. Summers & R. Chazan-Cohen (Eds.), *Understanding early childhood mental health: A practical guide for professionals* (pp. 59–78). Baltimore, MD: Paul H. Brookes Publishing Co.

Murphy, E.S., & Lupfer, G.J. (2014). Basic principles of operant conditioning. In F.K. McSweeney & E.S. Murphy (Eds.), *The Wiley Blackwell handbook of operant and classical conditioning* (pp. 167–194). New York, NY: Wiley.

Neilsen Gatti, S., Watson, C., & Siegel, C. (2011). Step back and consider: Learning from reflective practice in infant mental health. *Young Exceptional Children, 14*(2), 32–45.

Norman-Murch, T. (1996). Reflective supervision as a vehicle for individual and organizational development. *Zero to Three, 17,* 16–20.

Norman-Murch, T. (2005). Keeping our balance on a slippery slope: Training and supporting infant/family specialists within an organization context. *Infants and Young Children, 18*(4), 308–322.

Norman-Murch, T., & Ward, G. (1999). First steps in establishing reflective practice and supervision: Organizational issues and strategies. *Zero to Three, 20*(1), 10–14.

O'Donnell, K., Glover, V., Barker, E.D., & O'Connor, T.G. (2014). The persisting effect of maternal mood in pregnancy on childhood psychopathology. *Developmental Psychopathology, 26*(2), 393–403.

Ong, K.K., Emmett, P.M., Noble, S., Ness, A., & Dunger, A. (2006). Dietary energy intake at the age of 4 months predicts postnatal weight gain and childhood body mass index. *Pediatrics, 117*(3), 503–508. doi: 10.1542/peds.2005-1668

Osofsky, J.D. (2009). Perspectives on helping traumatized infants, young children, and their families. *Infant Mental Health Journal, 30*(6), 673–677.

Osofsky, J.D. (2011). Introduction: Trauma through the eyes of a young child. In J.D. Osofsky (Ed.) *Clinical work with traumatized young children* (pp. 1–8). New York, NY: Guilford Press.

Owens, J.A., & Dalzell, V. (2005). Use of the "BEARS" sleep screening tool in a pediatric residents' continuity clinic: A pilot study. *Journal of Developmental and Behavioral Pediatrics, 6,* 63–69.

Patient Protection and Affordable Care Act of 2010, PL 111-148, 42 U.S.C. 18001.

Patterson, G.R. (1982). *Coercive family process.* Eugene, OR: Castalia.

Pawl, J. (2000). The interpersonal center of the work that we do. *Zero to Three, 20,* 5–7.

Pawl, J., & St. John, M. (1998). *How you are is as important as what you do.* Washington, DC: ZERO TO THREE/National Center for Clinical Infant Programs.

Perera, D.N., Short, L., & Fernbacher, S. (2014). "It's not that straightforward": When family support is challenging for mothers living with mental illness. *Psychiatric Rehabilitation Journal, 37*(3), 170–175.

Popp, T.K., & Wilcox, M.J. (2012). Capturing the complexity of parent–provider relationships in early intervention: The association with maternal responsivity and children's social-emotional development. *Infants and Young Children, 25*(3), 213–231.

Potegal, M., Kosorok, M.R., & Davidson, R.J. (2003). Temper tantrums in young children: 2. Tantrum duration and temporal organization. *Developmental and Behavioral Pediatrics, 24*(3), 148–154.

Price, S.K., & Masho, S.W. (2014). What does it mean when we screen? A closer examination of perinatal depression and psychosocial risk screening within one MCH home visiting program. *Maternal and Child Health Journal, 18*(4), 765–771.

Rader, N., & Zukow-Goldring, P. (2012). Caregivers' gestures direct infant attention during early word learning: The importance of dyadic synchrony. *Language Sciences, 34*(5), 559–568.

Ramchandani, P.G., Domoney, J., Sethna, V., Psychogiou, L., Vlachos, H., & Murray, L. (2013). Do early father–infant interactions predict the onset of externalizing behaviors in young children? Findings from a longitudinal cohort study. *Journal of Child Psychology and Psychiatry, 54*(1), 56–64.

Repachouli, B., & Gopnick, A. (1997). Early reasoning about desires: Evidence from 14- to 18-month-olds. *Developmental Psychology, 33*(1), 12–21.

Rice, K.F. & Groves, B.M. (2005). *Hope & healing: A caregiver's guide to helping young children affected by trauma.* Washington, DC: ZERO TO THREE Press.

Riley, S., Brady, A.E., Goldberg, J., Jacobs, F., & Easterbrooks, M.A. (2008). Once the door closes: Understanding the parent–provider relationship. *Child and Youth Services Review, 30,* 597–612.

Roben, C.K.P., Cole, P.M., & Armstrong, L.M. (2013). Longitudinal relations among language skills, anger expression, and regulatory strategies in early childhood. *Child Development, 84*(3), 891–905.

Romano, E., Baillargeon, R.H., & Cao, G. (2013). Hyperactive behaviors among 17-month-olds in a population cohort. *Infant Mental Health Journal, 34*(5), 406–416.

Rothbart, M.K., & Bates, J.E. (2006). Temperament. In W. Damon & R.M. Lerner (Series Eds.) & N. Eisenberg (Vol. Ed.), *Handbook of child psychology: Vol. 3. Social, emotional, and personality development* (6th ed., pp. 99–166). Hoboken, NJ: Wiley.

Rothbart, M.K., & Posner, M.I. (2006). Temperament, attention, and developmental psychopathology. In C. Cicchetti & D.J. Cohen (Eds.), *Developmental psychopathology: Vol. 2. Developmental neuroscience* (2nd ed., pp. 465–501). Hoboken, NJ: Wiley.

Ryan, R., Martin, A., & Brookes-Gunn, J. (2006). Is one good parent good enough? Patterns of mother and father parenting and child cognitive outcomes at 24 and 36 months. *Parenting Science and Practice, 6*(2–3), 211–228.

Samuels, J., Shinn, M., & Buckner, J.C. (2010). *Homeless children: Update on research, policy, programs, and opportunities.* Washington, DC: Office of the Assistant Secretary for Planning and Evaluation, U.S. Department of Health and Human Resources.

Sattler, J. (1998). *Clinical and forensic interviewing of children and families: Guidelines for the mental health, education, pediatrics and child maltreatment fields.* San Diego, CA: Author.

Scheeringa, M. (2004). Posttraumatic stress disorder. In R. DelCarmen-Wiggins & A. Carter (Eds.), *Handbook of infant, toddler, and preschool mental health assessment* (pp. 377–399). New York, NY: Oxford University Press.

Scheeringa, M. & Zeanah, C. (2001). A relational perspective on PTSD in early childhood. *Journal of Traumatic Stress, 14,* 799–815.

Schellinger, K., & Talmi, A. (2013). Off the charts? Considerations for interpreting parent reports of toddler hyperactivity. *Infant Mental Health Journal, 34*(5), 417–419.

Schön, D.A. (1983). *The reflective practitioner.* New York, NY: Basic Books.

Schön, D.A. (1987). *Educating the reflective practitioner.* San Francisco, CA: Jossey-Bass.

Seligman, S. (2014). Attachment, intersubjectivity, and mentalization within the experience of the child, the parent, and the provider. In K. Brandt, B.D. Perry, S. Seligman, & E. Tronick (Eds.), *Infant and early childhood mental health: Core concepts and clinical practice* (pp. 309–322). Washington, DC: American Psychiatric Publishing.

Shahmoon-Shanok, R. (2006). Reflective supervision: Its meaning and significance for integrated practice. In G.M. Foley & J.D. Hochman (Eds.), *Mental health in early intervention: Achieving unity in principles and practice* (pp. 343–381). Baltimore, MD: Paul H. Brookes Publishing Co.

Shahmoon-Shanok, R. (2010). What is reflective supervision? In S. Scott Heller & L. Gilkerson (Eds.), *A practical guide to reflective supervision* (pp. 7–24). Washington, DC: ZERO TO THREE.

Sheridan, A., Murray, L., Cooper, P.J., Evangeli, M., Byram, V., & Halligan, S.L. (2013). A longitudinal study of child sleep in high and low risk families: Relationship to early maternal settling strategies and child psychological functioning. *Sleep Medicine, 14,* 266–273.

Shonkoff, J., & Phillips, D.A. (2000). *From neurons to neighborhoods: The science of early childhood development.* Washington, DC: National Academies Press.

Siegel, D.J. (2013). *Reflections on the mindful brain.* Retrieved from http://www.open ground.com.au/OG-SITE-ARTICLES-2013/Siegel-article.pdf

Slade, A. (2005). Parental reflective functioning: An introduction. *Attachment and Human Development, 7*(3), 269–281.

Slade, A. (2007). Reflective parenting programs: Theory and development. *Psychoanalytic Inquiry: A Topical Journal for Mental Health Professionals, 26*(4), 640–657.

Slomski, A. (2012). Chronic mental health issues in children now loom larger than physical problems. *Journal of the American Medical Association, 308*(3), 223–225.

Stepp, S.D., Whalen, D.J., Pilkonis, P.A., Hipwell, A.E., & Levine, M.D. (2012). Children of mothers with borderline personality disorder: Identifying parenting behaviors as potential targets for intervention. *Personality Disorders: Theory, Research, and Treatment, 3*(1), 76–91.

St. James-Roberts, I., Sleep, J., Morris, S., Owen, C., & Gillham, P. (2001). Use of a behavioural programme in the first 3 months to prevent infant crying and sleeping problems. *Journal of Paediatrics and Child Health, 37,* 289–297.

Substance Abuse and Mental Health Services Administration. (2009). *Family psychoeducation: The evidence.* Rockville, MD: Center for Mental Health Services, Substance Abuse and Mental Health Services Administration, U.S. Department of Health and Human Services. Rockville, MD: Author.

Substance Abuse and Mental Health Services Administration, Center for Behavioral Health Statistics and Quality. (2014a). *The NSDUH report: State estimates of adult mental illness from the 2011 and 2012 National Surveys on Drug Use and Health.* Rockville, MD: Author.

Substance Abuse and Mental Health Services Administration. (2014b). *Results from the 2013 National Survey on Drug Use and Health: Summary of national findings.* NSDUH Series H-48, HHS Publication No. (SMA) 14-4863. Rockville, MD: Author.

Tandon, S.D., Mercer, C.D., Saylor, E.L., & Duggan, A.K. (2008). Paraprofessional home visitors' perceptions on addressing poor mental health, substance abuse, and domestic violence: A qualitative study. *Early Childhood Research Quarterly, 23,* 419–428.

Thompson, R.A. (2008). Early attachment and later development: Familiar questions, new answers. In J. Cassidy & P. R. Shaver (Eds.) *Handbook of attachment: Theory, research, and clinical applications* (pp. 348–365). New York, NY: Guilford.

Thompson, R.A., & Goodvin, R. (2007). Taming the tempest in the teapot. In C.A. Brownell & C.B. Kopp (Eds.), *Socioemotional development in the toddler years: Transitions and transformations* (pp. 320–341). New York, NY: Guilford.

Tomlin, A.M. (2002). Partnering with parents with personality disorders: Effective strategies for early intervention providers. *Infants and Young Children, 14*(4), 68–75.

Tomlin, A.M., & Viehweg, S.A. (2003). Infant mental health: Making a difference. *Professional Psychology: Research and Practice, 34*(6), 617–625.

Tomlin, A., Weatherston, D., & Pavkov, T. (2014). Critical components of reflective supervision. Responses from expert supervisors from the field. *Infant Mental Health Journal, 35*(1), 70–80.

Touchette, E., Petit, D., Paquet, J., Boivin, M., Japel, C., Tremblay, R.E., & Montplaisir, J.Y. (2005). Factors associated with fragmented sleep at night across early childhood. *Archives of Pediatrics and Adolescent Medicine, 159*(3), 242–249.

Tracey, T.J., Bludworth, J., & Glidden-Tracey, C.E. (2012). Are there parallel processes in psychotherapy supervision? An empirical examination. *Psychotherapy, 49*(3), 330–343.

Tremblay, R., Nagin, D., Seguin, J., Zoccolillo, M., Zelazo, P., Biovin, M.,…Japel, C. (2004). Physical aggression during early childhood: Trajectories and predictors. *Pediatrics, 114,* 43–50.

Trivette, C.M., Dunst, C.J., & Hamby, D.W. (2010). Influences of family-systems intervention practices on parent–child interactions and child development. *Topics in Early Childhood Education, 30*(1), 3–19.

Ursache, A., Blair, C., Stifter, C., & Voegtline, K. (2013). Emotional reactivity and regulation in infancy interact to predict executive functioning in early childhood. *Developmental Psychology, 49*(1), 127–137.

Vallotton, C.D., & Ayoub, C.A. (2011). Use your words: The role of language in the development of toddlers' self-regulation. *Early Childhood Research Quarterly, 26*(2), 169–181.

Watson, C., & Gatti, S.N. (2012). Professional development through reflective consultation in early intervention. *Infants and Young Children, 25*(2), 109–121.

Watson, C., Gatti, S.N., Cox, M., Harrison, M., & Hennes, J. (2014). Reflective supervision and its impact on early childhood intervention. *Early Childhood and Special Education, Advances in Early Education and Day Care, 18,* 1–26.

Weatherston, D. (2000). The infant mental health specialist. *Zero to Three, 21,* 3–10.

Weatherston, D. (2001). Infant mental health: A review of the relevant literature. *Psychoanalytic Social Work, 8*(1), 39–69.

Weatherston, D. (2005). Returning the treasure to babies: An introduction to infant mental health service and training. In K.M. Finello (Ed.), *The handbook of training and practice in infant and preschool mental health* (pp. 3–30). San Francisco, CA: Jossey-Bass.

Weatherston, D.J., & Barron, C. (2010). What does a reflective supervisory relationship look like? In S. Scott Heller & L. Gilkerson (Eds.), *A practical guide to reflective supervision* (pp. 63–82). Washington, DC: ZERO TO THREE.

Weatherston, D., Kaplan-Estrin, M., & Goldberg, S. (2009). Strengthening and recognizing knowledge, skills, and reflective practice: The Michigan Association for Infant Mental Health competency guidelines and endorsement process. *Infant Mental Health Journal, 30*(6), 648–663.

Weatherston, D., & Tableman, B. (2015). *Infant mental health home visiting: Supporting competencies/reducing risks.* Southgate, MI: Michigan Association for Infant Mental Health.

Weatherston, D., Weigand, R.W., & Weigand, B. (2010). Reflective supervision: Supporting reflection as a cornerstone for competency, *Zero to Three, 31*(2), 22–30.

Webster-Stratton, C. (2001). *The Incredible Years: Parent, teachers, and children training series. Leaders guide.* Seattle, WA: The Incredible Years.

Weinfield, N.S., Sroufe, L.A., Egeland, B., & Carlson, E. (2008). Individual difference in infant-caregiver attachment: Conceptual and empirical aspects of security. In J. Cassidy & P.R. Shaver (Eds.), *Handbook of Attachment: Theory, research, and clinical applications* (pp. 78–101).

Weitzman, C., Edmonds, D., Davagnino, J., & Briggs-Gowan, M. (2014). Young child socioemotional/behavioral problems and cumulative psychosocial risk. *Infant Mental Health Journal, 35*(1), 1–9.

Weitzman, C., & Wegner, L. (2015). Promoting optimal development: Screening for behavior and emotional problems. *Pediatrics, 135*(2), 384–395.

Weldum, J.R., Songer, N.S., & Ensher, G.S. (2009). The family as foreground. In G.L. Ensher, D.A. Clark, & N.S. Songer (Eds.), *Families, infants, and young children at risk: Pathways to best practice* (pp. 39–58). Baltimore, MD: Paul H. Brookes Publishing Co.

Wesley, P.W., & Buysse, V. (2001). Communities of practice: Expanding professional roles to promote reflection and shared inquiry. *Topics in Early Childhood Special Education, 21*(2), 114–123.

Wessel, M., Cobb, J., Jackson, E., Harris, G., & Detwiler, A. (1954). Paroxysmal fussing in infancy, sometimes called colic. *Pediatrics, 14,* 421–435.

Weston, D. (2005). Training in infant mental health: Educating the reflective practitioner. *Infants and Young Children, 18*(4), 337–348.

Wiggs, L. (2001). Sleep problems in children with developmental disorders. *Journal of the Royal Society of Medicine, 94,* 177–179.

Wight, V., Chau, M., & Aratani, Y. (2010). *Who are America's poor children? The official story.* National Center for Children in Poverty Policy Brief. Retrieved from http://www.nccp.org/publications/pdf/text_912.pdf

Williams, D.S., & Fraga, L. (2011). Coming together around military families. In J.D. Osofsky (Ed.), *Clinical work with traumatized young children* (pp. 172–199). New York, NY: Guilford.

Wittmer, D. (2008). *Focusing on peers: The importance of relationships in the early years.* Washington, DC: ZERO TO THREE.

Woods, J.J., Wilcox, M.J., Friedman, M., & Murch, T. (2011). Collaborative consultation in natural environments: Strategies to enhance family-centered supports and services. *Language, Speech, and Hearing Services in Schools, 42,* 379–392.

Yoches, M., Summers, S.J., Beeber, L.S., Jones Harden, B., & Malik, N.M. (2012). Exposure to direct and indirect trauma. In S.J. Summers & R. Chazan-Cohen (Eds.), *Understanding early childhood mental health: A practical guide for professionals* (pp. 79–98). Baltimore, MD: Paul H. Brookes Publishing Co.

Zeanah, C.H., Berlin, L.J., & Boris, N.W. (2011) Practitioner review: Clinical applications of attachment and research for infants and young children. *Journal of Child Psychology and Psychiatry, 52*(8), 819–823.

Zeanah, P.D., Larrieu, J.A., & Boris, N.W. (2006). Nurse home visiting: Perspectives from nurses. *Infant Mental Health Journal, 27*(1), 41–54.

ZERO TO THREE. (2005). *Diagnostic classification of mental health and developmental disorders of infancy and early childhood* (revised ed.). Washington, DC: ZERO TO THREE Press.

Zimmerman, M., Rothschild, L., & Chelminski, I. (2005). The prevalence of DSM-IV personality disorders in psychiatric outpatients. *American Journal of Psychiatry, 162,* 1911–1918.

Index

Tables, figures, and boxes are indicated by *t*, *f*, and *b*, respectively.